THE SWEET SPOT

THE
SWEET
SPOT

HOW AUSTRALIA MADE ITS OWN LUCK – AND COULD NOW THROW IT ALL AWAY

PETER HARTCHER

Black Inc.

Published by Black Inc.,
an imprint of Schwartz Media Pty Ltd
37–39 Langridge Street
Collingwood VIC 3066 Australia
email: enquiries@blackincbooks.com
http://www.blackincbooks.com

The National Library of Australia Cataloguing-in-Publication entry:

    Hartcher, Peter.

    The sweet spot : how Australia made its own luck and could now throw
    it all away / Peter Hartcher.

    ISBN: 9781863954976 (pbk.)

    Notes: Includes index.

    International economic relations--21st century. International business
    enterprises--21st century. Australia--Economic policy--21st century.
    Australia--Foreign economic relations--21st century. Australia--Social
    policy--21st century.

    338.994

Typesetting: Duncan Blachford
Index: Geraldine Suter

Printed in Australia by Griffin Press. The paper this book is printed on is certified
against the Forest Stewardship Council® Standards. Griffin Press holds FSC chain
of custody certification SGS-COC-005088. FSC promotes environmentally
responsible, socially beneficial and economically viable management of the
world's forests.

FSC
www.fsc.org
MIX
Paper from
responsible sources
FSC® C009448

CONTENTS

for Mindanao

GOLD

Two centuries before the first British flagstaff was crunched into the sandy soil of Botany Bay, Europeans speculated that the mysterious Great South Land might be the biblical Ophir, trove of untold riches. Ophir, a land where the very rocks and mountains were said to be made of solid gold, was the fabled source of the precious metal that had been lavished on King Solomon's temple in Jerusalem.

As the European powers conquered one land after another, they were disappointed that they hadn't yet found Ophir. The unexplored southern Pacific became their last remaining hope.

Greedy for gold, Spain sent three expeditions into the southwest Pacific in the forty years from 1565. The existence of a continent in roughly the position of Australia had been long spoken of, but never confirmed.

The fever was so strong on them that when the Spanish happened upon a group of tropical islands near the equator, so confident were they that they had discovered the source of Solomon's gold that they named them accordingly.

But the Solomon Islands were not the mysterious *Terra Australis Incognita* that they had been sent to find, and they were not Ophir. (It turns out that there was gold in serious quantities under the soil there, but the Spaniards were destined never to find it. It wouldn't be mined for another 400 years.)

After their third attempt to find the southern continent, the

Spanish captains and crew, frequently lost on the world's biggest ocean, plagued by disease and divided by bitter rivalry, gave up.

Other Europeans eventually stumbled on Australia. Once settled, they scratched Australia hard enough to uncover even more gold than Ophir had supplied to Solomon's Temple, which is quite a feat. The Old Testament speaks of 100,000 talents of gold, which we would measure as some 3,400 tonnes – at today's prices that's worth $140 billion. Still, the combined output of Australia's goldmines delivers this much of the precious metal every fifteen years at modern production rates.

Gold has been important in Australia's history. So have all the other resources scraped from the bowels of the earth. But it was not the gold rushes of the nineteenth century or the resource booms of the twentieth that have made Australia the standout success of our time.

Australia today is closer than it has ever been to fulfilling its promise as a golden land, even the most golden of all lands. It is the only developed nation on earth that has not suffered a recession in the last two decades.

It used to be said that when America sneezed, Australia caught a cold. Instead, Australia has proved to be the rich country most immune to the economic ailments of the US and, indeed, everywhere else. Australia sailed through the Asian economic crisis of 1997–98, prospered through the US stock-market bust and recession of 2001 and continued to grow through the savage global financial crisis of 2008–09.

Going into 2011, Australia's unemployment rate of 5 per cent was half that of Europe or America. "Australia astonishes," was the 2010 summary by France's *Le Monde* newspaper, which carried a front-page cartoon of smiling kangaroos standing next to the Sydney Opera House and flashing V-for-victory signs as a chart showed Australia's exceptionally resilient rate of growth.

Australia has a higher average income per head of population than Germany, Japan, Singapore or France, surpassing that of its "mother country," Britain, by one and a half times. And in 2008, Australia passed a major milestone. For the first time since World War One, its income per head surpassed America's. A decade ago, Australia lagged 40 per cent behind the US. By 2010, it was well ahead – by about $15,000 per head, or almost one-third, in fact.

If this achievement were a sporting triumph, Australians would have erupted in a frenzy of celebration. If the Aussies had beaten the Yanks in the medal tally at the 2008 Beijing Olympic Games, the country would have gone wild with ticker-taped self-congratulation. In the event, Australia's athletes won half as many medals as did the US in Beijing, but the country was still thoroughly pleased with itself.

Yet surpassing the country regarded as the benchmark of prosperity in the key measure of income was not even noted in the mainstream media. Winning sporting gold is a national triumph. Winning real gold, the gold of high incomes and high living standards, is, apparently, trivial.

Perhaps we needed a medal ceremony to get people's attention?

History shows that Australians developed their outsized pride and enthusiasm for sport partly as a national consolation prize. The country might not have been able to compete with its colonial master, Britain, for wealth or artistic accomplishment, or with its great and powerful friend, America, for prosperity or power, but it could always walk tall on the sporting field. For most of the last century, the Aussies could reliably thrash the Poms at cricket or rugby and make the Americans sweat for their prizes in tennis or swimming.

Perhaps it's too new, or too incredible, for Australians to absorb, but the country has now become so successful as a prosperous modern power that it can afford to take a little credit for winning the real prizes of international life, rather than just the consolation ones.

It's more than income. In its annual ranking of all the countries on earth, the United Nations combines measures of income, education and health to create the Human Development Index. The UN describes it as a way of measuring how well "people can develop their full potential and lead productive, creative lives in accord with their needs and interests." In its 2010 assessment of 194 countries, Australia scored second only to Norway in enjoying the best living conditions available to the human species. The two countries scored near-identical tallies of 93.7 for Australia and 93.8 for Norway. If the index incorporated climate, of course, Norway would have to vacate the dais.

This was the highest ranking Australia had achieved since the index was first published in 1990. In that year, Australia was placed seventh in the Human Development Index. Also in that year, Australia's per capita income rated it fifteenth in the world. Today it's seventh according to 2010 figures from the International Monetary Fund, behind Luxembourg, Qatar, Denmark, Switzerland and Norway. The long list of 176 countries that follows after Australia begins with Sweden, the US, the Netherlands, Canada, Ireland, Austria, Finland and Singapore.

But then Australia, ranked second in the world in the Human Development Index, went one better. In late 2010, and even without an adjustment for the weather, the UN published an updated tally which ranked Australia ahead of Norway and, indeed, every other country on earth. In an improved measurement that it called its "hybrid" Human Development Index, combining its traditional items with new data measurements, Australia was awarded a score of 93.82 and Norway 92.89. Australians, in short, enjoy the benefits of living in the world's superpower of living standards.

Want a second opinion? In 2011, the Organisation for Economic Co-operation and Development (OECD) published a new index measuring living conditions in the world's thirty-four developed countries. It was called the Better Life Index. This survey covered a much broader set of measurements including not only health, education and income but also personal security, working hours and community connections. It found that Australia's overall living conditions were the best. This was not a back-office, after-lunch, hands-up for a tabloid magazine but an objective study painstakingly prepared by an expert multinational staff in Paris, reporting to thirty-four governments. So both the UN and the OECD, one measuring all countries and the other comparing rich countries, found that the country offering the best living conditions in the world was Australia. Could this be mere coincidence? Or is all of this evidence telling us something?

The term "The Lucky Country" was applied famously by Donald Horne in his 1964 book. He intended it ironically. Yet by the time he died in 2005, he had come to the conclusion that Australia had changed. Australia had started to make its own luck.

One of the perversities of Australia's ascendancy as the superpower of living conditions is that its people have shown a striking insouciance about it. At two consecutive national elections – in 2007 and again in 2010 – the voters refused to re-elect the governments that presided over these conditions. This is at odds with history. These are the only occasions since 1949 on which the Australian people have rejected a national government at a time of economic growth.

It seems that two decades of unbroken expansion have created the sense that this is situation normal, and that no one should get any special credit. Yet both in Australia's own history and in world experience, such a long run of prosperity is unique.

Nor was it accomplished by digging gold and other resources

out of the ground. Australia reformed and renovated and emerged as a successful new model before the latest resources boom arrived. By the time the commodities boom of the 2000s began its first phase in 2004–05, Australia had already developed a flexible, high-performance economy that was consistently outstripping US growth. The Nobel Prize–winning American economist Paul Krugman said as early as 1998 that Australia's impressive new resilience made it "the miracle economy of the world financial crisis."

By 2005, the OECD reported that "in the last decade of the 20th century, Australia became a model for other OECD countries." Australia was a model in two ways. First, in the sense that it had crafted a unique set of conditions. These settings made it distinct from the two models that had dominated twentieth-century policy choices for democratic countries – the American model and the European. There was now a new model. Australia combined the best elements of each, American freedom with European fairness. And it adopted the worst elements of neither, avoiding the worst of America's inequality and the oppressive cost of the European welfare state.

Australia was not only different, but also highly successful. This is the second way that Australia is now considered a model, a good lead for others to follow. One of the distinctive characteristics of the Australian model was that it achieved all this – sound growth, high living standards and the protections of a social security net – while living within its means. The Australian government was running consistent budget surpluses, not deficits, for the ten years from 1998. This set Australia apart from the main economies of the developed world – the US, Europe and Japan. And it was happening years before the mining boom was even a glint on the horizon. The federal government paid off the last dollar of national debt in 2006.

But surely Australia is now so dependent on mining that it must owe everything to the commodities boom? Not at all. Ask yourself this: how big a part of the economy is Australia's mining sector? From the rhetoric of our politicians and commentators, Australians formed the impression that it accounts for about a third, according to a survey by the Australia Institute. In fact, even in the full flush of the boom, Australia's entire energy and mining sectors together constituted only 8.4 per cent of the national economy in 2010.

That's not a misprint. Only one dollar in every twelve generated in the Australian economy in 2010 came from the combined industries of oil, gas, coal, iron ore, gold and other minerals. The finance industry is bigger, accounting for 10.6 per cent of the total economy. So is manufacturing at 9.3 per cent. And mining is one of the smallest jobs generators. Of the nineteen industry categories counted by the Australian Bureau of Statistics, mining is the second-smallest employer, employing just 1.5 per cent of working Australians. Even the "arts and recreation services" industry hires more. Mining's strength is its contribution to exports – a little over half the national export earnings comes from energy and mining. But you can't build a successful modern nation on an industry that accounts for only 8 per cent of the present-day economy and employs just 1.5 per cent of the workforce. If the country depended on mining and energy, it'd be a Third World nation. And even 8 per cent might be too big for Australia's good.

On balance, the resources sector has been helpful to Australia over the last two centuries as a source of work and wealth. But when prices take off and boom arrives, it is not so much blessing as curse. A sudden gusher of money poorly managed can be as harmful for an economy as winning the Lotto can be for an unprepared wage-earner. As the head of the Treasury, Ken Henry, said at the end of 2010: "We are having to grapple with the consequences of what could very well turn out to be the largest external shock to the Australian economy in its history."

Hardly had the shiny new Australian model been noted internationally when a cataclysm loomed on the horizon in 2008 – the world's most wrenching economic event since the Great Depression of the 1930s. It was the ultimate stress-test for the new Australian arrangements. It tore away from many countries the flimsy façade of success. In one country after another, it turned out that prosperity was not real because it had been borrowed, and borrowed at unsustainably high levels. They could get away with it only until adversity struck.

Some of the star performers of the world economy before the Great Collapse of 2008–09, the countries that were vaunted as outstanding success stories, had been dependent on high levels of private debt. They were suddenly horribly exposed when the easy credit stopped. Ireland, once the so-called Celtic Tiger, and Iceland and Latvia are now in painful states of withdrawal from their addiction to performance-enhancing debt. It gave them the exhilaration of brief bursts of speed, and the agony of the inevitable letdown.

Other apparent successes turned out to have been built on unsustainable government debt. Australia eliminated its national debt before the crisis struck and, even though it resumed borrowing to stimulate growth through the 2008–09 global crisis, its liabilities are so small as to be almost trivial. As the principal powers of the world sink beneath the crushing weight of national borrowings in 2011, Australia's government debt is feather-light. If you picture the national debt as a lead belt handicapping an athlete, measuring net government debt as a percentage of each county's GDP, the European Union was wearing a 67-kilogram weight around its waist at the end of 2010, the US 65 kilograms and Japan 120. Australia's was 5 kilograms.

The weighted-down world powers will spend at least a decade

recovering fully from the global financial crisis of 2008–09. Australia is stripped down to run ahead with Asia rather than fall back with the West. History sped up in the three years following the crisis. Indeed, it now appears to have been a civilisational inflexion point. The decline of the West accelerated and the rise of the developing powers became nearer and more assured. When the crisis broke out in 2008, the world already had a two-speed economy – the rich countries were out for a gentle stroll while the rising poor countries were at a sprint. Both parts of that trend have sharpened now that the acute phase of the crisis has passed, and both look set to sharpen further in the years ahead.

The global crisis was a shock for countries everywhere. What was the result for the newly built Australian model? Australia only increased its advantage over the rest of the world's developed countries.

The founder of modern Singapore, Lee Kwan Yew, made the famous prediction that Australians were destined to become "the poor, white trash of Asia." That was in the 1980s.

Two decades later, in 2007, the then treasurer of Australia, Peter Costello, was entertaining Lee at a private dinner. He wanted an update on Lee's thinking. Lee, by this time bearing the title of Minister Mentor in the cabinet of Singapore, replied: "You have changed. Your country is a different place now." Since then Australia has only stood out further among the ranks of the world's rich countries.

Australia's accomplishment is far greater than generating wealth and services for an elite. The rich can live well in any country. That is no achievement. The wider picture is that Australia is one of the world's fairest countries, one of the most tolerant, and one of the safest.

This will jar with the image that many Australians have of their country. We have been told again and again that inequality has grown worse, that the rich get richer while the poor get poorer, that racial and religious intolerance has sharpened, and that the crime rate is on the rise. In short, that society is in decline. And while you can always find anecdotes to support any argument, the hard and comprehensive evidence is that none of these claims is true.

Against the tide of events elsewhere in the world, Australian income inequality has become less unequal. The rich have got richer, but the poor have not got poorer, and the gap between them has actually closed. This has not been constant or unequivocal, but it did occur in the eight years to 2008. As the international experts at the OECD reported in a major 2008 study of thirty rich countries: "Income inequality in Australia has fallen quite sharply since 2000. It is now below the OECD average for the first time."

As Australians have become wealthier, they have not become more selfish. The proportion of private incomes that is given to charitable purposes has doubled in the last decade, according to the *Giving Australia* report. After the Irish, Australians are the most generous donors in the world, on the OECD's count. And the rate of giving of time and energy – volunteering – has also been rising.

The crime rate has been falling fairly consistently for twenty years now. This, too, is hard for many to accept. Andrew Leigh, an economist who became a Labor MP in 2010, wrote that, "Most Australians – particularly those whose major source of information is talkback radio – believe that crime is not only high, but on the rise." The truth is the opposite. The rate of murder, the most serious crime and a proxy for crime more generally, doubled between the 1950s and the late 1980s. But since then it has fallen back, almost to the level of the 1950s. In international rankings, Australian crime rates are not among the best, but neither are they among the worst. They are about average for a developed country.

Australia is one of the most ethnically diverse societies on earth. No country has been more successful in building a harmonious national pool from so many diverse streams. Riots at Sydney's Cronulla Beach in 2005 raised hard questions about whether Muslim immigrants could peacefully live in Australia. The conviction in 2010 of five Muslim men for plotting terrorism raised yet more. While anxiety still surrounds the Islamic integration challenge, 2011 began with a promising portent. A young immigrant from Pakistan, Usman Khawaja, became the first Muslim to represent Australia in cricket. He won his place on the national team with his brilliant batsmanship, but he has been embraced for his character – he's the most popular member of the NSW squad, according to its captain. His father remarked: "It shows that it's a fair system and whoever puts in effort can achieve anything in this country."

So Australia has managed to become one of the richest countries in its financial wealth, perhaps the richest of all in its living conditions, and also rich in its spirit of fairness and cohesion.

This book will surprise most Australians and shock some. A great many will resist its central observation. Why? Because Australians are long accustomed to assuming that they are second-rate at anything but selected sporting events. Because the voices of disgruntlement are louder and more emphatic than the quiet contentment of the satisfied. And because humans become as deeply invested in their grudges and gripes as they do in their pleasures, and will not easily let go of a well-rehearsed complaint.

This book points out what the serious observers in the rest of the world have noticed but that most Australians have not: Australia has become one of the most successful countries on earth. By some of the most important measures, it is the most successful of all. Australia is perhaps the Ophir of our time. But then again, Ophir turned out to be a myth.

2

SUCCESS AND FAILURE

If you think that a country's fate is decided by its geography, its natural resources, its climate, the skin colour or the ethnicity of its inhabitants, then I have five words for you: North Korea and South Korea.

No pair of countries could be more similar in essential ingredients, yet so stunningly different in outcomes. They were a single country – plain Korea – for half a millennium until the end of World War Two. They occupy the same peninsula, inhabited by the same people, many of whom have family across today's massively fortified demilitarised zone (DMZ). Identical in their genes, their history, their language, their customs, they are one people.

At the time the peninsula was divided into north and south, they were in a very similar condition – war-torn and dirt-poor, the same category of desperate poverty as the states of sub-Saharan Africa. If either side had any starting advantage over the other, it was the North, which commanded almost all of the natural resources of the Korean peninsula. While the South had no significant reserves of any energy or minerals, the North had big deposits of iron ore, coal, zinc, uranium and the world's largest known reserves of magnesite, an ore for making manganese, essential in constructing lightweight alloys for high-tech industries such as aircraft and electronics. The South Korean Chamber of Commerce and Industry in 2008 estimated the value of the resources lying in North Korea's soil at US$2 trillion.

Yet consider the differences now. A night-time satellite photo of the Korean peninsula is an eloquent statement of relative wealth. North of the thirty-eighth parallel is blackness. South is a dazzling landscape of light. North Korea has so little electricity that it is carefully and grudgingly rationed. Even most of the scant energy that it does enjoy is supplied at concessional rates by its only major ally, China. The people lack power to warm themselves, and most lack the food to feed themselves adequately most of the time. A famine in the late 1990s killed an estimated 2 to 3 million people, or about one in ten of the national population. While North Korea has kept its people in abject poverty and misery for decades, the South has built itself into one of the most prosperous countries on earth. South Korea produces twenty times as much electricity as the North.

Democratic and capitalist, South Korea's citizens enjoy income per head an estimated 1,600 per cent higher than that of their brethren across the DMZ. A South Korean can expect to live seventy-eight years. On the other side of the border, life expectancy is an estimated sixty-four years. The difference – fourteen years – is a damning indictment.

North Korea, a dictatorship with an old-fashioned communist economy where the state owns and controls everything, forbids its people to export to the outside world. Instead, it extorts money from the outside. It prints counterfeit of other countries' banknotes, trafficks heroin and pirated Viagra, and demands that other governments give it money in return for delaying its nuclear weapons program, then goes ahead and produces nuclear bombs anyway. While the North has developed its government to resemble an organised crime ring, the South has become a successful trading nation that wants for nothing and has given rise to some of the world's most thrusting multinationals, such as Samsung, Kia and LG.

Why the difference? It can't be the geography, the climate, the language, the culture or the people, because they're identical. The difference is that North Korea has a bunch of bad policies and South Korea good. That's the difference that policy can make. It's the difference between national success and national failure, between assertive people with prosperity and opportunity on the one side, and servile people living in a state of hungry subsistence on the other.

Of course, there is a lot more involved in how each country came to have its existing set of policies.

North Korea's first premier, the Soviet-sponsored Kim Il Sung, the self-styled Great Leader, created a political dictatorship and surrounded himself with a Maoist-style personality cult. Under this quasi-religious totalitarianism, bad policy was implemented and there was no system for admitting failure and adjusting the approach. One of the Great Leader's tenets was a fierce kind of self-sufficiency called *juche*. Mao embraced the same concept under a different name. It is impractical, sentencing the people to permanent shortages of everything. The two leaders took the same approach and it led to the same disastrous outcome.

In China during the Great Leap Forward, the country suffered famine and mass deaths – an unacknowledged national catastrophe. The estimated toll of Mao's unnecessary famine is 30 to 45 million deaths, making it by far the deadliest episode of the deadliest century. But it's also the least publicised of the twentieth century's great atrocities, the one most successfully hushed up.

The point of departure between China's self-inflicted disaster and North Korea's is that when Mao died, the regime changed and policy changed with it. Deng Xiaoping, whom Mao had exiled to work in a tractor factory in the provinces, returned to Beijing, took power and launched China's economic opening in 1978. Instead of quixotic socialist self-sufficiency, China entered the world trading system. It was a corrective that allowed China to trade its way out of poverty into wealth – perhaps the most consequential act of postwar world history.

But when Kim Il Sung died, power transferred to his son, Kim Jong Il, the self-styled Dear Leader, in the manner of a monarchy. It was the first dynastic transfer of power in any communist regime. And even in death, Kim Snr retained the title of president in perpetuity. This allowed no opportunity for a reconsideration of North Korea's big policies. The Great Leader had been worshipped. Now the Great Leader and his son were both to be worshipped. The Dear Leader, like the Great, was infallible. Mistakes could not be admitted. The national desperation only worsened. When the Soviet Union collapsed and Moscow ended its subsidised supplies to Pyongyang, the full force of *juche*'s stupidity was allowed to bear down upon the people of North Korea.

So, as China demonstrated, dictatorship alone does not explain bad policy. Beijing's communist dictatorship has enough internal flexibility to allow for the correction of bad policy. North Korea's does not. The outlook for North Korea's long-suffering people is bleak.

South Korea, operating under US military protection, started life as a military dictatorship masquerading as a democracy, with a state-directed form of capitalism that delivered early economic success. But the people rose up and demanded that the generals give them freedom as well as rising incomes. With Molotov cocktail-throwing students in a tireless vanguard, the middle class eventually joined the street protests in 1987. The generals retreated. The people got what they wanted.

Democracy and its handmaidens – freedom of speech, freedom of association, freedom of worship and the separation of powers – have allowed for a constant process of trial and error, producing strong institutions and a winning combination of good policies.

Where the North fears its people and represses their skills as well as their aspirations, the South serves its people and develops their skills in pursuit of their aspirations. The people rise, and, with them, the nation.

But just as dictatorship does not guarantee bad policy, democracy does not guarantee good. Under either political system, countries make choices. It is, of course, entirely open to democracies to choose bad policy. And all do, at some point. The question is, can countries learn the right lessons from the experiences of good and bad policy? Can they keep the good and abandon the bad? Can countries learn from the experiences of others?

Australia's pathway to renovation and success is instructive to others as a good example, a model. It should give hope to others. Australia has its own unique history, but the good policies that it chose are not uniquely applicable to Australia. The question now facing Australia is whether it can learn the lessons of its own recent experience. Does Australia have the perspective to comprehend what it has done? And does it have the maturity to persist with the good ideas and abandon the bad?

3

ASHES AND ORE

One of Australia's great national rituals is the Test cricket series played against England. For Australians, it's a chance to re-create the day in 1882 when Australia's team gave England a shock from which it has never really recovered. It was the first time that anyone had ever beaten the British at their own game. The Australian victory meant that English cricket had died, as one observer wrote, and "the body will be cremated and the ashes taken to Australia." For Australia, it was a defining moment in crafting a national identity. For Britain, it was a hurtful blow to imperial pride.

As the annual ritual was being played out on the field in Sydney in 2007, a line formed outside the men's room at the Members' Stand. There was nothing unusual about that. It's a standard part of the ritual. But there was something very telling about the toilet queue on this particular day. The line included, among other citizens, the country's prime minister, John Howard. It also included the leader of the opposition and future prime minister Kevin Rudd. The Catholic archbishop of Sydney, Cardinal George Pell, was also biding his time. The three holders of high office took their places and waited patiently with the other patrons. None made any attempt to claim special privilege, pull rank or send a security detail to clear a path. And none of the ordinary mortals in the line felt any obligation to step aside for their leaders. In Australia, there was nothing unusual about that either.

This entrenched egalitarianism is one of the two defining strands that run through Australian attitudes. Citizens know that some among them will have more power and money than others. That's the natural and inevitable condition in any society. But according to the unspoken national ethos, no Australian is permitted to assume that he or she is better than any other Australian. How is this enforced? By the prompt corrective of levelling derision. It has a name – the "Tall Poppy Syndrome." The tallest flowers in the field will be cut down to the same size as all the others. This is sometimes misunderstood to mean that anyone successful will be destroyed. Not so. It isn't success that offends Australians. It's the affront committed by anyone who starts to put on superior airs.

The heir to the British throne, Prince Charles, had a taste of it when he was sent to high school in Australia for a couple of terms. "I have gone through my fair share of being called a Pommy bastard, I can assure you of that," he said in a speech to a crowd of Australians in London in early 2011. It was an experience that Charles hadn't encountered in a deferential, class-conscious Britain, and would never expect to. "But look what it has done for me. By God, it was good for the character. If you want to develop character, go to Australia." If Australia keeps its current constitutional arrangements, Charles, one day, will be its king. His treatment at the hands of his Australian schoolmates illuminates a key difference between Australian social attitudes and British.

Talk of egalitarianism in Australia is sometimes reduced to a discussion of the concept of "mateship." This is a subject that politicians love to discuss at every opportunity, because they can be fervently in favour without ever spending a cent on it. A society has different realms of egalitarianism. One is the egalitarianism of manners, and here, as the equal-opportunity toilet queue and Charles's schoolboy experience attest, there is an established equality in the way people mingle and deal with each other.

The point was illustrated in caricature in 2005 when a memo to security staff in Australia's Parliament House instructed attendants to greet all visitors respectfully "and not address them as 'mate' or use similar colloquialisms." When this was reported in the media, it produced a political storm. In a bipartisan show of indignation at the attempt to stifle this most Australian expression of instant familiarity, the prime minister, John Howard, denounced it as "absurd and ridiculous," while the opposition leader, Kim Beazley, defended the salutation "mate" as "a great part of Australian culture." Be warned. Any attempts at creating the appearance of class distinction, at putting on airs or tolerating them, will be rubbed out ruthlessly.

But beneath the manners and mannerisms, egalitarianism has a deeper and harder identity. It's called fairness. This has several manifestations. One is the fairness of outcomes. Another is the fairness of opportunity. A third is the fairness between one generation and another. Why does fairness matter? One reason is a basic truth about human nature. An American authority on financial crises, the late Charles Kindleberger, illustrated it this way: "In my talks about financial crises, I have polished one line that always gets a nervous laugh: 'There is nothing so disturbing to one's well-being and judgment as to see a friend get rich.'" Human beings are inherently sensitive to inequalities. One of the biggest global forces of the last century was a movement designed to eradicate inequality – it was called socialism and it convulsed world affairs for a century. Inequality and its obverse, equality, or fairness, are deeply powerful forces in human affairs.

Fairness is central to human happiness. It's well established that rising wealth adds to human happiness, but only up to a point. For a country as a whole, that point is a per capita income of around US$25,000 a year. Australia passed this level only about a decade ago, but is now more than double it. Beyond that point, income goes up but the national average level of self-declared "happiness" stalls. "After basic needs are met," writes the economist Carol Graham in her book *Happiness Around the World*, "other factors such as rising aspirations, relative income differences, and the security of gains, become increasingly important, in addition to income." It matters whether people are keeping up with the Joneses.

For instance, Graham compares a person from a poor country, Honduras, with one from a middle-income country, Chile. Each is among the poorest group in his country. The Chilean has twice as much income as the Honduran. Yet the Honduran, while poorer, is happier. Why? Because the fellow from Honduras isn't very far below the average for his country, but the Chilean is well below average for his. In other words, the number of dollars in your income isn't as important to your happiness as your perception of how you are faring compared to those around you. People don't seem to compare themselves to those in other countries but to the people they see around them – friends, family, neighbours, work-mates, the bloke in the car next to theirs.

The disquieting power of inequality is not a new discovery. Two centuries ago Napoleon Bonaparte said of religion that "it introduces into the thought of heaven an idea of equalisation, which saves the rich from being massacred by the poor." When a critical mass despairs of a fairer future, the poor throughout history have indeed murdered the rich. Even where unchecked inequality does not lead to revolution, it has corroded societies throughout history. "Since inequality grows in an expanding economy, a society may find itself divided between a cultured minority and a majority of men and women too unfortunate by nature or circumstance to inherit or develop standards of excellence and taste," wrote the husband-and-wife team of Will and Ariel Durant in *The Lessons of History*. They go on: "As this majority grows it acts as a cultural drag upon the minority; its ways of speech, dress, recreation, feeling, judgment, and thought spread upward, and internal barbarisation by the majority is part of the price that the minority pays for its control of educational and economic opportunity."

Inequality has not only led to "internal barbarisation" in the past. It is contributing to social ills and problems of quality of life today. An impressive body of new research demonstrates that it aggravates a broad range of our most troubling problems. Violent crime, depression, mental illness, obesity, educational failure and personal debt are among the social ills of wealthy societies that grow worse as inequality grows, and improve as equality increases. With some 200 published peer-reviewed papers testing the link between income inequality and health, and more than fifty on the link between income inequality and violence, "it is clear that greater equality, as well as improving the wellbeing of the whole population, is also the key to national standards of achievement and how countries perform in lots of different fields," the epidemiologists Richard Wilkinson and Kate Pickett wrote in their groundbreaking book *The Spirit Level*. This was not some starry-eyed socialist notion but an empirical reality. As Britain's Conservative prime minister, David Cameron, said in 2009: "Per capita GDP is much less significant for a country's life expectancy, crime levels, literacy and health than the size of the gap between the richest and poorest in the population ... We all know, in our hearts, that as long as there is deep poverty living systematically side by side with great riches, we all remain the poorer for it."

As I noted earlier, egalitarianism, including the concept of fairness, is one of the two defining strands running through Australian attitudes. The other is freedom. This is the right to make your own choices in life. Freedom, of course, includes political and legal rights. In the modern world, it also includes the freedom to choose a course of study or a field of work or to start a business.

Consider the extraordinary story of Andrew "Twiggy" Forrest, a sun-weathered entrepreneur from Western Australia. He was a little man in the business world, with a history of business failure and bankruptcy. His assets weren't much more than tremendous personal drive and, remarkably for a man who laboured under a childhood stammer, a silver tongue. But he had a plan.

In 2003 he bought into huge, undeveloped deposits of iron ore lying under the red deserts of West Australia. The ore was scattered across an area the size of Switzerland: 40,000 square kilometres. He decided that he would mine it to sell to a voracious China. The problem? There were two. He would need to raise several billion dollars. And he would be challenging two mighty conglomerates: Rio Tinto and BHP Billiton were two of the world's three biggest iron ore producers. These behemoths were not only the biggest companies in the country with combined revenues of $39 billion; at the time, they enjoyed control of the West Australian iron ore industry.

In fact, Forrest's mining licences were for prospects that Rio and BHP had once owned but allowed to expire – their rejects, in short. He was seeking to build a business on their rubbish. They also happened to own all the railway lines connecting the region of Forrest's prospects, in the Pilbara area, with the coast some 300 kilometres away. These twin problems were so daunting that no new producer had entered the region in forty years.

A West Australian mining magnate, Michael Kiernan of Territory Resources, recalled the initial reaction to Forrest's plan: he "comes up and says, 'I am going to be the third force in iron ore' when we already have two gorillas in BHP and Rio. Everyone said at the time, 'Get real, there are things you cannot do.'" The investment community agreed. Shares in his company, Fortescue Metals Group, traded for 2 cents apiece.

Forrest raised $3 billion from overseas investors. He built a mine, a port, an ore-crunching plant and the heaviest capacity railway line in the world. Cyclones disrupted progress and killed two construction workers. Machinery broke. The Establishment jeered. But he ended the gorillas' duopoly and created a multi-billion-dollar export business in record time. He went from drilling ore samples in the West Australian desert to shipping the first load of iron ore to China in just forty-two months. The company's share price hit $13 before tumbling in the global recession. But the shares were still valuable enough that "Twiggy" Forrest's 31.3 per cent share made him the third-richest man in Australia, with a net worth of about $6 billion in the 2011 *Business Review Weekly* rich list. In three years, he had vaulted over the three-generation fortune of James Packer.

With his new wealth and standing, Forrest launched an initiative to create 50,000 jobs for the country's perennially disadvantaged Aboriginal people. He also declared a plan to double his firm's iron ore output, which would make Fortescue a bigger producer than either Rio or BHP. When asked whether he felt vindicated, Forrest said, "For my part we have done no more than what we said we would do. No more and no less." He knows enough not to put on superior airs.

"Twiggy" Forrest is extraordinary. Yet he is also emblematic. He happened to have spotted his opportunity in the resources sector, the object of a global boom. But many other entrepreneurs have taken advantage of Australia's commercial and legal freedoms to succeed in fields other than mining.

To the longer-standing success stories of the bionic ear inventor, Cochlear Ltd, and the sleep apnea treatment innovator, ResMed, Australian entrepreneurs have added stories like that of CSL Ltd, formerly known as the Commonwealth Serum Laboratories. This federal government agency was privatised in 1994, transformed from a sleepy manufacturer of vaccines for the government to become a global biopharmaceutical firm generating billion-dollar annual profits. Another case study in entrepreneurial transformation is Orica. Founded to sell dynamite to the diggers on the Victorian goldfields in the 1850s, it had entered a long stagnation as the British-controlled Imperial Chemicals Industries (ICI). But when its British parent spun it off as an Australian firm in 1997, it recast itself and is now another $1 billion-a-year profit maker. Instead of just selling chemicals, it has become an innovative supplier of the services to go with the chemicals. So it doesn't just sell explosives to mines, for instance, but also the more profitable blast systems.

Professor Ian Frazer's pathbreaking work produced the world's first vaccine designed to prevent cancer. Cervical cancer had been estimated to kill about a quarter of a million women a year worldwide. Now women can vaccinate themselves with Frazer's treatment, sold under the tradenames Gardasil or Cervarix, and millions do every year. Frazer is now working on a vaccination against skin cancer.

Why does this commercial and entrepreneurial freedom matter? Because an entrepreneur invests money and hires people to conduct a business. If it prospers, they will invest more money and hire more people. Not only are they creating investment, jobs and wealth; they are also creating further opportunity, further freedom and further wealth, jobs and investment, a virtuous circle of expanding reward and opportunity. For the individual, it's important to have the opportunity of productive work. For the society, a country needs a thriving private sector to supply the tax revenues to pay for a high-quality public sector. Without tax revenues from private wages and profits, there can be no road and rail, law and order, schools and hospitals, water and sanitation.

Isn't all that entirely obvious? It may seem so today, but it was hotly contested for much of the twentieth century. The idea that economic freedom led to economic growth first flourished when it was put forward by Adam Smith in his 1776 magnum opus, *An*

Inquiry into the Nature and Causes of the Wealth of Nations. Free markets, secure property rights and limited government would incubate prosperity and growth.

How did freedom produce growth? It wasn't entirely obvious that a man busily working away at his own money-making would contribute to anything greater than his own bank account. But Smith conceived of an "invisible hand." In turning his own efforts towards making as much profit as possible, "every individual necessarily labours to render the annual revenue of the society as great as he can," wrote Smith. A man "intends only his own gain, and he is in this ... led by an invisible hand to promote an end which was no part of his intention." The invisible hand turned selfish pursuit of money into the greater good of the society, individual greed begetting a social good.

One of history's little jokes was that the man who conceived this marvellous invisible hand of the free market actually earned his livelihood as the very visible hand of the state, collecting customs monies for the government.

Smith's idea won wide acceptance among economists for a century or so, but then it came under severe challenge. As industrial capitalism grew, so did the brutal exploitation of many factory workers. In capitalism's early laissez-faire form, unchecked and unregulated factory owners went too far in creating exploitative inequality. The free market appeared to be creating more misery and suffering than social good.

Socialism and communism were history's responses to the slums, poorhouses and callous industrial maimings and deaths. The invisible hand of the market was directly challenged by the idea that the iron fist of central planning and socialism was more efficient and led to greater growth and fairer outcomes.

When the Soviet Union's economy boomed in the 1940s and '50s, state-directed planning appeared to have a good case. Soviet communism raised a poor agrarian society to the status of a major industrial economy in just three or four decades, with growth rates matching those of the US and Japan. Central planning can work to quickly raise the development of a poor country by commandeering labour and capital and funnelling it into a few chosen sectors. New industries can spring up where none previously existed. But where central planning has proved useful for helping some poor countries make quick leaps when playing industrial catch-up, it is no use whatsoever once they have caught up. Once a country reaches the middle-income rank, centrally controlled approaches have nothing to offer. Growth slows and economies stagnate, because public officials are poorly placed to decide how to allocate labour and capital in the most productive and profitable ways. That was the Soviet Union's fate, showing that the invisible hand of the market is better at responding to subtle shifts in demand and profitability than the iron fist of a state ministry.

China watched the Soviet sclerosis, recognised the problem and reformed in time to save itself from the same fate. With the Chinese flair for colourful metaphor, the central figure in China's economic opening, Deng Xiaoping, said: "It doesn't matter if a cat is black or white, so long as it catches mice." Ideological arguments over the superiority of socialism over capitalism are unimportant, Deng was saying. All that matters is performance. He wanted economic growth and prosperity. In a supreme act of political pragmatism, China embraced the free market from 1978. This decision raised more people out of poverty more quickly than at any time in human experience. It also powered China to rise from being a poor, weak and economically unimportant nation to become the world's second-biggest economy in just three decades.

The former US president Ronald Reagan liked to say that economists are people who see something that works in practice and say, "Yes, but will it work in theory?" If the real-world evidence were not enough, economists have indeed found that what appears to be a relationship between freedom and growth is not just coincidence but actually a strong and consistent link. A landmark study by James Gwartney, Robert Lawson and Walter Block, *Economic Freedom of the World: 1975–1995*, published by Canadian think-tank the Fraser Institute, showed a strong correlation between freedom and growth. Of the 102 countries studied, they found that the ten which had made the most progress in economic freedom increased their per capita income by an annual average of 2.7 per cent, after inflation. This group comprised Hong Kong, New Zealand, Singapore, the US, Switzerland, Britain, Canada, Ireland, Australia and Japan. All of the countries that moved toward economic freedom "achieved positive growth rates" of per capita income, they reported. In contrast, the countries with the largest reductions in economic freedom experienced an average decline in per capita GDP of 1 per cent per year. Only two of these countries were able to achieve positive rates of economic growth. This group was Zaire, Iran, Algeria, Syria, Nicaragua, Brazil, Burundi, Romania, Uganda and Zambia.

Much study since then has affirmed the relationship. If you want growth and prosperity, you need economic freedom. There is academic debate over whether a country needs to make continuous movement towards greater economic freedom to increase its growth performance – this would lead ultimately to a libertarian fantasy of extremely little regulation and tiny government with very few public services – or whether it's enough to achieve a certain threshold level. The global economic crisis of 2008 suggests powerfully that there is a threshold point of economic freedom required for good levels of growth, and that going much beyond that point can actually set growth back. The US, Britain and Europe suffered a disastrous banking collapse because of inadequate regulation, not because of excessive regulation. The academic world has yet to catch up with this real-world experience. But the conclusion seems to be that there is a commonsense threshold for creating enough economic freedom to foster a thriving private sector.

Fairness and freedom are the essential themes in Australia's history during the 110 short years since it became a unified country. All countries make their way by navigating these twin currents. In making practical choices of policy, the two are usually opposed: it's an established tenet of economic policy that equity and efficiency are to be traded off against each other. Perfect equity in incomes policy, for instance, would give everyone the same income, but fail to reward initiative and effort. The economy would wither. Perfect efficiency, on the other hand, would create a society of huge inequality. With no social safety net to catch the most vulnerable, exploitation and suffering would go unchecked. The key to crafting a country lies in setting the balance.

Abstract? Not at all. This is a subtler version of the same great clash that electrified the world for the half-century of the Cold War. Marxist communism seeks perfect equity by allocating all resources equally. Free-market capitalism seeks perfect efficiency by allocating all resources according to price. The polarisation of the world into capitalism and communism, efficiency and equity, is now extinct.

Capitalist countries responded to the threat of communist revolution by accommodating the demands for greater fairness. Governments took the harsh edges off capitalism to make it less brutal and more equitable. Public education, public health, labour laws, welfare support and other measures protected citizens from capitalism that was red in tooth and claw.

Communist states either collapsed and vanished or accommodated the need for more market efficiency. All countries now combine the concepts of efficiency and equity in some way. But the classic dilemma in making policy, the contest between equity and efficiency, remains. How has Australia chosen between them?

Since federation, Australia has alternated between an emphasis on one or the other. There have been only three broad phases. Equity was the dominant consideration from 1901 until 1983, from federation to the advent of the Hawke–Keating era. This was the nation-building phase. Fairness, equal treatment and social cohesion were paramount. In the second phase, efficiency was dominant. This ran from 1983 to 2007, from the beginning of the Hawke–Keating governments to the end of the Howard–Costello years. It was a repair phase. The nation had been built, but now its economy needed renovation. Third is the current phase, beginning in 2007 with the end of the Howard era and the advent of Labor under Kevin Rudd and Julia Gillard. It's too early to be definitive, yet the evidence to date suggests that the pendulum has swung back to favour equity.

Somewhere in the balance between fairness and freedom, equity and efficiency, the ashes and the ore, lies the explanation for what has emerged as the Australian Model. Just how fair is Australia today? And how free?

4

COME THE REVOLUTION?

Napoleon said that "religion is what keeps the poor man from murdering the rich." In the modern world, it's government. This occurs not so much through the police force, although that helps. Rather, the greatest protection for the rich is the acquiescence of the poor: the acceptance of their right to accumulate and enjoy wealth. It's up to governments to engineer the conditions for that acquiescence, by keeping society acceptably fair and keeping open the possibility that everyone has an opportunity to get at least reasonably rich.

Ever-increasing financial inequality is the normal and natural state of affairs in human society. And, through history, violent revolution has been the ultimate cure for this. "Since practical ability differs from person to person, the majority of such abilities, in nearly all societies, is gathered in a minority of men," observed Will and Ariel Durant in *The Lessons of History*. "The concentration of wealth is a natural result of this concentration of ability, and regularly recurs in history." It may reach a point "where the strength of number in the many poor rivals the strength of ability in the few rich; then the unstable equilibrium generates a critical situation, which history has diversely met by legislation redistributing wealth or by revolution distributing poverty." They conclude that "all economic history is the slow heartbeat of the social organism, a vast systole and diastole of concentrating wealth and compulsive recirculation."

To manage the tide of money flooding to the rich, governments everywhere set up policy structures to stand against the flow and keep it in check. The most familiar of these is the progressive income tax, with higher rates imposed on bigger incomes. Part of those taxes goes towards common goods that everyone enjoys equally – clean air and water, national security, absence of epidemics. And part is redistributed to help redress inequalities, paying to support the unemployed, the disabled, lower-income families. Other common levelling structures are property taxes, capital gains taxes, regulated wages, labour conditions, consumer protection laws and the means testing of welfare payments to exclude the rich. Governments everywhere do all of this, but there are wide differences in how they do it and the outcomes they create.

Australians are tough judges of the fairness of their society. Consider the following criticisms.

"Australian society is increasingly polarised," said Dr Greg Martin, an academic at the University of Western Sydney, in 2008, to the point where it had created "a new breed of underdog." He argued that "the 'disrespect' shown individual consumer-citizens who are disadvantaged by the prevailing predominance of the market is 'un-Australian,' since it runs counter to quintessentially Australian values such as a fair go for all and concern for underdogs." His academic paper on the subject, in a play on the idea of the Lucky Country, was titled "Tough luck!"

In the same year the *Australian Financial Review* published a piece headed: "Australia and the American way of life." Emma Connors reported that "the evidence appears to be firming that Australia is now more economically divided than just a few decades ago." Losing its egalitarian streak, Australia increasingly resembled America, increasingly unfair and with increasingly rigid segregation of rich and poor.

In 2011 the leader of one of the more important unions, Louise Tarrant of United Voice – formerly known as the Liquor, Hospitality and Miscellaneous Union – said in a speech that economic growth "has proved a spectator sport for the millions of workers left behind." And in 2010 a business columnist with the *Age*, Leon Gettler, wrote: "There is something unsettling about the latest revelations from Credit Suisse that Australia is the third-richest country in the world."

Finally, the head of the country's peak social welfare body, Dr Cassandra Goldie of the Australian Council of Social Security, issued a statement in March 2011 headlined "Inequality is growing in Australia." She said that Australia needed to "find ways to deal with these growing problems and reverse the current trend of growing inequality which threatens to make us poorer as a nation."

With all of this expert opinion expressing so much concern, surely Australia is suffering a serious problem of inequality? How bad is it really? Let's look at the particular angles taken by each expert.

Dr Greg Martin explains that his argument is based on "a personal narrative or 'autoethnography' ... used to illuminate these issues via the author's own experiences of renting accommodation in Sydney." Martin tells his personal tale of tough luck with a landlord and extrapolates it into an assertion about the state of the entire society. We are left to wonder at whose "tough luck" he's really writing about, Australia's or his own. He actually published this as an academic paper. This is an object lesson against allowing your view of an entire country to be determined by narrow personal experience alone.

The *Financial Review*'s Emma Connors, concerned that Australia was now living "the American way of life," reported that sales of Krug and Dom Perignon champagnes had soared, and so had sales of fancy yachts. "Such conspicuous consumption is partly responsible for a widespread belief that Australia is drifting away from the notion that this is a fair place for all. The data is inconclusive but poll your average weekend barbeque and you'll find most agreeing that this country is more divided than it was just a few decades ago." This is quite accurate. The "widespread belief" is one thing, the data another. A consensus cooked up around the barbeque does not necessarily equate with hard fact.

What about the point by union leader Louise Tarrant that economic growth "has proved a spectator sport for the millions of workers left behind"? It's a good line and she won some headlines with it. It was created, however, in another country. As she acknowledged, Tarrant took the line from the US economist Paul Krugman, who wrote it in his *New York Times* column in 2006. He was making the point that in 2004 the American economy grew by 4 per cent yet the purchasing power of the median American family fell. Like Connors, Tarrant is casually assuming that Australian experience is following American. But Australia's experience in this has not been America's. No matter how much time Australians spend looking at America, we are not America. These are examples of how conflating Australia with the US can be quite misleading.

It was Australia's run-up in wealth that caught the attention of Leon Gettler. And it is, indeed, striking. It's been one of the most rapid in the world: private wealth per adult tripled from $103,000 to $320,000 in the ten years to 2010, according to the international wealth survey by the bank Credit Suisse. This is the value of all cash and shares and bonds and real estate and other investments, minus debt. The wealthiest people on earth on this measure were the Swiss with an average $370,000 per adult, followed by the Norwegians with $326,000, and Australians in third place. Next came Singaporeans and the French, each with $255,000.

But why should Gettler find this "unsettling"? Shouldn't it be a welcome development that the people of Australia have improved their relative wealth, their ability to provide for themselves, their independence? Isn't this a source of national strength, not a source of worry? And $320,000 might be a lot by international comparison, but it's still only about half the average price of a house in Sydney or two-thirds the average price of a house in Melbourne.

Gettler runs through two main reasons why he finds the private wealth of Australians "unsettling." First, because it's what he calls "housing-centric." Sixty-four per cent of Australian private wealth is held in the form of housing, making it vulnerable to the vagaries of the housing market. This is true but not terribly meaningful. Australians do hold more of their wealth in real estate than the global average of 49.5 per cent. But so do many others. The French proportion is the same as Australia's. New Zealand's 74 per cent and India's 83 per cent are much higher. But so what? Housing wealth is indeed vulnerable to falls in the market, but other forms of wealth are just as vulnerable. Share values rise and fall with the stock market. Cash holdings are subject to changes in inflation and taxation. Overseas investments are vulnerable to currency swings. This is an excuse, not a reason, to be unsettled by rising wealth.

Second, Gettler says that he's troubled because of the inequality involved. Of course private wealth is held unequally. It's what defines rich and poor. But in Australia, it's held less unequally than in almost all of the other countries at the top of the table. This is detailed in the Credit Suisse data, and we'll see the key figures on this shortly. But Gettler didn't mention this important point. And one of the very reasons that it's better distributed in Australia is because home ownership is relatively high at around 70 per cent. Widespread home ownership helps spread the wealth. This is an advantage of Australia's "housing-centric" wealth. For someone concerned about inequality, as Gettler seems to be, this is surely a reason to be reassured, not unsettled.

Finally, there was the claim by Dr Cassandra Goldie, the head of the social welfare lobby group ACOSS, that inequality in Australia is growing. Is she right?

Let's consider the evidence. There are several kinds of inequality. One is the inequality of outcomes. Another is the inequality of opportunity. A third is the inequality between one generation and another.

Taking each in turn, first, how equal are outcomes in Australia? Here we will look at income and wealth in particular. There are two common ways of looking at income inequality. One is to look at the trend through time, to see if incomes are growing more or less equal. On this measure, Australian incomes have indeed grown more unequal in recent years. Goldie is right.

The authoritative source on this, the Australian Bureau of Statistics, compared income distribution over the twelve years from 1995–96 and 2007–08. This happens to have been almost precisely the term of the Howard government, which ran from March 1996 to November 2007. The bureau looks at three chunks, low-, middle- and high-income households.

In the first decade of the Howard era, inequality actually narrowed. This was completely at odds with the rhetoric about Howard, who was routinely accused of waging a neoliberal war against working people. In fact, largely because of his family payments system, Howard actively redistributed income from the richest to the middle- and lower-income brackets. In net terms, only one Australian worker in four was paying any tax. Most were receiving government payments and benefits bigger than their tax bills. But in the last couple of years of the Howard term, inequality worsened. The reasons for this are not dissected by the bureau, but probably include the first wave of the mining boom, which boosted mining-related incomes, and the final Howard–Costello tax cuts, which favoured better-paid workers.

The disposable income of the lowest-paid segment of the population rose by 12 per cent in those twelve years, adjusted for inflation and for the number of people per household. In other words, the 12 per cent measures the change in actual buying power of a household.

The middle-income household enjoyed an average improvement in buying power of 14 per cent. For the upper-income group, the improvement was 20 per cent, the bureau calculated. So the group with the highest incomes enjoyed the biggest improvement in its command over goods and services. The lowest-income group enjoyed the smallest. The middle group was in the middle. So the gap between the best- and worst-paid segments widened.

Another way of analysing the same information is to look at shares of income. The low-paid group was paid a total of 11 per cent of all household income in 1995–96. By 2007–08 that had shrunk slightly to 10.1 per cent. The middle's share fell slightly from 17.7 to 17 per cent. The top group's share rose from 37.3 to 40.5 per cent.

So by either measure, income inequality has grown. By how much? The statisticians of the world have a yardstick to reduce inequality measures down to a single number. It's called the Gini Index, named after its Italian inventor, Corrado Gini. It's a statistical measure of the divergence between rich and poor. Where income distribution is perfectly equal, the Gini Index is 0. In a perfectly unequal society it would be 1. Australia's score in 2007–08 was 0.319. Using this index, the bureau concludes that income inequality in Australia increased by 7.7 per cent in those dozen years.

So it's not a big increase, but it's real. Interestingly, inequality increased more sharply than this in the years of the Hawke and Keating Labor governments. An important point to note is that Australian inequality was not on a steady worsening trend. It has oscillated, sometimes improving, sometimes deteriorating. Whether it has grown better or worse depends on where you draw your measuring points. So it worsened in the twelve years to 2008, but, as the OECD noted, the gap narrowed sharply in the eight years to 2008.

How unequal are Australian incomes compared to the rest of the world? This is the second common way of looking at income inequality. Among the developed countries, Australia is in the middle. Using the Gini index, the UN ranks Australia's level of income equality twentieth among the forty-two countries that it groups together as enjoying "very high development." On this measure, Australian incomes are more unequal than those in Norway, Ireland, Canada or Japan, for instance, but more equal than incomes in Britain, the US, Italy or Singapore.

So Australia's inequality of incomes is mid-range among the rich countries of the world, and grew slightly more unequal in the twelve years to 2007–08. While we're on the subject of inequality of outcomes, what about wealth? How great is Australian inequality on that measure?

The latest authoritative data from the ABS is for the two years to 2006. In that time average net household wealth – assets minus debt – in Australia grew by 14 per cent to $563,000. Households in the poorest fifth saw an average gain of 6 per cent to $27,300 in wealth, those in the middle gained 9 per cent to $341,700, and those in the richest fifth gained 18 per cent to $1.72 million. The richest profited most because they held the type of assets enjoying the fastest run-up – shares and superannuation accounts. (This isn't some traditional class-based measure of wealth, by the way. The definition of "rich" in these years includes homeowners in the main mining states, Western Australia and Queensland, and those who always do best in wealth measures, people aged 45 to 65.)

But then the global financial crisis hit. The Reserve Bank estimated that the crisis had something of a levelling effect, with the richest losing an average 15 per cent of their wealth and the rest losing 10 per cent in 2008. The wealth of the richest fifth would have been taken back to a little below its 2006 level, the bank estimated, while the rest would have stayed a little ahead. In the time since, we can assume that those same types of asset favoured by the rich have recovered fastest, but we await further statistical studies to bring us fully up to date.

So by income and by wealth, inequality in Australia has widened in the last decade. But it is not true that the rich got richer and the poor got poorer. In both income and in wealth, all income groups improved their lot considerably. The rich got richer, but the poor didn't get poorer. In fact, the poor grew less poor.

Here is the key thing that divides the Australian experience from the American. While the middle-income and poorer segments actually suffered cuts to incomes and wealth in the US, in Australia all groups gained in income and in wealth. No group – bottom, middle or top – grew worse off for having lived in Australia. The purchasing power of the average Australian income grew by 70 per cent in the decade to 2010, and the average household wealth doubled, despite the global financial crisis. Australia's performance was among the strongest anywhere in the world. And every group benefited from that national enrichment. They didn't benefit equally, but all benefited.

Australian household wealth is obviously held unequally. But how does this inequality compare to the rest of the world? On this measure, Australia ranks tenth out of twenty-one developed countries cited by Credit Suisse. The distribution of Australian household wealth is not as equal as in Norway, Canada or Austria, but it's more equal than in Sweden, Switzerland, France or Singapore. So with equality of wealth, as with income, Australia sits in the middle of the rich countries.

The second major category of fairness is the equality of opportunity in a society. This is not a matter of whether citizens have equal outcomes, but whether they have equal opportunities to improve their outcomes by dint of effort, to move from lower to upper levels of income and wealth.

Consider the mobility of people in poverty. A common definition of a person in poverty is someone receiving less than half the national median income. A major survey by the Melbourne Institute tracked a panel of Australian households over several years. It found that 12 per cent of households met this definition of impoverishment in one year. But only 6 per cent had an income this low for two years running. After three years, just 4 per cent were still under the line. This outcome, published in 2005, shows a high degree of mobility.

Where you end up need have no relationship to where you begin.

As the OECD reported in 2008: "Australia is one of the most socially mobile countries in the OECD. What your parents earned when you were a child has very little effect on your own earnings. Australia's performance in this respect is much more like those of Denmark and Canada, not Italy, the United Kingdom and the United States, where there is much less mobility. Similarly, the educational attainment of the parent affects the educational achievements of the child less than in most other countries."

The third principal category of fairness is one that is usually overlooked – how fair one generation is to another. If today's adults help themselves to future income streams by running up the national debt, we leave a bequest of debt to tomorrow's adults. It means that our children and grandchildren are paying for our self-indulgence. And they are powerless to resist our present depredations on their future earnings. It would be a cruel parent who bought himself a fancy house by pledging the future wages of his infant children to service the mortgage. But that is exactly what the people of most countries are doing. It's known as intergenerational equity, or, more accurately, inequity.

It would be a myopic discussion of inequality that didn't look at it, because it is an enormous problem across most of the world. Who could be a more powerless victim than someone not yet born, not old enough to understand, or not old enough to vote? But this is exactly the reason that it's usually carefully ignored in discussions of inequality. It's extremely unfair, it's very uncomfortable, and the victims aren't complaining about it. Yet.

A country's government debt reaches a tipping point. Until that point, the debt is whatever a government adds to it, plus interest payments. But when it hits the tipping point – with the cumulative effect of the debt, interest payments on it and the interest that becomes payable on the interest – it is transformed. It starts to snowball, with the compounding interest adding endlessly to the total owed. A government doesn't need to add another cent in borrowings. The debt just grows of its own accord. When's that critical point? The World Bank estimates it to be when gross government debt hits the equivalent of about 80 to 90 per cent of the Gross Domestic Product (GDP), varying with the rate of interest payable.

How do countries measure up to this? The average debt for all countries of the world is about 60 per cent. Some countries, with sovereign default looming, threw themselves in 2010 on the mercy of the International Monetary Fund and the European Union to stay solvent. These include Ireland, Greece and Portugal. According to a uniform measure by the OECD, when these countries lost control of their debts, Ireland's gross government debt was the equivalent of 105 per cent of GDP, Greece's was 129.2, and Portugal's was 92.9.

Now consider the world's major developed economies. In 2011, gross government debt as a percentage of GDP reached 81.3 in Germany, 85.5 in Canada, 88.6 in Britain, 97.1 in France, 98.5 in the US, 132.7 in Italy and 204.2 in Japan. In other words, all the world's biggest developed countries have reached, or are approaching, the tipping point where their national debts will take on a life of their own. Without dramatic intervention, these countries will not be in control of their debts – rather, the debts will be in control of the countries. "We project that gross general government debt in the advanced economies will rise from an average of about 75 per cent of GDP at end-2007 to about 110 per cent of GDP at end-2014," projected the IMF's deputy managing director, John Lipsky. This even eclipses the fiscal crisis that followed World War Two, when the cost of the war and reconstruction peaked in 1950.

Yet the US, Japan and Western Europe were able to overcome their 1950 debt burdens pretty successfully. Can't they do it again? Lipsky made this point: "This surge in government debt is occurring at a time when pressure from rising health and pension spending is building up." Not only do the main powers of the West have huge and unsustainable debt burdens but their people have high expectations. The voters expect their living standards will only improve and their entitlements are secure. There are aging populations in the main powers of Europe and Japan, though the problem is milder in the US. This coming demographic tsunami is "not a transitory wave like the baby *boom* many affluent countries experienced in the 1950s or the baby *bust* that they experienced in the 1930s," said the Centre for Strategic and International Studies in its 2008 report, *The Graying of the Great Powers*. "It is, instead, a fundamental shift with no parallel in the history of humanity." The last time public debt burdens were this heavy, not a single country in the world had a median age higher than thirty-six. Today, half of Western Europe has one over forty. This means bigger health and welfare costs with a smaller base of taxpaying workers to fund them.

The only solutions are for these countries to perform drastic surgery on the living standards of their people – with big tax increases, dramatic spending cuts, or both – or be forced into austerity by the financial markets or the IMF. The young people of today, and the generation about to be born, are going to inherit this legacy of indulgence and incompetence. They will get the bills without enjoying the benefits. This is profoundly unfair. And how does Australia compare? Gross Australian government debt as a proportion of GDP in 2011 was 25.9 per cent and the OECD projected it to rise to 26.8 per cent in 2012. Our Treasury projects that it will taper off after that. That is the lowest among OECD countries and compares very happily to the OECD average of 102.8 per cent. The Australian government budget is projected to be running a surplus from 2012–13, and it plans to use the surpluses to pay off its debt fully by 2018–19.

The grown-ups of today's Australia are, in this sense, perhaps the only true grown-ups of the developed world. They will leave their younger generations no crushing debt burdens, no expensive unpaid bills for sumptuous meals eaten long ago. Today's older generations in Australia are leaving an inheritance of a debt-free future just as the Americans, the Japanese and the Western Europeans – the principal powers of the Western bloc – are bequeathing painful shortfalls to their coming generations. All countries have rising generations. Some will be trying to rise under the crushing burden of accumulated government debt. Younger Australians, almost uniquely among the rich countries, will not. This intergenerational fairness is a big and lasting achievement.

On the first type of fairness, the fairness of outcomes, Australian inequality has been widening in recent years. Measured as inequality of income and inequality of wealth, Australian policies have allowed the rich to move further ahead of the poor. There is scope for governments to redress the seemingly inexorable encroachment of inequality. But no income group has been left out of the wealth increase. It is not true, as it is in America, that "growth has proved a spectator sport" for those at the bottom.

The incomes and the wealth of the low-, middle- and upper-income groups have all been rising in the last decade or so in Australia. And by international standards, Australian economic equality is in the middle. On the second type, the fairness of opportunity, Australians have ample opportunity to move out of poverty, to transcend their parents' income category, to build the lives they choose for themselves. Economic equality is not enforced in Australia, but it is enabled. By international comparison, Australia's performance has improved in recent years to be better than the average for the rich countries. On the third type, the fairness of how one generation treats another, Australia's performance is exemplary, and almost uniquely so. Australia's fast-rising prosperity has been enjoyed unequally, but fairly. The revolution seems no closer. Could it be fairer? Yes. But perfect economic equality is impossible, even, as recent history teaches us, in communist societies. And trying to get there would allow no room for the other essential quality in the creation of a successful modern society, freedom.

5

LOW-FAT COUNTRY*

If you have too much cholesterol or other fat build up in your arteries, you feel feeble and you could die prematurely. Doctors may decide to insert stents into your arteries. A stent is a tiny metal cage that slides inside an artery, crushes the fats into the artery walls and opens it to restore normal blood flow. You don't need the stents after a few weeks or months, but doctors leave them in because it's too traumatic for you to go through more surgery to have them out. This is usually fine, though a small fraction of people, about one in 200, will develop dangerous thrombosis because of the stents. But a US company, REVA Medical, invented a better way – clever plastic stents that gradually dissolve harmlessly into the bloodstream after a few years. No surgery required. When REVA wanted to raise money on the stock market to finance its venture, it could have chosen to list its shares in the US, London, Hong Kong, Canada or pretty much anywhere. The company decided to list in Australia. Why?

A few years earlier, the obvious market for a start-up medical technology firm would have been New York's NASDAQ exchange, the world's preferred nurturer of plucky entrepreneurs. NASDAQ would list anything that seemed like a good idea, and many that didn't, whether the venture was generating any money or not. But investors had suffered searing losses in the 2008 financial crisis, and many of the very worst wipeouts were among the NASDAQ

---

* Guaranteed to contain less fat than most competing brands.

start-ups that were making little or no revenue. And this was starting to look like more than a casual one-off. Following the mass financial bloodshed of the 2000 tech wreck, when the NASDAQ's dotcom craze ended in disaster, it was looking like a trend. In a belated bid for greater investor confidence, NASDAQ toughened its listing rules and decided it would no longer list companies with under US$100 million in revenue. REVA Medical didn't clear that hurdle, so it looked elsewhere. It wanted a big exchange, preferably a prestigious main board rather than a secondary one, with credibility and deep liquidity. As a bonus, a country with a well-developed medical establishment would help with clinical trials. Another advantage would be a country with established investment ties to Asia.

In London the firm would have been forced onto the secondary board. In Hong Kong it would have had to pay at least $5 million, and as much as $10 million, in fees to lawyers and accountants. Canada would have suited, but lacked the connections to Asia that Australia's exchange offered. So REVA Medical ended up listing in Sydney, the sixth most heavily traded stock exchange in the world and the second most traded in Asia, behind Tokyo and ahead of Hong Kong and Shanghai. The company listed on the main board, with deep liquidity, low fees and strong subscriptions. Australian investors put up an initial $40 million, British investors another $20 million, Americans $15 million and Hong Kong investors a further $10 million for a total of $85 million. Its shares floated at $1.10 apiece and traded around $1.30 thereafter, gratifying its owners and its backers. When it listed two days before Christmas 2010, it was the world's biggest initial public offering of any company not yet generating revenue, according to Kim Jacobs of Inteq in Sydney, a corporate adviser whose clients include REVA. "Australia overall is a good platform. Australia is recognised internationally for its medical standards. Approval from Australia's TGA [Therapeutic

Goods Administration] is well recognised. The reputation of our financial markets is excellent, and we have an established super-highway to Asia," says Jacobs. "Companies like this can incubate in Australia and list elsewhere when they're ready. They love us."

These advantages rest on other foundations that are so obvious that they are easily overlooked: the rule of law and an independent judiciary so that investors know contracts are enforceable; an overall level of regulation that is at least no more onerous than in comparable countries; high-quality professionals at internationally competitive rates so that legal and financial support services are adequate; and manageable levels of tax.

REVA wasn't the first innovative US medical device company to choose to list its shares in Australia. The manufacturer of the world's smallest heart pumps, Heartware, went before it, a $32.4 million Sydney listing that is now capitalised at $1.3 billion on the US exchanges. Its pumps are today keeping more than 800 people alive.

And REVA won't be the last. GI Dynamics is to follow in 2011. It's a company with a startlingly promising treatment for two modern epidemics: obesity and Type 2 diabetes. After having a sock-like filter, the so-called EndoBarrier, inserted into their intestines with an endoscope, obese people lost an average 20 to 25 kilograms (based on 450 people who have so far undergone clinical trials). And in 95 per cent of the people suffering Type 2 diabetes, their disorder came under control. After a year, the EndoBarrier is removed in a five-minute operation and need not be revisited for three to five years. The treatment costs some $4,000. The exact working of the EndoBarrier is not understood, but the European Union has granted it medical approval. Its potential market, 52 million obese people, is worth $200 billion. It will list its shares on the Australian stock exchange for the same reasons that REVA Medical did.

This isn't because Australia is any sort of competitive threat to the US. It's not. Or that Australia has mastered the art of creating masses of high-tech start-ups. It hasn't. The point is that Australia has the advantages as well as the freedoms that allow first-rate opportunities for entrepreneurs, even American ones. And they're not always in the areas you'd expect. Some of the key Australian attractions for these companies are longstanding. Others, like the advantage over NASDAQ in listing rules for start-up firms, have only just emerged after the global financial crisis. But the old dirge about Australia as some sort of hopelessly over-regulated, over-taxed horror story for international business is no longer true.

Of the ten richest Australians, six made their fortunes themselves. Only four inherited any real wealth. This is a telltale sign that Australia is not a nation of entrenched wealth and limited opportunity but one of openness and economic mobility. While James Packer, Anthony Pratt and Gina Rinehart inherited billions from their dads, and John Gandel got off to a running start as heir to his parents' Sussan clothing chain, the other six among Australia's richest billionaires started with little or nothing.

Before he founded Westfield, Frank Lowy was a Czech refugee from Hitler's Europe who started in business by opening a small-goods store in Sydney's western suburbs. Before the success of Fortescue Metals Group, Andrew Forrest was a determined Perth prospector recovering from a business failure. Harry Triguboff, the son of refugees fleeing Chinese communism, worked a northern Sydney milk round to finance his first block of real estate before parlaying it into the Meriton Apartments empire. Clive Palmer, son of a cinema-owning small businessman, dropped out of a journalism degree to start small-time speculation in Brisbane real estate before moving into the iron ore trade. Chris Wallin was a salaried geologist with the Queensland Mines Department before striking out on his own to find coal in vast quantities. Ivan Glasenberg, who started life in South Africa, is another self-made success. Son of a Lithuanian luggage maker, he was intrigued by the possibilities of trading when he saw a merchant profit by sourcing wax from South America to sell to Japan. He worked his way up through the commodity trading business to become chief executive of Swiss-based Glencore, which has been dubbed the biggest company you've never heard of. When the firm went public in 2011, his share was worth $8.8 billion.

For comparison, of America's ten richest, six inherited wealth and four made it themselves. While Bill Gates, Warren Buffett, Larry Ellison and Michael Bloomberg are self-made men, David Koch, his brother Charles Koch and the four Waltons – Christy, Jim, Alice and Rob – all inherited their fortunes. This is just one rather limited measure of economic freedom, but more systematic studies also find that Australia is among the freest economies in the world.

By the leading international measure, Australians enjoy a freedom of enterprise even greater than the fabled American entrepreneurialism. A conservative US think-tank, the Heritage Foundation, and a pro-capital US newspaper, the *Wall Street Journal*, collaborate annually to compare 183 countries. "Economic freedom is the fundamental right of every human to control his or her own labour and property," say the authors of this Index of Economic Freedom.

The ranking in 2011 scored Hong Kong first, Singapore second and Australia third. They were followed by New Zealand, Switzerland and Canada. Rounding out the top ten were Ireland, Denmark, the US and Bahrain. Many Australians will be surprised that their country's private sector is so lightly burdened. They usually hear only the complaints from business about the obstacles, not the ease. Industry, always anxious to make more money for less effort, will never spend precious public airtime thanking its host country. It uses its access to the public consciousness to demand more advantage. Nor will companies give credit to host countries or governments when chief executives can take the credit themselves.

In its overview of Australia, the Index of Economic Freedom says: "Australia's modern and competitive economy performs well on many of the 10 economic freedoms. The country has a strong tradition of openness to global trade and investment, and transparent and efficient regulations are applied evenly in most cases. An independent judiciary protects property rights, and the level of corruption is quite low." Of the ten categories, Australia's strongest scores were for financial freedom, labour freedom, property rights and business freedom. Its weakest scores were for trade freedom, investment freedom, government spending and fiscal freedom. Its scores on monetary freedom and freedom from corruption were middling.

The component that will embarrass both sides of Australian politics is the measure of labour freedom. Australia's employers and their lobbies, like the Australian Chamber of Commerce and Industry, and their political proxy, the Liberal Party, routinely complain about the restrictiveness of labour laws. Employers always want to drive down the cost of labour. Their champions will always push for better terms for their constituents. But the Index of Economic Freedom found that Australian employers actually have very little to complain about compared to those in the rest of the world.

Labour laws handcuff employers more tightly in every country of the world bar four. The only countries with more relaxed labour laws are the US, Singapore, Bahrain and Montenegro. The Index's authors wrote of Australia: "Highly flexible employment regulations enhance employment and productivity growth. The non-salary cost of employing a worker is moderate, and dismissing a redundant employee is costless. Unemployment remains well below the OECD average." The business lobby and political conservatives will not want this broadcast because it shows that they have succeeded so well that there is very little left for them to demand, relative to labour laws in the rest of the world. And the unions and their political proxy, the Labor Party, will want this kept quiet because it suggests that they could have done much better at winning more protective working conditions for their members.

So it's inconvenient for both sides of politics, but true nonetheless, that in the spectrum of real-world possibilities Australian employers have a great degree of freedom in the hiring, firing and managing of their workforces.

The World Bank, the big Washington-based international institution through which rich countries lend to poor, has a similar index, its Ease of Doing Business Index. It rates Australia lower, in tenth position, but still assesses its business conditions as easier than those of 173 other countries. Where the Index of Economic Freedom covers broad areas, the World Bank's index is a narrower tally of nine very specific indicators. Of these nine indicators, Australia stands out in the ease of starting a business. While it takes an average of two weeks in the OECD countries to get official permission to register a business and start operating, in Australia it takes only two days. While registration costs an average of 5 per cent of annual per capita income, in Australia it costs just 0.7 per cent, otherwise known as $400. And while the average developed country requires a business owner to put up 15 per cent of their per capita income to start a company, in Australia it's zero. Only in New Zealand is it easier to start a firm. Australia's worst performance among the nine indicators is in dealing with construction permits, where the country ranks sixty-third. Why? Because it takes an average of eighty-four days to get the electricity connected, and ninety days and $2,900 to file a development application.

The nine countries listed ahead of Australia for the ease of doing business in this ranking are Singapore, Hong Kong, New Zealand, Britain, the US, Denmark, Canada, Norway and Ireland. The ones immediately following Australia are Saudi Arabia, Georgia, Finland, Sweden, Iceland, South Korea, Estonia, Japan, Thailand, Mauritius and Malaysia.

Does Australia have troublesome and costly regulations? Absolutely. No one has put a credible overall price tag on them, but we have a few sketchy indicative points of the recent costs of regulation. First, the OECD estimated in 1998 that complying with all regulations cost small- and medium-sized Australian firms an annual $17 billion in total. Second, in 2001–02 the federal government spent $4.5 billion on the administrative costs of its regulatory bodies. Third, in Victoria alone there were sixty-nine separate state-based bodies regulating business in 2004.

The Business Council of Australia published an eye-opening and influential report in 2005 that found the national parliament had passed as much legislation in the four years from 2000 to 2003 as it had in the first seven decades of Australian federation. Commonwealth primary legislation was proliferating at the rate of 350 pages for every week of parliamentary sitting. This puts an entirely new complexion on the argument that Australian politicians should spend more time in parliamentary sittings. There is a persistent popular notion that unless parliament is sitting, the politicians are somehow not working hard enough. But when parliament does sit, this is what it does – it makes new laws. And at a very great rate.

The annual rate of growth in the sheer volume of national legislation was 10 per cent, more than twice as fast as the national economic growth rate. And this was under a conservative government, supposedly the enemy of big government and the regulatory state.

The Business Council report helped galvanise both sides of politics. The Howard government in 2006 set up an Office of Best

Practice Regulation and introduced a requirement that all national agencies assess the regulatory impact of any new legislation before presenting it to the parliament. The Rudd Labor Party took power in 2007 with a promise to cut one existing regulation for every new one that it introduced. Neither pledge was fully delivered, but these plus other improvements put new points of scrutiny into the system of regulation. The national effort was also introduced to the states through the Council of Australian Governments, and in 2010 the OECD was sufficiently impressed to declare: "Australia represents in many ways a 'role model' for OECD countries in its proactive approach to regulatory reform." And even the Business Council, in its annual scorecard of regulatory performance, though troubled that the effort at the national level was sagging, awarded the federal government and every state government a rating of at least "adequate," with the national government and most states winning an "adequate to good" score.

It is the standard complaint of every business person that taxes are too high and the compliance burden too great. Yet corporate Australia has less to complain about than its counterparts in most countries. Among the thirty-four developed countries of the OECD, Australian firms benefit from the tenth lowest tax burden, according to the World Bank's 2010 comparison of taxes on commercial profits.

This is not a simple comparison of the formal corporate tax rate. The standard rate on company profits in Australia is 30 per cent. On this simple measure, Australia taxes company profits a little more heavily than the OECD average rate of 28.5 per cent, but more lightly than the average rate of OECD countries weighted according to size, which is 35.6 per cent. But these simple rates of tax don't allow for the multitude of deductions and charges and allowances and refunds and credits that are applied with wild variations from country to country.

The World Bank's comparison puts a standard framework across all countries to measure "the amount of taxes and mandatory contributions payable by businesses after accounting for allowable deductions and exemptions as a share of commercial profits." It excludes taxes withheld by companies, like PAYG or GST, to be later remitted to the tax authorities. And it finds that Australian companies pay 47.9 per cent of their commercial profits in tax, much higher than the pro forma tax rate of 30 per cent. It shows that Australia's private sector pays a much higher share of profits in tax than New Zealand's 34.3 per cent or Britain's 37.3 or Norway's 41.6. But it also shows that the Australian rate is quite similar to the US rate of 46.8 per cent. It's also lower than Germany's 48.2 or Spain's 56.5 or France's 65.8. Taking developing countries into account, Australia's corporate tax burden is also much lighter than China's 63.8 per cent. Seven countries actually taxed their companies more than they earned. That is, they paid tax at an effective rate of over 100 per cent. You certainly wouldn't want to try to turn a profit in the Republic of the Congo, where you'd have paid $3 in tax for every $1 in profits. Which may be why just about nobody does.

The burden of time it takes to calculate and prepare and pay tax is also lighter for Australian companies than for those in most other countries, as measured by the World Bank. In Australia's case it was 109 hours in 2010, making it the fifth shortest among the thirty-four OECD nations. The least troublesome jurisdiction among the developed countries was Luxembourg with a 59-hour tax task. Overall, including the developing countries, the unchallenged winner was the Maldives, where it took exactly no time at all. This South Asian archipelago nation with only 400,000 people relies on tourism taxes for 90 per cent of all revenues. It's also the first country to hold an underwater cabinet meeting, a gimmick to draw international attention to its plight as one of the world's lowest-lying nations. Global warming is an existential threat to the

Maldives, which has an average elevation of just 1.5 metres. The ease of tax compliance is probably poor consolation. Just behind Australia was Britain with 110 hours and then much further down the list, after Belgium, Sweden, France, Haiti and Sudan, was the US at 187 hours.

Australia's economic liberty is not restricted to corporations. The individual in Australia not only enjoys the political and social freedoms of one of the world's oldest continuing democracies, but also great economic freedom. An Australian typically pays a relatively light tax bill, has readier opportunity to find work than almost anywhere in the developed world as the unemployment rate suggests, and enjoys enormous economic and social mobility.

"A light tax bill?" I hear outraged voices exclaim in incredulous indignation. You bet. Once again, there is the simple tax rate and then the real story. An Australian earning the average income in 2010 of $62,700 paid notional tax of 35.5 per cent, assuming a single person without kids. Based on a simple comparison of the pro forma tax rate, this made Australia look something of a heavy taxer. On this measure, Australia was the fourteenth biggest taxer among the OECD's thirty-four nations. The average was 34.4 per cent across all countries.

But look again. Once all money movements, not just the headline tax rate, are taken into account, the picture is a very different one. In its international survey "Taxing Wages," the OECD calculates something it calls the "tax wedge" for each type of taxpayer in each country. The tax wedge is the actual imposition of the state on a worker's pay, minus any handouts the worker gets from the state. It also takes into account compulsory contributions for social security or superannuation. In other words, it is a comprehensive net measure of how much a worker actually pays.

Australians turn out to be one of the less taxed peoples in the developed world. The single earner on average income with no kids is actually the eleventh most lightly taxed among their counter-parts in the thirty-four OECD countries. The Australian paid 39.3 per cent tax, but the average for the rich countries was heavier at 43.5 cents in the dollar. The Australian paid more tax than the American's 34 or the Swiss's 27, but less than the Belgian's 66 or the Italian's 53.

"Australia is among the OECD countries that levy a low tax burden on labour income," the Paris-based intergovernmental think-tank reported in 2010. "The tax wedge is about 8 to 13 per-centage points below the OECD average for most families." For lone parents with two children on a low income, the net tax take was a whopping 27 percentage points below the average. "The tax wedge decreased strongly for all family types as a result of tax cuts implemented over the past 11 years," the report added.

Like REVA Medical's pioneering work with human arteries, Australia has managed to work out how to intelligently keep the arteries of economic life open, and the fatty build-ups of regulatory interference under control. Even as it delivers a relatively high degree of fairness in society, it has also improved the level of free-dom in its economy. It is the happy equilibrium of this balance that is the source of Australia's modern emergence as a model, a success in its own right and an example to others. How did it happen?

6

DESTINED TO FAIL

In one of the better-known Irish jokes, an English traveller stops a local to ask the way to the Irish town of Balbriggan. The Irishman chastises the visitor: "Well, if I was going to Balbriggan, I certainly wouldn't start from here." That Australia has emerged as an outstandingly successful modern society invites a jest in the same vein – you wouldn't have started with our origins!

On the contrary, Australia seemed destined to fail as a European settlement. It was peopled by Britain's criminal outcasts. It was set up as the world's biggest prison. A rapacious army staged a successful military coup on the colony's twentieth birthday. The colony was set in the world's most fragile natural environment, with less rain than any continent except Antarctica. The country was founded on principles of racial discrimination and exclusion. And it was far from the centres of commerce. If a successful country can be crafted from these ingredients, it must give hope to others. A poor beginning does not fate a country to a bad ending.

Charles Darwin was confident that Australia's convict genes were its destiny. Even after free settlers had been added, he couldn't see much hope. He visited Australia as part of his famous five-year world voyage on the HMS *Beagle*. Although he thought that the colony at New South Wales had managed to turn "vagabonds" from the northern hemisphere into "active citizens" of the southern, and that "a new and splendid country" had sprung up, he was pessimistic about its future. He could not see how it could ever prosper. The great English naturalist could not see how the society could elevate itself as it was forever rooted in the toxic soil of its convict beginnings. The good would always be poisoned by the bad. He found the people quarrelsome, materialistic, uncouth.

After inspecting New South Wales in 1836, when the convict proportion of the population had greatly diminished, Darwin wrote:

> I was disappointed in the state of society. The whole community is rancorously divided into parties on almost every subject. Among those who, from their station in life, ought to be the best, many live in such open profligacy that respectable people cannot associate with them. There is much jealousy between the children of the rich emancipists and the free settlers, the former being pleased to consider honest men as interlopers. The whole population, poor and rich, are bent on acquiring wealth: amongst the higher orders, wool and sheep-grazing form the constant subject of conversation.
>
> There are many serious drawbacks to the comforts of a family, the chief of which, perhaps, is being surrounded by convict servants. How thoroughly odious to every feeling, to be waited on by a man who the day before, perhaps, was flogged, from your representation, for some trifling misdemeanour. The female servants are of course much worse: hence children learn the vilest expressions, and it is fortunate if not equally vile ideas.

Any advantage that Darwin noticed was, to his mind, immediately cancelled out by the presence of convicts. For instance: "Settlers possess a great advantage in finding their sons of service when very young. At the age of from sixteen to twenty they frequently take charge of distant farming stations. This, however, must happen at the expense of their boys associating entirely with convict servants."

Darwin then declared his prediction for the Australian colonies: "I am not aware that the tone of society has assumed any peculiar character; but with such habits, and without intellectual pursuits, it can hardly fail to deteriorate." He added insult to the injury: "My opinion is such that nothing but rather sharp necessity should compel me to emigrate."

Darwin would go on to develop the theory of evolution, but the great man was unable to imagine that Australian society could evolve. The genetic beginnings of Australian society cast a veto on any possibility of improvement. In this, Darwin was no pioneer. This was the mainstream view among respectable Englishmen at the time. New South Wales was "a nest of vipers" that would form "a nucleus of contagion" in the South Pacific, as a parliamentarian and one of the leading evangelical figures of the time, William Wilberforce, told Britain's House of Commons.

English evangelists shipped Bibles to Australia with the convicts; the convicts tore the pages out to make playing cards. They made black and red markings on them from soot and blood. Soot, blood and blasphemy must have seemed a fitting metaphor for the depravity of the damned colonies of Australia.

Establishing colonial Australia as the world's first and only continent-sized jail, and setting it under military rule, was not a promising portent for a free society. Beginning with Captain Arthur Phillip in New South Wales in 1788, the colonies were administered by a governor, always a military or naval officer. They were absolute rulers, in theory at least, for the first forty-six years of the colony. Yet their rule did not always carry absolutely, notably when it clashed with the will of the notorious rascals of the NSW Rum Corps. This was the body of English soldiers that was raised specifically for garrisoning New South Wales. They were wilful and corrupt. They were derisively given their name because they operated a monopoly on the de facto currency of the day. In the absence of any coin or paper currency, rum became the medium of exchange. The Rum Corps staged Australia's first and only successful military coup.

The colony was exactly twenty years old when, on January 26, 1808, the date today celebrated as Australia Day (it coincided with the date of the First Fleet's arrival in 1788 at Sydney Cove), the army rose up against the governor and seized power. The conflict started with a relief operation. After serious flooding along the Hawkesbury River north of Sydney, the new governor, William Bligh, the same Bligh of the famed mutiny on the *Bounty*, ordered supplies and loans to be given to the affected farmers. This gave relief to the farmers and also brought down the price of food throughout the colony. Why should this trouble the Rum Corps? Because the traders in the corps had been profiteering from the food shortages, selling supplies at exorbitant prices.

Governor Bligh had been chosen to rule New South Wales precisely because he was tough enough to confront the rogue Rum Corps, which had defied successive previous governors. He was expected to tame not only the army, but also the increasingly demanding wealthy entrepreneurs of the colony. Chief among them was a former officer and paymaster of the Rum Corps, the rich and powerful settler John Macarthur. Today he is celebrated as the pioneer of the Australian wool industry. Back then he had angered the British government's adviser on Australia, the famous botanist Sir Joseph Banks.

Banks had travelled with Captain James Cook on his voyage of the British discovery of Australia in 1770. From London, the influential Banks remained active in NSW affairs for decades. Banks had counselled against the establishment of a wool industry in New South Wales, but Macarthur defied him and broke the law by importing the first merino sheep from the king's flock. Macarthur had also used personal contacts in London to win vast grants of prime land in defiance of the NSW governor. Macarthur had antagonised Banks, and now Banks sought retaliation by choosing William Bligh as the new governor. As soon as Bligh took office in Sydney, he clashed with Macarthur. The two were in constant dispute for all of Bligh's tenure. And it wasn't just Macarthur. The wealthy and powerful of New South Wales had been accustomed to receiving generous land grants from governors. This was central to their standing; land was the chief wealth of the colony. Macarthur had done very well, and so had the commander of the Rum Corps, Major George Johnston. Bligh brought the largesse to an end. Where the previous governor, Philip King, had handed out 24,000 hectares, Bligh granted a mere 1,600. Aggravating this injury to the pride of Australia's bunyip aristocracy, Bligh generously awarded half of that to himself and his daughter. "So the rebellion is important as the first major crisis in the fight between government and capital in Australia," wrote the journalist Michael Duffy.

The conditions for the coup were set when Bligh, following instructions from London, ordered an end to the use of rum as currency. Although the army had earlier lost its monopoly on sales, it was still the dominant supplier of the fiery spirit. Now it was to be deprived of its greatest source of income. The Rum Corps had successfully defied the two previous governors, Hunter and King, on this core interest and it was now ready to defy Bligh. The mutiny was later named the Rum Rebellion for this reason. But it was not rum that provided the actual trigger for the coup.

The flashpoint was Bligh's order for the arrest of John Macarthur over a disputed fine. Macarthur was brought before a court, but the court, composed of one civilian judge and six officers of the Rum Corps, took his side. This was improper but unsurprising. Major Johnston had a longstanding friendship and business partnership with Macarthur. Indeed, in his time as the Rum Corps' paymaster, Macarthur had been the man who organised the finance that first put the Corps into the rum business. Johnston and Macarthur were in alliance, a parodic Australian precursor of what the US president Dwight D. Eisenhower would later describe as the "military-industrial complex."

A furious Bligh demanded to see Major Johnston on January 25, but the army chief excused himself due to illness. He had crashed his horse-drawn gig the previous night returning home from a big dinner. (This is thought to have been Australia's first drink-driving accident.) Instead, on the next day, January 26, 1808, Johnston took the initiative. He demanded Bligh's resignation. He sent troops, with a military band in attendance to supply all the pomp of a colonial soundtrack, marching on Government House.

The defiant governor was defended only by his indignant daughter armed with a parasol. He was arrested by the troops which were supposed to be serving him. A military junta took control of the colony and wild celebrations took place that night in The Rocks area of Sydney. The junta kept Bligh under arrest and luxuriated in its privileges. The imperial authority eventually got around to cleaning up, but it took two years before it purged the junta and restored legitimate government to Australia. The logistics of long-distance rule were tricky. London was on the other side of the world, a round trip of six to sixteen months.

This early overthrow of legitimate authority might have set a fatal precedent, sending the colony into the sort of endless cycle that has trapped many countries in perpetual instability and poverty, one of many potential disqualifiers to the successful development of a stable, prosperous, free nation.

Major Johnston was eventually court-martialled in London. Apart from being discharged from the military, he went unpunished. This was exceptionally mild. He returned to Sydney to enjoy the wealth he had accumulated in the Rum Corps. He lived as a respected citizen and was later a member of the first NSW Legislative Council. The broad main street through Sydney's Annandale is just one of the places named after him. His ally in corruption and coup-making, John Macarthur, fled Australia for eight years to evade an arrest warrant, but later won a pardon from London. He too returned to Sydney to enjoy wealth and social respectability.

William Bligh eventually returned to London and was promoted, twice, but never again given any sort of command. In a remarkable record, he had been subject to four mutinies in his life as a commander. First was the famous mutiny against the harshness and abusive outbursts that accompanied his rule on the HMS *Bounty*. Next he was in command of a naval vessel during a widespread industrial-style sailors' strike. Britain's sailors refused to put the country's Channel Fleet, including Bligh's ship, to sea, demanding better conditions and their first pay rise in a century. It was called the Spithead mutiny. The government met the sailors' demands and the strike was settled peacefully.

Bligh was also in command of a ship caught up in a similar widespread revolt, the mutiny at the Nore, that was inspired by the success of the Spithead strike. This revolt was more radical. The mutineers blockaded London and threatened to defect with their ships to France, with which Britain was at war. It ended badly for the mutineers when they were routed. The government made no concessions. The ringleaders were hanged. Others of the rebels were sent to New South Wales.

And New South Wales was then the site of the fourth and final mutiny against Bligh's command. "Bligh is perhaps the only English captain to be credited with having an entire continent rebel against him," according to the BBC.

*

Nature's stocking of the colonies was, like the human convict stock, not promising for the Europeans. Australia's environmental fragility has more recently moved Jared Diamond, professor of geography and environmental health sciences at the University of California, to choose it as one of four leading showcase candidates for systemic, national, environmental catastrophe.

In his 2005 book *Collapse*, Diamond asks whether Australia will one day be considered in the same category as the ancient overgrown Mayan ruins or the abandoned jungle-bound city of Angkor. The overexploitation of a country's environment to the point of collapse he calls "ecocide."

His four candidates for ecocide are Rwanda – where, he argues, overpopulation has already contributed to genocide – Haiti, China and Australia: "Ecologically, the Australian environment is exceptionally fragile, the most fragile of any First World country except perhaps Iceland." And while Diamond's critics, such as the professor of archaeology Tim Murray of La Trobe University, accuse him of alarmism, they do not disagree with his diagnosis.

It's not a new problem. At first glance, the Australian landscape looked to the first English settlers to be lush and ripe for farming. Tall forests and long grasses suggested rich soils and plentiful rains. But it was a hoax of nature on an unprepared people. The towering blue gums they saw in Victoria's Gippsland, for instance, were bigger than anything the colonists had ever seen, perhaps the tallest trees anywhere in the modern world at up to 130 metres. But when they cut them down, they were frustrated to discover that the forest did not grow back as quickly as it would in Europe, but instead took an uneconomically long time. Indeed, we're still waiting two centuries later for those old native forests to recover fully.

It was the same with the grass, with crops, with European agriculture of all types. It was a misapprehension that nearly wiped out the colony in its earliest years. Only emergency food supplies shipped from the other side of the world saved New South Wales from total starvation. It was a misapprehension that meant that New South Wales was periodically dependent on food aid arranged by the mother country until the 1840s, more than fifty years after the First Fleet arrived. Farms were scratched into the earth, and, after just a few harvests, commonly abandoned as the settlers discovered the hidden poverty of the soil.

"Australia is the most unproductive continent," writes Diamond, "the one whose soils have on the average the lowest nutrient levels, the lowest plant growth rates, and the lowest productivity. That's because Australian soils are so old that they have become leached of their nutrients by rain over the course of billions of years."

Australia's soils are not only low in naturally occurring nutrient, they are high in salt. In the nation's main food bowl, the low-lying Murray-Darling Basin, the sea has repeatedly invaded the area over millennia. Each time it retreated, it left salt behind in the soils. When the land is cleared or irrigated, salt is drawn to the surface, crimping or killing crops. This problem of salinity emerged quickly in colonial Australia. Today one hectare in ten of cleared land in Australia is so saline as to be useless. The problem grows worse.

Water is another ever-present problem for farming. Rain in Australia has always been scant, compared to the other continents. It enjoys about a third less than the next-driest continent, Asia. Seventy per cent of Australia's surface area is classed as "arid." That is, it's too dry to grow crops or timber. And most Australian farmland gets only enough rain to grow a crop to maturity in less than one year out of every two, on average. The unpredictability of rain compounds the problem of scarcity. "Averages are just statistics in Australia," write Libby Robin and Tom Griffiths of the Australian National University. "They do not represent a reliable amount of rain on any sort of seasonal basis. An 'average annual fall' is usually the result of one major annual fall amidst many years of 'below average' falls."

The English colonists might have adapted to the land they found, eating the lean and tasty meat of the plentiful kangaroo, for example, or learning about the naturally occurring foods from the people who had got an early table at Chez Australie. But they were utterly determined to do it the other way around. The colonists wanted to adapt Australia to their own ways rather than adapt themselves to the new reality that they found. Holding the native people in contempt, they closed their minds to learning from the locals.

Australia's history of eating has been "one continuous picnic," in the memorable title of a book by restaurateur Michael Symons. Australians have always carried their food in with them, rather than draw on the surrounding offerings, he contended. The staple diet of the rural workforce until well into the twentieth century, for example, was the "Ten, Ten, Two, and a Quarter," a monotonous weekly ration of ten pounds of flour, ten pounds of meat, two pounds of sugar, a quarter-pound of tea, plus salt. This was the diet of crews of builders and bushmen, sailors and sawyers, road workers and rail gangers, miners and farmhands, soldiers and shearers. It was a country living on prison rations, long after it had ceased to be the world's biggest prison. The striking feature of the meat-based diet? It was overwhelmingly beef and sheep, European beasts that exacted a heavy cost on the Australian environment, rather than the native animals and seafood.

*

When the separate British colonies federated to form the new Commonwealth of Australia, the first moments of nationhood were not very promising for a society hoping to develop any sort of tolerance. The two racial verities of the first century and a half were that the native people were inconsequential, and that the Chinese were unbearable.

When Captain Arthur Phillip led his party ashore to set up the first settlement, the natives couldn't work out the gender of these covered-up creatures. Wary Eora men on the beach demanded by gesticulation to know whether they were men or women. Catching their meaning, Phillip ordered a hapless sailor to lower his trousers. The Aboriginal men were pleased. They called to the beach their women folk, who had been hiding in the dunes of Botany Bay. The locals offered their women to the visitors, an unmistakably warm welcome for the colonists. Phillip declined the offer. Race relations only went downhill after that.

The Australian Aboriginal population was crushed by design and by neglect. By taking possession of their land, the colonists took their everything. They owned no possessions other than those scant few they carried with them in their nomadic lives. Tens of thousands of years of continuous occupation were cancelled in an instant.

When the six states federated to form the Commonwealth of Australia on January 1, 1901, the original Australians were explicitly written out of the constitution. It was not enough to deny them any claim to their ancestral land. They had to be denied political rights, too.

This founding document of the new nation declared that in the national census, "aboriginal natives shall not be counted." This wasn't just so they would be overlooked. It was a more active exclusion. It was to make sure they were not counted for the purposes of creating parliamentary electorates or for qualifying states for grants that were to be calculated on a per capita basis.

The constitution denied the Commonwealth the power to make laws for Aboriginal people. Why? Because they were subject to laws made expressly for them, to be decided by the state

governments. This was essentially a licence for the states to dis-
criminate against their Aboriginal populations. In Queensland, for
instance, state law required them to work without pay, and denied
them the right to their own traditional cultural practices and to
Western practices too, such as playing cards or drinking alcohol.
And in Queensland and Western Australia, they were forbidden to
vote in state or federal elections. After federation in 1901, the
native people were theoretically entitled to vote under a federal
law, but in practice the administration of the electoral rules kept
many away from the ballot box.

The economic exclusion of Aboriginal Australians was brutal
too. The black worker was an indispensable part of the rural economy, supplying 55 per cent of the total workforce in the Queensland cattle industry, for instance, in 1886. Their quality as
stockmen was as good, or better, than their European counterparts,
according to the views of white station owners and managers
reported in the Queensland Parliamentary Papers of 1904. But
their exploitation, officially sanctioned, was so acute that they were
effectively barred from entry to the mainstream economy.

A historian, Dr Rosalind Kidd, after studying the Queensland
Government files of the time, describes a "huge, nameless army of
unpaid and underpaid Aboriginal labour" on which much rural
wealth was built, "generations of workers who even now are rarely
acknowledged." The situation of Aboriginals who were assigned a
job by the Queensland Government in the first half of the twentieth century was grim: if they were paid at all, their money flowed
straight to the "Chief Protector," with workers forced to apply for
permission to spend it. According to Kidd:

> In Queensland until 1968 in rural areas and until 1979 on
> government settlements, Aboriginal legislation overrode the
> whole raft of industrial protections enjoyed by every other

Australian worker. Consider the facts from the government's own files. By 1907 in Queensland, there [were] more than 3,000 contracted Aboriginal workers, many working where white labour was unavailable. Often regarded as more reliable and superior stock riders and bushmen – and that's on the files – than their white counterparts, but they were sold to the pastoral industry for about 3 per cent of the white rate. In 1921, the Chief Protector admitted shelter for many Aboriginal workers was, and I quote, "worse than they would provide for their pet horse, motorcar, or prize cattle."

If the Aborigines were repressed because they could be, the Chinese were expelled because they couldn't be. The stories of the goldfields clashes between Europeans and Chinese are famous. The reason for the hostilities? The Chinese worked ores that the whites had deemed uneconomic, and made them economic. The Chinese were an absurdly small minority. In an era when 1.3 million immigrants rushed to Australia to make their fortunes, fewer than 40,000 Chinese arrived. But the enmity grew fierce. Commonly forced out of prime prospecting areas, the Chinese miners worked abandoned areas and discarded tailings that the Europeans had left as worthless. But Chinese tirelessness and teamwork often yielded gold. Extracting gold where the Europeans could not, or would not, infuriated the whites. Anti-Chinese violence on the goldfields culminated in the notorious Lambing Flat riots where some 3,000 whites chased about 1,000 Chinese off their diggings until the authorities restored order.

A less well-known fact is that the Chinese also competed with Europeans in the wider economy. The first sugar plantation in the Cairns district, the Hop Wah plantation, was financed by a syndicate of 100 local Chinese in 1879. Chinese entrepreneurs pioneered major banana plantations. The *Cairns Post* reported in 1889 that "in the theatre of agriculture the Chinese have the front seat while the whites sit behind them and admire their pigtails."

As the historian Henry Reynolds has recounted, a young Norwegian scientist, Knut Dahl, described the Darwin he found in the 1890s, where the Chinese ran the business community. In the European part of town, Dahl wrote, "the few business people and officials in the service of the Government were apparently in no hurry over their duties and adopted the cool and indolent habits peculiar to the majority of white men in tropical towns ... Chinatown, on the other hand, was a welter of life and activity. The very air smelt of business. You heard, saw and felt nothing but business. One had the feeling that the people one saw thronging the shops and streets, who bought and sold, and, busy as ants, carried on their trades, belonged to a race which slowly and securely was gaining opulence and power." And that was precisely the problem. The Chinese were formidable competitors with the European colonists.

Victoria's was the first government in Australia to impose restrictive immigration laws, in 1855. With growing numbers of Chinese arriving to join the throngs heading to the goldfields, Victoria imposed steep fees and a limit of one Chinese arrival for every 10 tons of cargo arriving on the same ship. Other colonies followed.

Sinophobia intensified in 1888, 100 years after the arrival of the First Fleet. The NSW premier Sir Henry Parkes had strategic concerns. He worried that China was "rapidly creating armies and a formidable navy" and that the apparently harmless Chinese hawker wandering through an Australian town with a basket of vegetables "represents here a great power ... which has risen up to be one of the most formidable powers in the world." The Chinese authorities had already protested against the Australian campaign to keep their people out of lands which the Europeans could not develop themselves. Three weeks after Parkes spoke these words, a ship, the *Afghan*, turned up with 268 Chinese on board. It was the trigger for an extraordinary wave of national demonstrations to shut the Chinese out. This populism fitted neatly with the loftier strategic concerns of the political leaders. The colonial governments met and all except Tasmania swiftly agreed to tighten the exclusion of Chinese. Victoria's restrictions were the toughest, where a ship would be allowed to land only one Chinese for every 500 tons of cargo it carried.

Aggressive racism was one of the strongest common bonds bringing the new states together in the creation of a federated Australia. In 1901, in an urgent act, one of the very first acts of the very first session, the new national parliament voted for a law prohibiting Chinese immigrants, the policy known as White Australia.

The first prime minister, Edmund Barton, declared that the entire country was determined to preserve the "purity of race." The leader of the Protectionist party, later to become the country's second prime minister, Alfred Deakin, declared of the new Commonwealth that "from now hence forward all alien elements within it shall be diminished." The federal Labor leader, John Watson, to become the third prime minister, railed against the "influx of coloured people." And the Free Trade Party's leader, George Reid, later the fourth prime minister, swore that the "current of Australian blood shall not assume darker hues."

The Immigration Restriction Act of 1901 was based on a ruse first devised in the apartheid system of South Africa. It was called the "Natal formula" because it was pioneered in that South African district in 1897. Ostensibly a neutral rule that tested only for linguistic skill, it didn't actually mention the Chinese or any other race. Instead, it defined a "prohibited immigrant" as "any person who when asked to do so by an officer fails to write out at dictation and sign in the presence of an officer a passage of fifty words in length in an European language directed by the officer." After Japan objected, even the reference to "European language" was later changed to any "prescribed language." The law, on the face of it, was racially neutral. It was not the statute but its application that guaranteed a White Australia. British applicants were not tested at all. A Chinese applicant, even if he spoke English, would be tested in Gaelic or some other impossibly obscure tongue.

This idea for the enforcement mechanism of a White Australia was first presented to Australia's premiers by the British secretary of state for the colonies, Joseph Chamberlain, at a meeting in 1897. Chamberlain was the father of Neville who, as British prime minister, would later appease Adolf Hitler. Chamberlain wanted to encourage Australia to be covert in its anti-Chinese discrimination. The reason? Britain had signed a treaty with China guaranteeing free access to each other's territories. When Beijing got angry with Britain for allowing its colony to exclude Chinese citizens, the British needed to have a cover story.

Australia pitched itself vociferously into this White Australia commitment when the Chinese population was at its peak, then and since, of 3.3 per cent of the national total. Between the beginning of the gold fever in 1852 and the end of the century, 40,721 Chinese arrived in Australia and 36,049 departed. The net influx, 4,672, was hardly the beachhead of an invasion, yet it was the basis for a new, united nation.

Criminal, brutal, militaristic, starving and racist. This wouldn't seem the most likely starting point for a country that emerges a little more than two centuries later as one of the world's outstandingly law-abiding, free, peaceful, fair, prosperous, tolerant societies. Yet, somehow, this is exactly what happened.

WOULD YOU LIKE SOME RIGHTS WITH YOUR FLOGGING?

Australia was the first country in the world to vote itself into existence. The referenda to federate the six separate British colonies into a new nation-state on the first day of the twentieth century, January 1, 1901, constituted a pioneering act of nation-building. It marked Australia as a uniquely democratic creation in the history of humankind.

Federation was consciously modelled on the American union, but also proudly different from the US experience. The man customarily described as the father of federation, Sir Henry Parkes, a long-bearded former journalist with chronic money problems, was premier of New South Wales when he ignited the federation movement with his famous speech in Tenterfield in 1889. With all the grandeur that could be mustered in small-town New South Wales, Tenterfield's mayor hosted Parkes at a banquet in the School of Arts. Some eighty dignitaries, including, we are told, "most of the prominent tradesmen" and "several ladies," were there. The report of Parkes' speech from the *Sydney Morning Herald* at the time ran: "Australia had now a population of three and a half millions, and the American people numbered only between three and four millions when they formed the great commonwealth of the United States. The numbers were about the same, and surely what the Americans had done by war, the Australians could bring about in peace … (Cheers)."

Till then, nation-states had been formed by top-down acts of will by great men, or organically through a long history of common ethnicity and encircling geography, or forged by war. And sometimes by all three. Others were born when rebel territories broke away from the centre, as the US broke from Britain.

But the federation of Australia was the first time that a nation-state had been created by an act of participatory democracy – a vote. The constitution had been drawn up by elected delegates. The people of each colony were then given a direct "yes" or "no" vote on whether to accept it. No one asked the American people to vote on the Declaration of Independence, the act of creation of the United States of America. The delegates from the thirteen states that issued the declaration, as the Second Continental Congress, were not democratically elected either. Some were self-appointed "committees for safety" and others were the result of small, impromptu public gatherings. So where the Australian constitution begins with the words "Whereas the people ... have agreed to unite," the US Declaration of Independence can only lay theoretical claim to be expressing the will of the people: "We, therefore, the Representatives of the United States of America ... in the Name, and by Authority of the good People."

By today's standards, the Australian referenda were not paragons of democratic participation. Voting was voluntary, and no more than 46 per cent of eligible voters turned out in any one colony. The definition of an eligible voter would not stand today. Women were allowed to vote in only two of the colonies, South Australia and Western Australia. And Aboriginal men and other "coloureds" were eligible to vote in New South Wales, Victoria, South Australia and Tasmania, but not in Queensland or Western Australia. Still, by the standards of the day, it was a unique and exemplary moment in the advance of democracy and the sovereignty of the people.

In a pattern that was to become all too common in Australian politics, the "no" campaign on federation was full of attempts to scare voters into rejecting change. For instance, NSW voters were told the fiction that they would have to pay an extra 22 shillings and sixpence a year in tax, which was about one week's income on the average of the day. As each colony held its referendum, the newspapers put up big tally boards in the streets to display the results to the public as they came in. Crowds gathered and cheered as the "yes" votes mounted. Those in favour of the bill to federate were known as "Billites." Opponents were "Anti-Billites."

In New South Wales, the final "yes" vote came in at 56.5 per cent. In Queensland, the "yes" vote was 55 per cent. In South Australia it was 79 per cent. "The people sent up cheers and triumphant shouts which proclaimed a decisive victory and sent a thrill through everyone with any emotional feelings," the *Adelaide Observer* reported. In Tasmania and Victoria the Billites won with an astonishing 94 per cent in each colony.

Western Australia's colonial government played brinkmanship. It charged high tariffs on goods from the rest of the continent. The premier, John Forrest, who in historical curiosity was the great-great-uncle of the iron ore entrepreneur Twiggy, didn't want to have to do away with the tariffs, a condition of federation; he needed the revenues that they raised. He argued that Western Australia's protected farms and factories would not be able to compete with the goods from the rest of the continent. So Western Australia stalled, refusing to hold a referendum. But the hordes living on the WA goldfields didn't appreciate this. They saw no benefit from WA protectionism. For them, it simply inflated the prices on all the necessities of life. Most of the goldfields folk were recent arrivals from the other Australian colonies, in any case, or "t'othersiders" as they were called. They felt more connection with their eastern home colonies than with Western Australia.

The mining communities founded federation leagues and threatened to secede from Western Australia to join the Commonwealth. Frustrated, in 1900 the folk of the goldfields presented a petition to Queen Victoria demanding to separate from Western Australia. The petition contained 30,000 signatures and ran to 2 kilometres in length. Forrest, embarrassed, finally conducted a referendum. The West Australians voted "yes" with a resounding 69 per cent. But it was so late, July 1900, that the British parliament had already enacted the bill to give force to the wishes of the other Australian colonies. This historical anomaly explains why the Australian constitution's opening sentence begins with a notable omission: "Whereas the people of New South Wales, Victoria, South Australia, Queensland, and Tasmania, humbly relying on the blessing of Almighty God, have agreed to unite in one indissoluble Federal Commonwealth ..."

Of course, the Americans were busy at war with Britain at the time of their declaration of independence. They didn't have the luxury of time or even security for popular deliberation. It was a desperate moment. Even the congress itself had to flee and relocate as British soldiers occupied Philadelphia. But while Australia was not born in a moment of national emergency, it was created, in large part, in anticipation of a possible national emergency. The six British colonies in Australia each maintained a separate army. A British officer, Major General James Bevan Edwards, had inspected them and recommended that they be organised into a single Australian force. This was plainly a sensible idea – if a foreign power were to invade one part of the coast, all the continental forces should be concentrated in resisting the attack for mutual security instead of sitting idle in their barracks in the pretence that an imaginary line would keep the invader contained within a single colony. But, as a reporter described Parkes saying at Tenterfield: "He would like to know what was to become of an army without a central executive power to guide its movements." No colony would allow another to direct its troops, nor would the colonies allow the imperial government in London to order their soldiers about in their home land. A continental army without a continental government was a nonsense.

Parkes set a second and related matter before the grandees of Tenterfield: "They had now, from South Australia to Queensland, a stretch of about 2,000 miles of railway, and if the four colonies could only combine to adopt a uniform gauge, it would be an immense advantage in the movement of troops." Who then could have guessed that even after Australia had voted itself into a united political entity, even 110 years later, it would still be operating a Balkanised system of six different rail gauges? The main interstate routes were standardised – passengers need no longer alight at the border between New South Wales and Victoria, for instance, for customs and immigration processing, and wait as all the goods on the train are unloaded from one train and loaded onto another with a different gauge. But even interstate standardisation took ninety-five years. Incredibly, the Melbourne–Adelaide track was only made seamless as late as 1995 by the Keating government. And the states still operate three different gauges – standard, Cape and Irish – for large sections of their networks, and another three gauges for more specific sections, such as the Queensland sugar trams.

The other important distinction between the US and Australian founding documents is that while the Americans were rebelling against an imperial overlord, Australia was declaring itself a united nation-state "under the Crown of the United Kingdom of Great Britain and Ireland." Australia was building a new room in an old house under a shared roof. So where the US was born as an independent nation as an act of revolution, Australian independence was evolutionary. And so was the democratic impulse that moved the Australian founding fathers to submit the proposed federation to a popular vote. The idea that legitimacy rested in the popular will was not born with the federation referenda but was already firmly entrenched in Australia at the time of federation.

Where did this democratic sensibility come from? Strange as it may seem, it had already put down roots in the Australian soil in the earliest, harshest and most tyrannical days of the colony. At the very time that Australia appeared to be setting itself up for an ugly future as a vast criminal purgatory under the permanent lash of a thuggish military, the colony was actually developing a strong sense of egalitarianism and fair play that would ultimately inform a deep democratic ethos.

There is evidence from as early as the Second Fleet. The British government did what today would be called "contracting out" of the second dump of convicts. It went so badly that it would have been no surprise if contracting out had ended then and there and become no more than an historical artefact in Australia. The private shippers, Camden, Calvert & King, formerly slave traders between Africa and North America, were paid a flat fee per head for delivering their human cargo, dead or alive. They treated the convicts dreadfully and, even as the dead and dying were being carted off the ships on arrival in Sydney Cove, the contractors opened a store in the colony selling food and clothing. Where did they get the goods from? They were the same food and clothing that the contractors had been supposed to give their passengers on the long journey from Britain. Of the 1,026 convicts shipped, 267 (or 26 per cent) died before arriving in Sydney. The Second Fleet had the highest rate of death in the history of transportation to Australia. And another 47 per cent of the Fleet's passengers arrived ill.

When news of this brutal treatment reached London it provoked outrage and an official inquiry. A result was improvement in the conditions of transportation. The future contractors were paid according to the number of convicts they delivered alive. Doctors were put on board the fleets and even given authority over ships' captains to protect the welfare of the convicts. One consequence was that it became safer for a convict to travel to Australia than for a free migrant to travel to America. The British politicians and authorities increasingly accepted a responsibility to show humanitarian concern for the convicts. And the convicts increasingly asserted rights.

The historian John Hirst has told the strange and surprising story of how convicts in New South Wales, far from being the slaves of popular impression, had more rights than slaves in America and, in some ways, even more rights than free servants in England. The early convict system contains not only the beginning of the democratic sensibility but also of labour rights and even of a market-based economy. Hirst differs with the common assertion that Australia began its life as a jail: "In many ways, such statements are seriously misleading. To the modern mind, a jail is a closed, well-ordered institution, rigidly divided into warders and prisoners. Society in early New South Wales was not at all like this."

Convicts were not slaves. They had fixed terms, not lifetime servitude. Their children were born free, not into bondage. They remained subjects of the Crown and retained important legal and political rights. Convicts had the right to petition the governor, and hundreds did, every year. And convicts enjoyed more legal rights than their English counterparts. For instance, in England convicts were not allowed to stand as witnesses in a court, or to bring civil actions in a court, or to own property. But in Australia, these restrictions on rights were ignored. A convict could give evidence against his own master. And convicts had complete freedom in their sexual relationships. English laws on bastardry, where a woman could be punished for giving birth outside wedlock and fathers obliged to support their children, were not enforced in Australia. On the contrary, convict women were actually exempt from work while nursing their babies and, when weaned, the babies were given a ration from the government store. The first government institutions built in the colony were orphanages where children deserted by their parents were accommodated by the state.

Hirst sketches the contrasting scenes in his book *Freedom on the Fatal Shore*. A wealthy aristocrat in London would head home in the confident expectation that there would be a footman there to open the door, that a housekeeper would have lit fires in all the grates, and that the cook would have dinner ready. But, writes Hirst, "A landowner heading back to his home or estate in New South Wales had no such certainty. His servants might be brawling or drunk, or some of them might have run away or been arrested for a robbery in the town."

If a servant to one of the Lords of England should happen to offend, he could be dismissed. And if dismissed without a reference, he would not be able to get another job. In addition to the power of dismissal, an English master could work his staff for long hours and pay them as little as the market would bear. In the colony in Australia, the offending convict could be sent to court and, if the magistrate so ordered, could be flogged. This sounds fearsome. And it was.

But already we can discern two surprising facts about the use of the lash by convicts' masters in Australia. First, a master could not decide to give a flogging, and he could not administer the flogging himself. It was a matter for a court. This set the colony in Australia apart. In America, a master had the power to beat or flog his slave. And even in England, common law gave a master the right to beat his apprentice, a ship's captain his crew, and teachers their students. But in Australia a master had no right to hand out physical punishment to a convict. After 1800, even a British officer in the colony was forbidden to beat or whip a convict on pain of court martial. There was no private right to administer corporal punishment. It was to be done impartially, the business of the state and the judicial system.

Second, the lash turned out to be an ineffectual way to manage convicts. Although it was in common use as a punishment – there was one lashing a year, on average, for every four convicts – it could inflict pain but it could not compel obedience. The story of the British missionary L.E. Threlkeld makes the point. He arrived full of sympathy for the natives and for the convicts. He was given a mission station at Lake Macquarie where he proselytised Aboriginal people. He was also given a farm with convicts to work it. The convicts were lazy and refused direction. The skilled men pretended not to know their trades and the others feigned sickness. They abused Threlkeld, told him they would never behave, and asked to be returned to the government. Against his better judgment, their master sent them to the magistrate at Newcastle, who ordered flogging and time in the cells. This cost time – days to fetch the constable, and days more to take the men to court – yet offered scant improvement in the men's conduct. Threlkeld tried withholding their rations of luxuries, tea, sugar and tobacco. But the convicts responded by working even less. And then they escalated the confrontation. They complained that their ration of meat was too bony, dumped it at the door of the store, picked the lock and robbed the store instead. Their master gave up and returned them to the government.

The most successful tactics for the management of the convicts were inducements rather than threats. The big inducement was a shortened term of servitude. The ticket-of-leave for a convict after three years of good behaviour was much more effective than floggings and even executions. The other key tactic was to allow convicts time to pursue their own interests. This was the concept of task work and "own time." The supervisor would set a convict a task – so many bricks made, so much land cleared – and promise them free time when it was done. While the colony's first governor, Arthur Phillip, initially resisted the idea, he ended up embracing it as a way of getting more work from them. The governor, far from being an absolute ruler, ended up negotiating with convict farm labourers over their hours, rations and workloads.

Some convicts used their "own time" for idleness or crime. Others used it to improve their lot. Australia's first profit-sharing venture depended on the aspirations of convicts working for extra reward in their own time. James Ruse, the first of the ex-convicts to become a settler, hired convicts to clear some of his land in return for the first year's crop. Soldiers and settlers hired convicts for extra work in the convicts' own time. The government was not the monopoly buyer of labour. The convicts were selling their labour on a market. This system prevailed for the first thirty-five years of the colony.

Convicts moved from servitude to ticket-of-leave and then full freedom. By the end of Lachlan Macquarie's term as governor in 1821, only thirty-three years after the arrival of the First Fleet, ex-convicts owned half of the wealth of the colony and were masters of many of its convicts, too.

If Australia was a slave society or a jail, then the question arises naturally – how did it transform itself into a free society? John Hirst's answer:

No one had a vote in New South Wales until transportation ended, but the making of a free society had been going on almost since the day it began. Free children had been born to convict parents. Convicts had been gaining their freedom; no bar was placed on their economic activities and they enjoyed the same legal rights as those who had come free ... When transportation ended no legal or institutional changes were required. The convicts still in bondage gradually progressed to freedom. The proportion of convicts in the labour force declined to zero.

One telling indicator of the success of the colony in creating rights for its convicts and ex-convicts: convicts started writing home to their friends and families urging them to join them in Australia. Some Englishmen committed crimes solely in order to be sent to their punishment in Australia.

The British authorities' responsiveness to the convicts' rights, combined with the assertiveness of the convicts themselves, created a broadly egalitarian and democratic ethos.

As the NSW colony grew and prospered and the number of colonies in Australia multiplied, the colonists began to tug at the imperial leash, insistently and persistently, for more power and more rights. The colonial elites sought, and were granted by London, a series of improvements in their degree of self-government. And as the colonies tugged at the empire for more power, so did the people tug at their rulers. The landowning class tugged at the colonial governments for more power sharing. And workers tugged at governments and employers for more rights. In modern parlance, it was the Australian Spring.

The first glimpse of formal democracy arrived in 1842. London agreed to give NSW property-owning men – including ex-convicts – the right to elect two-thirds of the parliament. Transportation to New South Wales was abolished eight years later, the gold rushes began and Victoria split off from New South Wales. One popular movement demanding more rights turned violent. The Eureka Stockade at Ballarat in Victoria began as a goldminers' protest against expensive mining licences in 1854, but it quickly took on a broader reformist thrust. Men with experience in the British Chartist movement, a workers' campaign for democratic rights, grafted political demands onto the miners' protest. Some 10,000 miners gathered on the goldfields to form the Ballarat Reform League. They voted to adopt the demand that "it is the inalienable right of every citizen to have a voice in making the laws he is called on to obey, that taxation without representation is tyranny." If their demands were not met, the men threatened to secede from Britain. Meeting with a stony response from the authorities, the miners built a stockade, hoisted the blue-and-white Southern Cross flag of the Eureka movement, and armed themselves. British troops put down the revolt in an efficient and brutal ten-minute assault. Twenty-two miners and soldiers were killed.

In an indication of where public sympathies lay, none of the rebels was found guilty and no one was punished. And the miners' demands for democratic reform were met within half a dozen years in Victoria, with the exception of their call for payments to members of parliament and annual parliamentary elections. Was this the result of the Eureka movement? No, the Victorian legislative council was already negotiating greater self-rule and wider voting rights with London. But these developments were all part of the ferment of the time. And Eureka was a powerful sign to the authorities that Australians' demands for rights were not necessarily limited to polite negotiations in wood-panelled meeting rooms. The Eureka rebels were the shock troops of Australian democracy. Though they were routed, their uprising was a warning to the negotiators in London and the colonial parliaments in Australia that the movement for greater rights was deadly serious.

It was as close as Australia came to a revolution. The Eureka Stockade was part of a popular restlessness, part of a continuum of assertive demands for a wider diffusion of workers' rights and political power. It was the most violent, but by no means the last.

The next year, strikes by stonemasons led to an important world-first. Following earlier strikes on two sites in Sydney – the Garrison Church at the Rocks and the Tooths Brewery on Parramatta Road – stonemasons all across Melbourne demanded that they be required to work no longer than eight hours a day. At that time, they were working ten hours or more. The stonemasons were a particularly hard-suffering part of the workforce. Dust inhalation killed them at an average age of thirty-six. But even so, the demand for an eight-hour day was radical. The French, after the 1848 revolution, had won the exceptional concession of a twelve-hour working day. And in England, the working day for women and children had been limited to ten hours a few years earlier. So eight hours a day seemed impossibly ambitious. But the strikers downed tools in the middle of a gold rush–led construction boom, striking on sites including Melbourne University. Their reluctant employers ultimately agreed. The working week was six days long at the time with only the Sabbath as a day of rest, so an eight-hour day equated to a 48-hour working week. It was the breakthrough moment that led to campaigns around the world for what became, eventually, the global standard.

When the next big wave of global labour and revolutionary activism launched, it took up the Melbourne stonemasons' achievement as its key objective for working people everywhere. The first congress of the First International, formally known as the International Workingmen's Association, met in Geneva in 1866 and declared: "The legal limitation of the working day is a preliminary condition without which all further attempts at improvements and emancipation of the working class must prove abortive, and The Congress proposes eight hours as the legal limit of the working day." The 48-hour week spread gradually in awards across Australian industries, but wasn't legislated in Victoria till 1916 and wasn't universal across the country till the 1920s. The stonemasons' campaign, like the Eureka Stockade, had been led by men with experience of the Chartist movement in Britain.

In 1855, the same year as the stonemasons' breakthough, the NSW and Victorian parliaments achieved another. After years of Australian campaigning and negotiating, London agreed to allow New South Wales to become a self-governing colony, and Victoria soon followed. The parliaments were to be elected by a vote of all male property-owners, and permitted to make their own laws and raise and spend their own revenue, although an anxious London retained the right of veto.

Another world-first soon took place. Voters were given the right to cast their ballots in secret, rather than in the open, in Victoria and South Australia in 1856. Victoria's was the first legislature any-where in the world to employ it. Why did it matter? Because voters can be watched and intimidated by political candidates, political parties or their supporters in an open ballot, and can then be tar-geted for reprisals. And they often were. The secret ballot is a vital protection for genuine democracy and is now universally accepted. It was another of the Chartists' demands, but it was achieved in Australia years before it arrived in London. When secret voting was later taken up in the US, it was known as "the Australian ballot."

Some ten thousand British women of all classes marched through the streets of London in 1908 to demand the right to vote and the right to stand for parliament. They were the Suffragettes. One of the banners they carried in their much-publicised proces-sion to Albert Hall displayed a striking painting of a tall, proud, thoughtful, middle-aged woman holding a trident and dressed in a full-length white dress of classical design, a red, white and blue cape flowing from her shoulders, a red-feathered helmet on her head. A slightly shorter, younger woman, also in classical white dress, touches her shoulder and bends forward toward her in an attitude of concern, her hand reaching for the hand of the regal older woman. She is adorned with a heraldic shield bearing the Southern Cross. The banner is titled: "Commonwealth of Australia." And the slogan in white letters on a dun-coloured background reads: "Trust the women mother as I have done." The banner is now displayed in Parliament House, Canberra, a proud reminder of the fact that while Mother England hesitated to recognise women's political rights, Australia acted.

Under self-government, the pace of reforms in Australia quickened. On one of the big reforms whose time had come – the franchise for women – the colonial government of South Australia was among the earliest in the world to act. In one key aspect, it was the very first. The South Australian parliament became the first legislature in the world where women could stand for election, a right granted by the Constitution (Female Suffrage) Act of 1895. This statute was approved by the narrowest possible margin on the floor of the parliament – a single vote, amid much controversy.

The main argument against women's entitlement to political participation was that females were too emotional, given to hysteria, and their minds too prone to the trivial, given to domesticity. A *Bulletin* magazine cartoon in 1894 portrayed a female mayor presiding over a council meeting in a very businesslike manner. Until a mouse is spotted in the council chambers. She shrieks, leaps onto a chair and adjourns the meeting. It's captioned "The Petticoat in Politics." It might have startled the cartoonist to think that in four generations the *Bulletin* would be defunct and that women would be serving as Australia's governor-general, prime minister, and deputy leader of the opposition. In two of the biggest states, New South Wales and Queensland, women would have held the posts of governor as well as premier. And in the biggest of the cities, the city that was home to the *Bulletin*, Sydney, a woman would have served as lord mayor as well. No one has ever accused any of these women of being fearful.

And in an argument where men accused women of being illogical, the women of the Victorian Women's Suffrage Society had logic on their side in their first pamphlet: "Are women citizens? Yes, when they are required to pay taxes. No, when they ask to vote. Does law concern women? Yes, when they are required to obey it. No, when they ask to have a voice in the representation of their country."

The first parliament to allow all adult women to vote was New Zealand's, in 1893. Second, as part of the 1895 Act, was South Australia's, which at the time was a separate British colony. Australia did not yet exist as a political entity, only as a geographical entity. Each colony on the Australian land mass was as a foreign country to the others. The South Australian bill to give political rights to women was passed by two houses of parliament, both exclusively populated by men. But before it could take effect, it needed the royal assent. That meant it needed the approval of Queen Victoria. She duly signed it during a Privy Council meeting on the Isle of Wight. It was supremely ironic that women could only win political rights through the act of a woman. At the national level, Australia gave women the franchise in 1902, almost as soon as the Commonwealth of Australia itself came into being.

It took a lot longer before Mother England was prepared to entrust women with political power. World War One broke the momentum of the Suffragette movement, even as it demonstrated in new ways the indispensability of women in society. It was not until 1928 that British women could vote for the national parliament, fully a generation after Britain's Antipodean colonies. In the US, though many states acted earlier, women did not win the right to vote in national elections until 1920.

The rising clamour for the recognition of workers' rights also led to another world-first. The Australian Labor Party, formed in 1891, became the world's first labour or socialist government in any parliament. Technically, this honour falls to the Labor government of Queensland in 1899 led by Anderson Dawson. But it lasted only a week. It didn't survive a single parliamentary sitting day and it certainly didn't accomplish anything. It was more an accident and a novelty than any sort of achievement. The world's first labour or socialist *national* parliamentary government was formed by Chris Watson, who became the first Labor prime minister in 1904. But he led a minority government, was frustrated in everything except passing supply bills, and resigned after less than four months.

The first substantive Labor government in Australia was under Prime Minister Andrew Fisher. And he also wins credit for being the world's first labour or socialist leader of any *majority* national government. He not only served three times as prime minister, but in two of those terms he led a government that enjoyed a majority in both houses of parliament and passed real and lasting reforms. He was one of Australia's nation-builders. Before emigrating from Scotland's coalfields as a young man in search of a better life, he had come to know the founder of the British Labour Party, Keir Hardie, and learned how to be a union agitator. But in the end, it was Fisher who showed British Labour and other workers' parties how to win and wield real power.

Fisher, who learned to write by scratching a slate with a piece of coal, created Australia's defence forces, its first paper currency, the trans-continental railway, the Commonwealth Bank and the national capital of Canberra. He introduced the national old-age pension, disability pension and maternity allowances. In these social and labour reforms he was "enshrining a sense of the 'fair go' in Australian politics," according to his biographer, David Day. He is also remembered as the prime minister who committed Australia to supporting Britain in World War One to "our last man and our last shilling." Fisher should be remembered, according to

Day, for "his historic importance as the leader of the first government in the world elected to represent the interests of ordinary people. The example set by each of Fisher's responsible, nation-building governments helped to calm the fears of voters in Britain and elsewhere who had panicked at the prospect of the workers taking power from their masters."

Another fundamental achievement of the Australian Spring was the enshrining of a minimum wage. It was a relatively new idea, "a concept which was virtually unknown in the remainder of the world," according to the historian Geoffrey Blainey. It was remarkable because it was not based on the ability of an employer to pay, and it was not based on a market rate. It was based on the reasonable needs of a family to support itself. That is, it didn't put private capital or the private market first. It put the worker and their family at the centre of the calculation.

Or, as the presiding judge and author of the so-called Harvester judgment, H.B. Higgins, put it, "the first and dominant factor" was "the cost of living as a civilised being." That's why it was intensely controversial at the time, and remains so to this very day. Higgins' starting point for deciding the needs of a "civilised being" was a horse. "If A lets B have the use of his horses, on the terms that he gives them fair and reasonable treatment, I have no doubt that it is B's duty to give them proper food and water, and such shelter and rest as they need." So an employer should do as much for his worker, plus clothing "and a condition of frugal comfort estimated by current standards." The Harvester judgment took its name from the company that brought the case before the court, the Sunshine Harvester Works in Victoria, one of the major enterprises in Australia in its day. Higgins said that a "fair and reasonable" minimum wage should be "something between a good wage and a living wage." That is, not generous, but not bare subsistence, either.

Higgins set the minimum wage for an unskilled worker with a dependent wife and "about three" children at 42 shillings a week. Adjusted for inflation, that would be worth $268.49 in today's money, according to the Reserve Bank's inflation calculator. The national minimum wage paid in 2010 was $569.90 a week. That means the minimum wage has risen by 112 per cent in real terms over 104 years. However, today's minimum wage earner with a dependent spouse and three children also qualifies for other welfare payments that didn't exist at the time of the Harvester case.

The concept of a minimum wage, the definition that it needed to be "fair and reasonable," was the high point of Australian egalitarianism in the view of the historian Keith Hancock. In his landmark work *Australia*, published in 1930, he wrote: "Manufacturers must learn to seek economy through efficiency, rather than efficiency through parsimony; they must make economic facts conform to the idea of justice."

The idea didn't spring from nowhere. It had developed in Australian society and politics, with strong influences from abroad, as the industrial relations academic David Plowman has pointed out. For two decades the unions had been agitating, organising huge demonstrations, rallies, deputations and exposés to put the case of the exploited worker and to demand a decent minimum wage. In 1890, seventeen years before the Harvester judgment, the premier of Queensland, Sir Samuel Griffith, had moved a bill for a minimum wage in his state. His bill proposed a wage that "can never be taken at a less sum than such as is sufficient to maintain the labourer and his family in a state of health and reasonable comfort." Griffith went on to become a father of federation and the first chief justice of the High Court. The Catholic Church strengthened the argument for action. Pope Leo XIII's 1891 encyclical *Rerum Novarum* on relations between capital and labour declared: "There underlies a dictate of natural justice more imperious and more ancient than any bargain between man and man, namely, that wages ought not to be insufficient to support a frugal and well-behaved wage-earner." And a bill for a fixed minimum wage went before the Victorian parliament two years later.

The concept of a worker-centric minimum wage was also part of a broader political settlement. The most contentious issue of federation was whether Australia should be built as a protectionist nation or a free-trading one. The leader of the Protectionist Party and future prime minister was Alfred Deakin. He proposed a policy of building support for protectionism by explicitly using it to ensure higher wages for workers.

Until federation, the individual Australian colonies – except for the free trade New South Wales – had each applied a protectionist policy to goods from each other and other countries. That is, they imposed taxes or tariffs on imports. It was done to create an artificial advantage for their local firms. One of the justifications for the policy was that the firms that benefited from this would be able to pay higher wages to their workers. Deakin called this "Old Protectionism." Now he proposed a policy he called "New Protectionism," which he declared to be more ambitious. As Deakin put it in the new federal parliament in 1907:

> The 'old' Protection contented itself with making good wages possible. The 'new' Protection seeks to make them actual. It aims at according to the manufacturer that degree of exemption from unfair outside competition which will enable him to pay fair and reasonable wages … It does not stop here. Having put the manufacturer in a position to pay good wages, it goes on to assure the public that he does pay them.

How to make manufacturers pay? The new federal government did not have power over wages. So Deakin would do it indirectly.

All firms would be forced to pay an excise on the goods they sold unless they won a special certificate of exemption. And they could only win this certificate if they could prove that they paid "fair and reasonable" wages to their workers. And when Deakin became Australia's second prime minister, his government implemented exactly this policy.

It was in pursuit of just this certificate of exemption that Sunshine Harvester had applied to Justice Higgins of the new Commonwealth Conciliation and Arbitration Court. And Higgins had chosen it to be his test case for defining the "fair and reasonable" wage. So the Harvester case was the judicial interpretation of a law introduced by the Deakin government as part of its New Protectionism policy. Higgins complained in court that he didn't want to be the one to interpret what the government meant by "fair and reasonable" but that the vagueness of the new law obliged him to try. It was Deakin's policy, but it was passed by parliament with the support of the party controlling the balance of power at the time, Labor.

The Harvester judgment was "Australia's first social justice statement," and "surely the noblest product of the early Commonwealth," according to the historians John Lack and Charles Fahey. "For workers, Harvester leavened the otherwise stale and bitter bread of Federation." That was for the workers who could afford any bread at all. The prelude to federation was one of the bleakest economic times in Australia's history. The 1890s was a decade of economic depression and human misery. The social welfare and wages measures, the rush of recognition of rights, were a political response to an economic failure and a social calamity. Australian egalitarianism and democratic impulses were already real forces in Australia. And the 1890s depression, coming just as Australia was federating, was an important force in giving expression to them. The need to respond to the hardships and suffering of the people shaped the political, welfare, wages and protection systems that were crystallising in the new country.

The people of this new country defined their rights not only by what they demanded, but also by what they resisted. The struggle against conscription in World War One was epic. It was brought to a referendum twice, the first time by Billy Hughes as a Labor prime minister and the second time by Billy Hughes as a Nationalist prime minister, and was defeated twice. It left Australia, with South Africa, as one of only two countries participating in the war that did not use conscription. (Australia has resorted to conscription for an overseas war only once in its history, during the Vietnam War.)

How did Australia develop from its origins as a brutal, military-run penal settlement to become a fair, free, tolerant, law-abiding country? Its early egalitarianism, democratic impulses and the people's assertion of expanding rights and freedoms go a long way toward supplying the answer. It's striking that Australia pioneered so many new rights and freedoms. Hyperbole at the time described Australia as a "working man's paradise." It was not that, especially during the depression of the 1890s, but it was something much greater than anyone could have imagined if they had paused to consider the first government structure erected in the new colony in 1788: a gallows.

*

Of course, rights and freedoms are necessary for a successful country, but not sufficient. There must be work for a people to build its worth and wealth for a nation to build its living standards.

But prosperity was the easy part for Australia, surely, guaranteed by the mineral wealth lying just below the ground. Didn't it give Australia a foolproof way of paying for high living standards? Not really. Coal, gas, oil, gold, copper, zinc, bauxite, uranium and diamonds are valuable commodities. But, in the long story of

humankind, it is normal that resource-rich societies end up failures. Not just most of the time, but virtually all of the time.
Resource wealth usually comes with high inflation, extreme
indebtedness, corruption and civil war. Professor Paul Stevens,
from the University of Dundee in Scotland, surveyed fifty-two
resource-rich developing countries and found that only four had
managed to extract a real national benefit from nature's bounty:
Chile, Malaysia, Indonesia and Botswana. That is a dismal record.

A large surge of money gushing into a fragile state will
almost always break it, not make it. Only a handful of truly
resource-rich nations have made it all the way through the obstacle
course to become First World countries: the United States, Canada,
Australia and New Zealand. Norway sits atop a gusher of oil, but
it was rich and stable long before it found its black gold in the
1960s. The common Anglo origins of these successful countries
hint at one of the explanations for their success. The neo-Britains
imported a ready-made set of helpful habits and institutions: a
concept of citizens' rights protected in the common law, the rudi-
ments of parliamentary democracy, an independent judiciary, the
right to private property, a strong work ethic and the structures
for capitalist risk-taking.

In starting afresh, these new societies also managed to leave
behind some of the worst aspects of their colonial mother. Australia
shrugged off the ruinous British class system, developing an aristocracy of merit rather than rule by an entitled idiocy. Egalitarianism
is a deep well of national strength. This constellation of forces
created strong states that were able to extract vast natural wealth
without destroying their societies and economies in the process.

Mining in Australian economic development was important,
but its role is exaggerated in the public mind. In the colonial
economy, pastoralism and agriculture held a bigger share. Towards
the end of the nineteenth century and into the twentieth, so did

manufacturing. Even when the gold rush was on, a mining event of global significance, with Australia providing a third of total world gold output, mining was the junior partner to primary production. In 1861, agriculture accounted for 22 per cent of Australia's estimated GDP, while mining was 17.5. Thirty years later, as Australia was nearing federation, mining had retreated to be 6.7 per cent of the total economy, while farming was 28.5 and manufacturing 16.6.

The chief effect of the gold rushes was to increase Australia's population. The prospect of finding the Biblical Ophir drew such a surge of immigrants that Australia's total population quadrupled from 430,000 in 1851 to 1.7 million in 1871. The need to house, transport and otherwise cater to the extra people gave a major boost to the housing and construction industries and the economy as a whole. This immigration effect lasted for years longer than the gold rushes themselves.

Farming was the biggest source of economic activity and the biggest source of exports in the colonial era and well beyond into federation. And of all the agricultural sectors, wool, famously, was the biggest. At first, Australian farm output grew because farmers were simply adding more farmland as they cleared the bush. The more land they had, the more produce they could grow. But this could not last forever, even in a continent as big as Australia. Around 1920, about 130 years after white settlement, the supply of new, quality, arable land ran out. There was another source of growth, however, that had already started to kick in. From about 1870, farmers had been applying two key new technologies. They seem so obvious and ordinary today that we don't even think of them as technologies, but they were transformative. One was the fence. Instead of having sheep roam free tended by shepherds, farmers started to fence the animals in. Hand in hand with the fence came the dam. With water to hand, there was less need to move the sheep around. Together, these innovations allowed a major intensification of wool growing and an exponential increase in output without having to find new land.

Further technological advance drove further agricultural breakthroughs. When shipbuilders started to use steel in vessels for the first time in the 1880s, ocean freight rates fell sharply. This suddenly made Australian wheat competitive on world markets. Then geneticists developed new breeds of disease-resistant wheat. Wheat output boomed. And the advent of refrigerated shipping made it possible to export butter, frozen meat and fruit. The growth in these industries, in turn, aided manufacturing growth, as farmers, traders, exporters and shippers needed more farm machinery, refrigeration equipment and food-processing plants. So agriculture and manufacturing expanded even as gold output sagged.

In defiance of its colonial origins, Australia was born a proudly democratic nation and a pioneer in the rights and freedoms of the people. And its burgeoning industries gave it the highest average incomes in the world. While the average per capita income in the US in 1890 was $3,396, in Australia it was $4,433, or 30 per cent higher, according to the late economic historian Angus Maddison. What could possibly go wrong?

8

THE RACKET

When Australia federated, the struggle between free traders and protectionists was quickly won. And it was the free traders who lost. The new country turned into a closed shop, sheltering itself from a competitive world and trusting in a benign Britain for its future. It might have worked as a transitional step, but protectionism led to a long-term stagnation as Australia became addicted to its sheltered existence. Much of Australian agriculture and manufacturing spent most of the twentieth century in a cosy, well-padded, expensive incubator provided by the government. It was all about preservation, not expansion, about equity, not efficiency. And it was a serious error of national strategy.

It was the economic analogue to the White Australia policy. Some of the rhetoric of federation disdained non-white peoples. "These races are, in comparison with white races," said the first prime minister, Edmund Barton, "unequal and inferior." But in spite of much of the propaganda of the time, the truth was that the new country's founders didn't look down on Asians as inferior. They were in awe of their competitive strengths. The real reason that the separate colonies had converged on racial exclusion before federation was that the Chinese were too tough as competitors: they were superior, not inferior, and the fathers of federation said so.

"They are not an inferior race," said Sir Henry Parkes. "They are a superior set of people. A nation of an old, deep-rooted civilisation.

It is because I believe the Chinese to be a powerful race, capable of taking a great hold upon this country, and because I want to preserve the type of my own nation, I am and always have been opposed to the influx of Chinese." And Alfred Deakin said: "It is not the bad qualities, but the good qualities of these alien races that make them so dangerous to us. It is their inexhaustible energy, their power of applying themselves to new tasks, their endurance and low standard of living that make them such competitors." The Chinese had outworked the whites on the goldfields of New South Wales and Victoria, out-traded them in the private economy of Darwin and outsmarted them in establishing the sugar plantations of Queensland. White Australia, like the tariff, was a protectionist measure. It was not an arrogant expression of self-confidence but a frightened retreat into self-doubt. Australia was a country in hiding.

So the early emphasis on rights was not just a matter of individual freedoms and labour rights. Through trade protectionism and labour arbitration, it was stamped on Australia's economic arrangements. It led to an emphasis on equity that gradually crowded out efficiency. Competitiveness stagnated and so did investment and innovation. By the early 1980s, Australia's minister for industry, John Button, declared that Australia was the proud host not to a manufacturing industry but an "industrial museum."

It started simply. Imagine a world with only two countries, as the economist W.A. Sinclair suggests, a way of simplification to show the main forces at work. One country is old and the other new. "The new region contains unused but potentially productive land whereas the older country is already using all its land and is undergoing economic growth. When the productive land in the new region is discovered, economic development may commence as a result of labour, capital and entrepreneurship flowing there attracted by [the] higher returns" that are available in a start-up land as opposed to an old and rigidly organised one. The old country, of course, is Britain, and the new one is Australia. This is how Australia's economy worked until about 1920, Sinclair argues.

In other words, Australia was simply an offshore extension of Britain, a new hinterland that fed the needs of the centre. Is this a major simplification? Yes, but it's an accurate one. And it moved from being the early de facto relationship between empire and colony into a deliberately structured economic policy. Australia was a part of the British imperial trade preference system, which meant that it was given preferential access to the British market for its exports. Less formally, British investors financed the great bulk of development in Australia. Together with the open-door immigration policy for UK immigrants, while the White Australia policy kept others at bay, Australia was very much an economic outpost of Britain. Of the foreign-born people in Australia at the time of federation, four out of five were from the United Kingdom. It was an enclave economy, sheltering in the larger empire.

Federation would have been the logical time for the new country to establish its own economic territory in the world. Instead, it continued as a British enclave. And it intensified and extended the concept of Australia as a closed shop. The six individual colonies already had their own separate White Australia policies. The new federation made them national. The six colonies had separate systems of tariffs and rules to protect their companies against those of the other colonies. Now, as they abolished those protections, the new federation built national ones. The separate colonies had recently introduced their own wage-setting bodies. Now the federal government introduced a national one that set national wages, and linked them to the tariff system. So the whole structure was interconnected.

The empire delivers the country a living, the country delivers industry a living, industry delivers the workers a living. White Australia keeps the distressingly industrious Asians out, while giving the British a comfortably familiar outpost. And Britain, in return, gets the land, the raw materials that the land yields, the opportunity to invest in the project and profit from the returns, and the strategic benefits of a South Pacific imperial base.

This is the arrangement that the journalist Paul Kelly has called "Australian settlement." He characterised it as five foundation principles of federation: White Australia, protection, arbitration, state paternalism and imperial nationalism.

At federation, New South Wales was essentially a free-trade state while Victoria was the champion of protectionism. The initial federal tariff rate was a compromise, set at 5 to 25 per cent, considered to be weakly protectionist at the time. These rates were doubled in 1908 because of the fear that the United States was about to dump heavily discounted wares on Australia and threaten Australian industry. By 1921 the tariff rate had doubled again. Commercial competitiveness was considered an optional extra. If an industry couldn't compete against foreign trade, the government would step in to preserve it. And so it did. Not only in manufacturing but also in agriculture. By the end of the 1920s, every major agricultural industry in Australia was being sheltered from world competition through government subsidies and marketing schemes, with the sole exception of the wool industry. It's often said that Australia, in this era, "rode on the sheep's back." It had to. Wool and wheat were the only parts of the agricultural sector that were growing unassisted.

Australian industry gradually grew addicted to protection from the outside world. With industry protection linked to wages, Australia had created a powerful national constituency for ever-increasing protection. And in 1921 the federal government created a Tariff Board to advise it. The board "was able to keep parliament supplied with a constant stream of recommendations for increased protection," as W.A. Sinclair put it.

The government liked protection because it collected revenue from the tariffs. Industry liked tariffs on foreign goods because it gave their local products an unearned competitive advantage. A 20 per cent tariff on imports, for instance, made the imported competing product 20 per cent more expensive than the local product. And the workers supported tariffs because they were part of a system that encouraged employers to pay "fair and reasonable" wages to their staff. The Brigden inquiry into the tariff system in 1929 found that "the tariff may be likened to a powerful drug with excellent tonic properties, but with reactions on the body politic which make it dangerous in the hands of the unskilled and the uninformed." The inquiry concluded that the tariff had reached its "economic limits." It advised against any further increases "without the closest scrutiny of the costs involved." And yet fifteen years later, the federal government had raised tariffs by a further 50 per cent on average. Australia had embraced what it called the "all-round tariff."

After World War Two, Australian protectionism, already rampant, was increased yet further. It was designed to create more jobs to accommodate the Italian and Greek immigrants who were allowed into Australia under the "populate or perish" rubric. The leader of the Country (later National) Party, "Black" Jack McEwen was a powerful advocate of more protection "all round" in the 1960s.

The effect of an ever-increasing tariff – simply a tax on imports – slowly choked Australia's appetite for goods from the rest of the world. While the tariff was a price mechanism, protectionism also deployed quotas and licences as ways to shut out import competition. After World War Two, quotas became the main tool of protectionism.

Was this healthy for economic vitality? No. If existing industries and jobs are locked in place, it may preserve the status quo, but it locks out the future. Capital and labour can't move to other, more promising industries. It is a very basic point, yet usually overlooked in arguments about protection. Why? Because it's easy to see the industries and the jobs of today, and hard to imagine the industries and jobs of tomorrow.

Was this healthy for the trade balance? No, because exporters use a lot of imports in making their products. On average, about a third of the cost of making an Australian manufactured product is in imported parts. So the tariff just made it more expensive for exporters to make their wares. This led to the adage that a tariff is a tax on exports. Protectionism made Australian exports more costly and penalised national competitiveness. Both imports and exports slowly shrank as a proportion of the economy as the century progressed.

The tariff was emblematic of the larger national state of mind. Australia was closing itself to the products but also the people of the world and many of its opportunities, and in return the world was growing without Australia. There came a moment in the 1960s when Australian intellectuals, economists and policy-makers realised that the country was in a deep malaise. Economists saw the emerging evidence that protectionism was stifling the economy, where policy-makers understood that White Australia was limiting both the economy and the society as well as constraining Australia diplomatically. It was increasingly difficult to justify a racist policy on moral grounds, but it was also a policy that penalised Australia's harder interests. In the 1960s Japan was dubbed a "miracle economy" and it soon became Australia's biggest trading partner. Yet under White Australia, a citizen could not marry a Japanese and sponsor him or her for citizenship. But protectionism and racism were such deeply established practices and so rooted in the federation pact that it was politically difficult to begin to open the closed shop.

And in the 1960s it was hard to demonstrate to the voting public that the country was not succeeding. Australia grew more slowly than the average rate for the OECD countries, but the world economy was thriving and Australian mining was booming and the economy was growing, even if it was lagging behind others. Average income per head grew at an annual average 3.2 per cent in the decade, its fastest rate since federation. Mining burgeoned on the national export account from just 3 per cent in the early '50s to 30 per cent in the mid '70s.

It was at this uncomfortable moment of realisation, when Australian elites were aware of the national dilemma yet politically unready to act, that Donald Horne wrote *The Lucky Country*, published in 1964. He captured the unease. The book is one of the toughest critiques of Australia ever written. His thesis was that Australia's good fortune in the form of mineral wealth had become a prop, an excuse and perhaps even a licence for a terrible national complacency. The nation's luck was its curse.

In the book's most famous passage, under the subheading of "Living on our Luck," Horne wrote: "Australia is a lucky country run mainly by second-rate people who share its luck. It lives on other people's ideas, and although its ordinary people are adaptable, most of its leaders (in all fields) so lack curiosity about the events that surround them that they are often taken by surprise." At its core, Horne said in a 2005 interview, the book was "a derivative-society thesis – the essential thing in the writing of *The Lucky Country* was derivativeness." Horne best captured this idea in a 1976 book, *Money Made Us*. "Overall, if, with exceptions, there was a scepticism towards original talent, even a hatred of it, the smart thing was to get the design of a proven success from overseas and then follow the instructions on the back of the packet."

This was a perfectly logical consequence of an economy built on protectionism. There was no incentive to take risks, to experiment, to thrust, to find a competitive edge in a system designed to reward a failure of competitiveness.

In its trade arrangements, Australia was still doggedly derivative of Britain. World War Two had exposed British dominance as a faded artefact. The supposedly unassailable British fortress of Singapore had folded without a fight before the onrushing Japanese. The British had signally failed to live up to their rhetoric on the defence of Australia. The Australian wartime prime minister, John Curtin, was forced to overrule London to order Australian forces home to defend the country against Japan. Churchill, who wanted to engage the Japanese in Burma, was reluctant to release the Australian troops. The postwar British economy was shrunken and damaged. And yet it was only when Britain joined the European Common Market in 1973 that Australia had to stop pretending that its economic future lay with the Mother Country.

On the Australian emphasis on entitlements, Horne wrote: "The general Australian belief is that it's the government's job to see that everyone gets a fair go – from old age pensioners to manufacturers. A fair go usually means money. Australians see government – which they both trust and despise – as an outfit whose job is to help them where they need help." The fair go, he wrote, "is essentially a non-competitive concept, a demand for protection, an attempt to gain security and certainty. Whether it is an underdog in a factory or a top dog demanding tariff protection the feeling is that justice lies in a guarantee of existence. To fight for existence in an open market must be avoided although one may use legal or other lurks."

Horne had detected and foreshadowed Australia's slide from the top ranks of the world's richest countries, arguing that luck and complacency were poor substitutes for originality and investment.

"Can the racket last?" he asked, immediately responding with a resounding "NO." He was, of course, correct, and it was a slippage that gathered pace in the '70s and '80s. How was Australia ever to emerge from its torpor?

The White Australia policy and trade protectionism both came under timid review in the 1960s. Import controls like quotas and licences were reduced, though the tariff remained. And the Liberal prime minister Harold Holt made an opening in immigration policy by relaxing entry for non-Europeans in 1966. The Labor government of Gough Whitlam eventually brought White Australia to an end in 1973, and Vietnamese refugees began to enter the country after 1976. This was the first substantial influx of any Asian nationality since federation. Whitlam also made an assault on protectionism by cutting all tariffs unilaterally by 25 per cent in the same year, later explaining, "The 1973 tariff cut ended an ethos of protection all round which took its antecedents from the time of Scullin," who was prime minister during the Great Depression. "McEwen used the tariff wall to establish a system of protection-on-demand. For decades this imposed a high flat tax on consumers."

Maybe, but Whitlam's tariff cut was soon followed by economic slowdown. The slowdown was blamed on the cut and this discredited the cause of free trade. Before the Whitlam cut, the average effective rate of protection was 35 per cent for manufacturing. But for cars it was 54 per cent, for clothing and footwear it was 83, and it ranged as high as 280 per cent for some basic metal products. So even after the 1973 cut, protection remained high. Whitlam abandoned the cause. And then protection started to increase once more. Not through the tariff now, but through quotas to limit car and clothing imports.

Australia remained addicted to its sheltered existence. The shop remained closed. Protectionism, and its supporting superstructure of controls on finance, controls on international capital flows and controls on labour, was comfortable but ruinous, like most unhealthy addictions. Australian average income per head slid inexorably from eighth place in the world all the way to eighteenth. Nation-building had included the creation and enshrining of rights and entitlements. But now the country had veered too far towards protecting rights and entitlements and had lost sight of the need for opportunity and competition. Equity had crowded out efficiency. Who would make the correction? Who would overcome the country's addiction? Who would break the padlock on the closed shop to let the world in and Australia out?

9

THE HEAVY ARMOUR

Paul Keating wanted to be chauffeured to his office one day in 1995. It's not a long journey from the Lodge to Parliament House, all of two kilometres. But the prime minister was infuriated to discover that his way was blocked by trucks. Very big ones. The TV news that night showed an angry Keating on foot, being ushered by his bodyguards between two monster logging rigs. He had to be restrained from taking a swing at the truck drivers. He didn't seem to notice that the loggers, blockading parliament in protest against a cut to the quota of forests they could turn into woodchips, were much bigger and burlier. The central characteristic of Keating was that he was utterly fearless. As far as the public knew, that was the end of the story of the loggers' blockade.

But once inside the prime minister's suite, Keating decided to escalate the argument. He ordered an aide to phone the Defence Department. He wanted the army to bring tanks to Parliament House immediately to clear the trucks. The aide complied and Defence began the bureaucratic process of deploying battle tanks. This train of events might have continued, and might have ended disastrously, but for two factors.

First was that other members of the Keating staff quietly cancelled the order. Second was the fact that the executive government of Australia was on covert permanent standby to contain the more erratic urges of Paul Keating. When the tanks didn't arrive, the prime minister made follow-up demands of his staff and his ministers to produce them. One senior minister who was involved in foiling Keating's insistence on calling in the army later explained: "We spent half our time containing the madness."

This was exactly the sort of person that Australia needed to break it out of its national torpor. He was utterly fearless, utterly determined, utterly indefatigable and, quite possibly, utterly mad, at least by the conventional political definition. Why? Because no sane self-interested politician would have taken the political risks that he did to reform the Australian economy. He didn't do it by himself, and he couldn't have. He needed ideas for reform. He needed a specific program to give body to those ideas. And he needed power, and enough time in power, to implement the program.

The ideas came courtesy of Margaret Thatcher and Ronald Reagan. The so-called conservative revolution was an Anglo-American ideological and political wave that rippled around the world. It also went by the names of neoliberalism or supply-side economics. Keating caught and surfed the wave in Australia. The specific program came from the Department of the Treasury, the economic policy arm of the federal government. And the power, ultimately the gift of the Australian voting public, was delivered to him by two other politicians. The man who gave Keating the job, the opportunity and the support he needed was Bob Hawke. As Labor leader from 1983 to 1991, Hawke won four elections, appointed Keating treasurer, and backed him on crucial decisions of the reform program. "It took two leaders, a former trade union leader and a high school drop-out, to transform Australia from a protected, insular country to an outwardly focused, globalised one," in the words of the Griffith Business School academic Tom Conley.

But there was one more man who delivered Keating the power he needed. He was John Howard. Although Howard was the leader of the opposition and the political nemesis of Labor, he also supported the Thatcher–Reagan revolution. He could have used his numbers in the Senate to block Keating's reforms. But on the critical measures, at the vital moments, he instead chose to support him. Without Howard's support, the reform program might have died on the floor of the Senate. With it, the program passed into law and became reality.

Thatcher, Reagan and Hawke–Keating all took power around the same time, the end of the 1970s or the early '80s, and all confronted similar economic conditions of sclerotic growth, high inflation, high unemployment and a paralysis of economic policy responses. They embraced neoliberalism, which a former US Treasury official in the Clinton administration, Brad DeLong, called "the only live utopian program in the world today."

Margaret Thatcher pioneered the pro-market revolution when she took power as British prime minister in 1979. She had a Keating-esque indomitable will. A former US Secretary of State, George Shultz, said: "If I were married to her, I'd be sure to have dinner ready when she got home." And of herself, the Iron Lady once said: "I am extraordinarily patient, provided I get my own way in the end." She took office with Britain stagnant and approaching national insolvency. The country was suffering high inflation, high unemployment, high taxes, a chronic budget deficit and chronic coal miners' strikes that periodically interrupted the electricity supply. Her solution was to "roll back the frontiers of the state," as she put it, and do the same to the union movement. She saw maximising individual choice as a moral issue, as well as a political and a philosophical one. This found expression, above all, in her economics: "There can be no liberty unless there is economic liberty." And in her most evangelical moment: "Economics are the method; the object is to change the soul." She was a deeply divisive figure in Britain and her economic shock therapy set off riots.

Ronald Reagan took the US presidency in 1981 with the same outlook: "The basis of conservatism is a desire for less government interference or less centralized authority or more individual freedom." Reagan lacked Thatcher's steely persona. He was affable to the point of being mocked as daffily absent-minded: "People here may be sharply divided over the Reagan administration's policies," said the Democrat senator Edward Kennedy, "but they all admire Ronald Reagan for not getting involved in them." Reagan was nonetheless, like Thatcher, a divisive leader. Like Thatcher, he confronted a powerful union and broke it. In Britain it was coal miners, in America air traffic controllers. Both leaders were subject to assassination attempts. They became close personal friends.

Bob Hawke and Paul Keating did not present their program in moralistic terms. They presented it as a practical matter of economic performance. After all, the Labor Party constitution committed it to the socialist objective of the "socialisation of industry, production, distribution and exchange." Hawke and Keating were now taking the party in precisely the opposite direction. It was called the "Hawke–Keating hijack" by one politics lecturer, Dean Jaensch. As a Labor minister of the time, Neal Blewett, later wrote: "Ideologically the Labor Party was not a natural vehicle for confronting the competitive imperatives of globalisation, which focused on the dead hand of protective tariffs, the distortions produced by industry subsidies, inefficient public enterprises, the sclerotic grip of financial regulation and the rigidities of the labour market."

Keating presented the problem simply. There were three crucial prices for the national economy, and in Australia they were "uncompetitive and wrong. The price of foreign exchange, the price of capital and the price of labour." To get the prices right meant allowing the market a much bigger say in setting them.

Why didn't the conservative party in Australia inaugurate the conservative revolution in Australia? The Liberals were in power under Malcolm Fraser from 1975 to 1983 but failed to embrace the pro-market reform agenda of Thatcher and Reagan. Fraser was a social conservative but an economic interventionist of the pre-Thatcher era. John Howard, the treasurer in the Fraser government, later explained that the Fraser Liberals suffered a failure of comprehension: "The economic setting had changed, and what worked in the 1960s no longer worked. I think there was a tendency, when the Fraser government got back into office – because so many of the people in it then had been in government before – to say, 'Well, we'll just go back to how we did things before.' But in that three-year period, which was quite short, the world had changed forever. We'd finally gone off the fixed exchange rate, broken free of the Bretton Woods world [of regulated international exchange rates and capital flows, in place since World War Two]. You'd had the oil shock; you'd had the impact of equal pay in Australia; you'd had a wages explosion; and you'd had a massive, foolishly-brought-about increase in government spending by the Whitlam government. I mean, in two years a 46 per cent increase in government spending – pretty savage. So we really had to adopt a different setting." But they didn't. Howard flirted with the idea as treasurer. He had commissioned an investigation, the Campbell Inquiry, into deregulating the financial system, but failed to act on its recommendations.

So the conservatives left the task of pro-market reform to Labor. Keating said that when he moved into Howard's office as the incoming treasurer, he found a copy of the Campbell Inquiry gathering dust on a shelf. The Coalition also left Labor an economic mess. Inflation was high and unemployment high at the same time. The recession of 1982–83 handed the incoming Labor government an unemployment rate of 9.9 per cent. The current account deficit was at its worst since the Korean War of 1950–53. The situation was so evidently bad that it gave Labor a licence for change.

Keating took up the task of reform with energy and conviction.

Perversely perhaps, Hawke and Keating turned out to be just the leaders for the task and for the time. They adopted the same basic tenets as Thatcher and Reagan, but without the moralising or the philosophising. "The logic of our economic policies leads to an expectation of smaller government," Keating, as treasurer, said in 1985. But there was no theology here: "Properly functioning, the market mechanism is a powerful engine for economic growth … I hold a very healthy respect for the advantages of market processes, but respect falls short of deification. Where they can be shown to assist our central economic objective of sound, sustained economic growth, market-based arguments will receive a receptive audience. Where they represent mere propaganda, they will go the same way as other dogmas which unnecessarily encumber our progress."

Although Labor's approach might have been less evangelical, it was in pursuit of the same objective – more play for market forces in the economy, with less protection, less rigidity and less government. The ten main policies of the neoliberals were set out in US economist John Williamson's "Washington Consensus": governments should run balanced budgets; governments should redirect subsidies away from politically favoured firms or industries and into the broader public goods of education, health care and infrastructure; taxation should be as low as possible and applied across as wide a base as possible; interest rates should be set by the market; so should exchange rates; trade should be as free as possible; so should international capital flows; governments should sell state enterprises and stay out of markets; governments should remove regulations except for those needed for safety, environmental protection, consumer protection and prudential supervision of the financial system; governments should provide secure legal title to property ownership at low cost.

The tenth of these was already in place in Australia, a product of the British legal system the colonists brought with them. Hawke and Keating made a good run at the other nine and succeeded in most but not all. The army stayed in its barracks, and Hawke exercised judicious political oversight, but Keating unleashed every ounce of personal and political firepower he possessed. One of Keating's ways of emboldening his colleagues in the Labor government in moments of doubt and fear was to pose this question: "What's the worst thing that can happen to you in this business? You could lose your job. So why be a mouse?" To most of his colleagues, this would have been a fearsome prospect. To Keating, it was trivial. Australia had found its reformer.

10

I DARE YOU

The cabinet had been unable to reach a decision. The treasurer was determined to make the reform and change the course of Australian history. But he could not get the support of his colleagues. Paul Keating would not relent; his colleagues would not acquiesce. After many hours of argument in the oppressively airless, dark-brown cabinet room of Old Parliament House, the prime minister, Bob Hawke, had asked his colleagues for licence to resolve the stalemate in a separate meeting with Keating. The group, relieved to have the burden lifted, agreed that Hawke and Keating should thrash it out.

Since the 1960s, when he was in his twenties, Keating had believed that Australia's income tax rates were too high. He wanted to cast the tax net wider to collect more revenue from a broader set of activities in the economy so that the government could cut the rates of income tax. It would increase Australia's efficiency and profitability and, though tax reform was always wildly controversial, it was now or never. The Treasury stood foursquare behind him.

Now, across the table from Hawke in the climactic meeting, with only their most senior advisers by their sides, Keating spent hours hammering Hawke with every possible reason that Australia needed to commit to ambitious tax reform. Several times he seemed to be close to winning the prime minister's go-ahead, but at the threshold Hawke hesitated and hedged.

Finally Keating was out of patience. He issued a dare. He held up a sheaf of papers, a draft cabinet decision. He said that unless Hawke specifically told him to stop, he was going to walk out of the room and go to the media and announce that the decision had been made to phase out protection for Australian manufacturing. Instructing his advisers, the Treasury secretary, Ted Evans, and his chief of staff, Don Russell, to gather their things, Keating stood up. He was defying Hawke to stop him. Hawke said nothing. Keating walked to the door. Still the prime minister said nothing. Keating opened the door and walked out into the hallway followed by Evans and Russell. Still no word from Hawke, as Keating tells the story. They closed the door. Hawke had not stopped them and Keating had triumphed. Don Russell delivered the punchline: "People wouldn't believe how we do things in this country." Although Russell himself has no recollection of this line, Keating polishes it like a family heirloom.

Keating didn't get the ambitious, sweeping tax reform he first sought. Hawke vetoed it when the unions and big business baulked. Keating was dejected for weeks. But he recovered and won very important changes nonetheless. As his former economics adviser John Edwards has quipped, Keating found victory in defeat. With Hawke, he did make income taxes lower and the tax base wider. Hawke and Keating cut the top marginal income tax rate from 60 to 47 per cent. Even after the conservatives took power in 1996, they made no further cuts to this rate for a decade. It would be sixteen years before the top personal tax rate set by Labor was cut, when the Howard–Costello Coalition government cut it from 47 to 45 per cent, in 2006. Another important reform by the Hawke–Keating government was the decision to end double taxing of dividends. Companies had previously paid tax on their profits, and then, when they paid those profits to their shareholders as dividends, the profits were taxed a second time. But Hawke and Keating introduced dividend imputation so that shareholders received a credit for the taxes the company had already paid. The profits were taxed only once. This favoured shares and it favoured investment in shares. And that meant that it favoured investment in Australian companies.

One of the reforms that Australia needed most was also perhaps the very hardest. Australia needed to engage with the world but was hopelessly attached to its security blanket of protectionism. It gave a warm feeling but was a flimsy substitute for a thriving economy. Paul Keating was determined to snatch it away. Keating and Hawke committed themselves to phasing out the tariffs and quotas that had protected Australian industry for almost a century. But to break the country from its addiction would be wrenching and unpopular.

The news of the tariff cuts was met with mighty uproar and a campaign of fearmongering and doomsaying that ran for years. The decision was opposed by both business and the manufacturing unions and it was unpopular in the polls. But Keating was resolute. In two steps, in 1988 and 1991, the government set out a plan for turning Australia from one of the more protected economies in the world into one of the freest. Labor had the luxury of support from the opposition. As opposition leader, John Howard endorsed the first step. John Hewson as opposition leader supported the second.

The withdrawal pangs were acute. In between the two steps, 132,000 jobs were lost in manufacturing, or one out of every nine. Most of these were unionised jobs, so it was a blow to the size, income and power of the unions. This made it especially painful for Labor. The temptations to relapse were strong, even as the second wave of reforms was about to take effect. When the economy went into recession in 1991–92 and unemployment rose to 11 per cent, with a million people out of work, most members of the government panicked. The unions and the Labor backbench demanded that the tariff cuts be cancelled or postponed. This would have been consistent with history – whenever the economy turned down, protectionism reared up. But the job was only half done. In one of the most heavily protected sectors, textiles, clothing and footwear, the government was giving the industry protection equivalent to an annual subsidy of $1.275 billion for an industry employing 55,600 people. That meant that the subsidy equivalent came to $22,931 per worker – more than they were actually paid in wages. So the economics for continuing to cut protection were compelling.

But the politics for freezing the cuts were equally forceful by 1992, after Keating had dispatched Hawke as prime minister. The government was in a dire position in the polls. Keating recalled the pressure building as the industry minister, John Button, the treasurer, John Dawkins, the leaders of the ACTU, Bill Kelty and George Campbell, all came to see him: "They all wanted me to abandon the policy. My view was that if you blink once, you will be lost. This was when we guaranteed the end of protection in the old Australian Settlement." Keating forced a reluctant party and government to continue with the painful therapy. In the final analysis, it came down to the determination of one man.

Certainly, he had allies outside the party. Agriculture had been through the same protectionism detox and come out of the program fitter, leaner and more competitive on the world market. An industry which had been unable to feed even the minuscule population of the early colony was able, two centuries later, to feed not only its own population but also to make it one of the world's top ten food exporters.

Australia, which took forty years to wean itself off emergency food shipments from the mother country, ultimately became one of the world's principal food suppliers. Big flows of foreign and local investment, the endless ingenuity of the farmer and the scientist, and the ruthlessness of the global marketplace drove a country with a fragile environment and low rainfall to become a world-leading producer. Capital, cunning and competition combined to defeat natural endowment. Farming became so successful and confident that it grew to resent the costly and cosseted manufacturers.

Farmers, after all, had to buy some of their machinery, tools, chemicals, fencing and other supplies from uncompetitive Australian manufacturers. And some of their taxes went to pay subsidies to the protected sectors. All this imposed a handicap on the hyper-competitive farmers, adding to their costs. Remember, a tax on imports is also a tax on exports. It was a burden they shouldn't have had to carry, and so their lobby group, the National Farmers' Federation, became an aggressive advocate of free trade in the 1980s. It was soon joined by the miners. If farming and mining could learn to thrive in a competitive global market, this might have given manufacturing some hope.

But protectionism is the hardest habit to kick. And it requires great faith in the marketplace and in the abilities of workers. Existing firms and jobs must be destroyed before new ones are created. It's impossible to know where they might emerge, or when, or how.

This was not the only reform of the Hawke–Keating era, but it was the toughest. Other reforms were essential handmaidens to the pro-market revolution. One was the 1983 decision to end regulatory control of the Australian dollar. By floating the currency, its value was set by supply and demand instead of officials at the Treasury and Reserve Bank.

This was vital because a freely moving exchange rate operates as a shock absorber for an economy. So when the Asian economic crisis of 1997–98 struck, the Australian dollar took a huge hit, falling from 78 US cents to 55, a depreciation of 30 per cent. This would not have been allowed to happen under the fixed-rate regime because it would have been deemed too disruptive and too inflationary. Australia would have gone into recession as the heart attack to the Asian economies sent demand for Australian exports into arrest. But the enormous adjustment to the exchange rate meant that Australian exports were suddenly 30 per cent cheaper than they had been. This gave them a competitive boost and allowed Australian firms to switch export sales rapidly away from the stricken Asian economies to other centres. Exporters managed the crisis well, the economy continued to grow uninterrupted, and the country sailed serenely through one of the great economic disruptions of the late twentieth century.

The float had been vigorously opposed by the Treasury secretary, John Stone. Why? He argued that the market would force up the value of the Australian currency, making exports ruinously uncompetitive. The force of Stone's convictions made Keating hesitate; this was an occasion where Hawke pressed Keating, who eventually agreed. They overruled Stone. Hawke at the time, with perhaps a flourish of excitement, called the decision "one of the most significant economic policy decisions of the era, if not in Australian history altogether." Stone's prediction was exactly wrong. The market pushed the dollar down, not up. In the year before the float, it averaged 98.6 US cents. A year after the float it was trading in the low 80s. The deregulation of the dollar actually delivered Australian exporters a competitive advantage. And it turned out that Australia had been overvaluing its currency for years. Its average trading value from the time of the float till the end of 2010 was 77 US cents. It took twenty-seven years for it to return to the same level as its pre-float regulated value of 98.6.

John Stone resigned some months after he'd been overruled. Soon after departing the Treasury, he recanted publicly: "I personally believe that the decision made by the present government on

9th December last [1983] will stand as its greatest achievement when all else has been forgotten." He could not have grasped the full scope of the pro-market reform program that Hawke and Keating would eventually impose.

Another reform was the deregulation of the financial system. Foreign banks were allowed to set up for the first time to compete with the local oligopoly. And financial markets were allowed to trade a wide variety of instruments. Markets started giving companies finance in place of bank loans, allowing big borrowers to go direct to the source of wholesale funds and cutting out the banking middleman. This reduced the role of banks in the economy.

The Hawke–Keating government also began a sweeping program of deregulation of industries. This included privatisation of state-owned firms. The Commonwealth Bank, Qantas, the Australian Wheat Board, Aussat Pty Ltd (which eventually became Optus) and a swag of others were sold to the private sector. But this was a subset of the larger set of measures to increase competition in the economy, including deregulation of the transport and telecommunications industries.

Finally, Hawke and Keating broke down some of the rigidity of the labour market. Till then, workers' wages and conditions had been highly centralised, with an annual national wage decided by an independent official commission. This body, the Conciliation and Arbitration Commission, set wages and conditions in considerable detail for each major industry. The same terms applied to all companies in the same industry, regardless of size, and allowed scant scope for individual firms to control their own ways of working. Instead, Hawke and Keating introduced a system where each company could negotiate the terms and conditions for its own workforce, within the larger framework of workers' protections. This was enterprise bargaining. It cut into the power of the commission, and it cut even harder into the power of the unions. In another time, this would have unleashed industrial mayhem as the unions struck to protect their fiefdoms. So why did they agree now?

Hawke–Keating's handling of the unions was the single most important difference between their approach to pro-market reform and the template laid down by Thatcher–Reagan. The Australian government did not declare war on the unions. Where Thatcher and Reagan pursued confrontation, Hawke convened a national summit with unions and business to craft a consensus. This concept was utter anathema to Thatcher: "To me, consensus seems to be the process of abandoning all beliefs, principles, values and policies. So it is something in which no one believes and to which no one objects."

Hawke and Keating went further than merely consulting the unions. In a historic first, they opened an experiment in explicit power-sharing with the unions. Hawke's grand bargain with the union movement, the Prices and Incomes Accord, and its successor agreements, was a co-operative project between government and organised labour for the macroeconomic management of the country. The unions agreed to help Hawke and Keating manage wages inflation. In return, they won a say in the reform process, and social and tax benefits for workers.

The Accord, the brainchild of a Hawke minister, Ralph Willis, turned out to be a powerful tool for managing reform without unrest or disruption. It was very controversial yet highly successful. Thanks to the Accord, Australia was able to break the wage–price inflationary spiral that had bedevilled the country for decades. In the past, when inflation rose, so did wages. The unions, naturally, wanted workers to keep, and improve, the real value of their wages, so they campaigned accordingly. The commission generally agreed with them. And where the unions were still unsatisfied, some routinely went on strike in pursuit of fatter settlements. So wages chased prices. Rising wages, in turn, increased costs for business.

So prices rose yet faster. A cycle developed. It was the wage–price spiral and it usually ended in recession. Just before Hawke and Keating took power in 1983, Australia had suffered a classic instance of the genre. The Liberal government of Malcolm Fraser and his treasurer, John Howard, presided over a wages breakout of 17 per cent and inflation of 11 per cent. It ended in the 1982–83 recession.

The Hawke–Keating breakthrough? In a remarkable act of forbearance, the workforce accepted a decade of stagnant wages, after allowing for inflation. Real wages rose by a total of just 1.2 per cent over ten years. In other words, the purchasing power of wages didn't budge for a decade. The wage–price spiral was broken. And the benefits that workers won in exchange? The government improved the so-called social wage, the overall level of payments and support that the government provides to the people. One example was the decision to re-introduce Medicare, with free public health available for everyone. Another was the decision to increase family allowances and introduce the family allowance supplement, cash payments to lower-income families.

One of the most notable benefits was a new system of superannuation, where employers were required to pay the equivalent of 9 per cent of salary into workers' accounts. This system of compulsory superannuation was denounced as a terrible impost on business. In truth, it ended up coming at the expense of traditional wage rises. There was a trade-off, in other words, as workers yielded on wage claims what they took in super. It was a useful reform as an enforced savings measure towards better-funded retirements. But it meant that workers were tolerating a great stasis in the real value of their pay in the interests of keeping their country economically stable.

The Labor Left was appalled. Labor had "abandoned its commitment to the people who are its true base – the workers, the dispossessed, the underclass of a capitalist society," wrote Dean Jaensch in his 1989 book *The Hawke–Keating Hijack*. "The Left argues that the policies of the government have out-liberalled the Liberal Party, that 'consorting with millionaires' is not a Labor approach, that the concentration on a deregulatory mode of economic policies, flirting with 'Thatcherist privatisation,' and a concerted pitch for middle-class support … are not within Labor traditions, and, in some instances, are positively anti-Labor."

And it was true that the advent of the Hawke–Keating government had some big effects not traditionally identified with the Labor Party cause. Its reform program had a big impact on wealth distribution. Since the 1920s, the trend in distribution of Australian income had been increasingly egalitarian. The highest-earning 1 per cent of the population received around 10 per cent of total personal incomes in the 1920s. That share had halved by 1980. The new pro-market reforms reversed this sixty-year trend. By 2002 the top 1 per cent was enjoying 9 per cent, returning almost to the level of 1921.

The Hawke–Keating reforms also created a renaissance in corporate profitability in Australia. This was vital because it is the prospect of profit that generates investment. A low-profit economy is a low-investment economy. And it is investment that creates new capacity, new industry, new technology, new jobs. Before the Hawke government took power, corporate profits made up 18 per cent of total incomes as a percentage of GDP, the so-called profit share in the economy. By 1989 it was 22 per cent. The wages share, by contrast, fell.

Although the fearmongering campaigns carried dire warnings that the government program would put Australian industry out of business, the Hawke–Keating reforms began a profit revival of historical proportions, with the full acquiescence of the labour movement.

Even today, the conservatives admire the Hawke–Keating profits turnaround. As opposition leader Tony Abbott told a Liberal Party gathering in June 2011: "We understand, in a way that Bob Hawke and Paul Keating grasped but that Julia Gillard and Kevin Rudd seem never to have learnt, that you can't have a society or a community without an economy to sustain it and that you can't have an economy without businesses that are allowed to make a profit."

There was one other key feature that distinguished the Hawke–Keating pro-market revolution from the Thatcher–Reagan equivalent. The Australian version of neoliberalism included a much more deft and discriminating approach to social spending. It will surprise most people to know that in all three of these pro-market revolutions – in Britain, in the US, and in Australia – government social spending rose. And not just a little. This jars with the popular demonisation of neoliberalism as a heartless, survival-of-the-fittest doctrine. But in practice, there's a worldwide pattern of governments increasing their social spending wherever they allow their economies to become more open to the world. The global marketplace can be a harsh disciplinarian and usually leads to increased inequality; governments, to sustain their countries' own social cohesion, need to take the edge off this with bigger social programs.

In Britain, government social spending as a proportion of the total economy rose from 16.4 to 19.4 per cent over the fifteen years to 1995. This included the eleven years of Thatcher's prime ministership. And in the US, the proportion rose from 13.2 to 15.4 per cent in the matching fifteen years. In Australia, it grew from 10.3 to 16.2 per cent in the same period. In other words, the growth in Australian social spending was much greater than in the UK and US as a proportion of GDP, which is the biggest of the big-picture measures. Against Britain's 3.8 percentage point increase, and America's 2.2, Australia's was 5.9.

Hawke and Keating, and more specifically the social services minister Brian Howe, took some measures to better target welfare spending, applying income tests, for instance. But their government did a great deal to increase welfare payments to families, which increased threefold as a percentage of GDP during their term in power. Hawke was lampooned for his 1987 pledge that "no Australian child will be living in poverty" by 1990. But expert assessment of the effect of Hawke's "family package" estimated that it cut the number of children in poverty by between 43 and 47 per cent.

To keep the government to its mission of increasing the play of market forces, the government also had to constrain its spending. Labor inherited a federal government deficit and a recession from the Fraser–Howard government. It managed eventually to turn the budget balance around and delivered surplus budgets in the three years from 1987–88. This was a much more fiscally conservative government than the nominally conservative one which had preceded it. Malcolm Fraser, with John Howard as treasurer, had managed to deliver only one budget surplus, and, even then, only just. Impressively, Keating cut federal spending from an initial sum equal to 28 per cent of GDP down to 23.3 per cent in his first five years. In a long-run international trend of ever-increasing government spending, this was a standout achievement. It returned government spending to its proportions of fifteen years earlier. And no treasurer since the Keating budget of 1989–90 has managed to return to this level of restraint – including even Keating himself in the six budgets that followed where he was either treasurer or prime minister. The recession of 1990–91 took the budget back into deficit and that's where it stayed for the rest of Keating's time in power. And he finally left office with government spending at 26 per cent of GDP. So he left spending smaller than he'd found it, but he also allowed a fiscal relaxation once he left the Treasury portfolio to assume the prime ministership.

Taken together, these seven key reforms – opening Australia fully to world trade, allowing a free-floating dollar, encouraging free flows of capital, cutting taxes on income and profits, deregulating and privatising industry, allowing a more flexible labour market, and restraining government spending – opened Australia's economy to the world and delivered the first part of the Australian version of the Thatcher–Reagan pro-market revolution. Neoliberalism had arrived courtesy of a new Labor. The fruits of reform were not entirely apparent for years, but it is now universally acknowledged that the Hawke–Keating reforms began a turnaround in the trajectory of Australia's national destiny. A long-running drift downwards in Australian competitiveness and relative living standards was finally arrested. The country was forced to compete in the wider world. And it emerged timorously only to discover that it could, indeed, thrive and prosper.

Keating's unyielding determination was a great asset and his greatest liability. Labor's research among voters consistently found that "a majority thought him 'strong'" but "the most common perception was of arrogance and aloofness," wrote one of his staff, the speechwriter Don Watson. "What strength the government had, he gave it, but he was also the government's greatest weakness."

Years later, Keating himself was proudly unrepentant: proud of his accomplishment, unrepentant of the enmity it had earned him. "When one undertakes," he said in 2004, "such a broad set of fundamental changes ... you virtually upset at some stage or another every sector: the labour market, the manufacturers, the car makers, the textile makers, the footwear makers ... the states, the electricity companies. I mean, not that one has a check-list, but you do get around to offending everybody. But somebody has to give the country a break."

But in his five years as prime minister, Keating was much less interested in economic reform than in his eight as treasurer. Indeed, once he'd taken an interest in what he called "the big picture," he relinquished further ambition for economic reform. Declaring that "I fixed the economy," he treated it more like a home requiring a one-off fix by renovation than a complex and ever-changing system. And in his years as prime minister, he became much sharper in rejecting the Thatcher–Reagan approach. As treasurer he was mainly concerned with forcing pro-market reform, but as prime minister in 1993 he wanted to emphasise the other great strand in Australian policy. Wishing to contrast himself against the then opposition leader, John Hewson, who proposed to extend Keating's pro-market economic reforms even further, Keating said: "There rarely has ever been a clearer choice: between the Australian traditions of fairness and equity and the economic and social jungle of Reaganism and Thatcherism which other countries have just abandoned." Keating retained his daring and determination, but it was now directed into driving Australia towards becoming a republic, into the arts, into Aboriginal reconciliation, into engagement with Asia, rather than into economic reform.

When Hawke and Keating took power in 1983, the average level of effective protection for the manufacturing industry was 25 per cent. By the end of Labor's thirteen years, it was down to less than 10. In the most heavily addicted sectors, protection remained much higher. For cars it was over 40 per cent and for textiles, clothing and footwear it was 50. The patient was certainly responding to treatment. Although there was a painfully dislocating restructuring, manufacturing exports were not wiped out as the doomsayers had grimly intoned. Instead, they took off. In 1983, exports of manufactures had been worth the equivalent of less than 1 per cent of GDP (excluding basic metal products, which are properly considered commodities). By the time Labor left, in 1996, this had grown to more than 2 per cent of GDP and was on an upward trajectory. Australian manufacturing was now more competitive. Keating left office with plans in place to continue the great national detox, but they had yet to be seen through to completion. Stripping away old rigidities was one thing, but new arrangements were needed to brace the new, open Australian economy. So even when Labor left office after thirteen years, the job was not yet finished.

11

ON OUR OWN

Peter Costello was deeply worried about the speculative attacks that drove the Australian dollar to dangerous new lows during the Asian financial crisis of 1997–98. The Reserve Bank had been spending as much as $1 billion a day, and losing. "The Reserve Bank ceased intervening essentially because our reserves were inadequate," Costello recalled later. "The hedge funds could see we didn't have the resources to turn the attack." The foreign exchange markets were shark-infested waters and perilous even for sovereign states. The Australian treasurer was so troubled that he eventually decided to ask the US for help. He would appeal to the Clinton administration. The experience was to leave a bitter taste in Costello's mouth. It changed the way he viewed the risks Australia faced in the world. And it changed Australia's economic future.

Costello attended a big meeting of finance ministers from around the Asia-Pacific in May 1999, on one of the Langkawi islands of Malaysia. Bill Clinton's Treasury secretary, Larry Summers, was there too. Costello took him aside during a coffee break at the APEC finance ministers' meeting and made his case.

He pointed out to Summers that the rules of the game were loaded against governments and in favour of hedge funds, multi-billion-dollar speculative vehicles for rich investors chasing super profits. The hedge funds were chiefly stocked with American money, and managed mainly from Wall Street, but were legally domiciled outside the US. So long as they didn't solicit funds from the American public, they were exempt from the normal rules of reporting and disclosure.

While the speculators were allowed to remain veiled in secrecy, central banks were required by the International Monetary Fund to disclose the size of their foreign exchange reserves. So the Reserve Bank was vulnerable to attack from shadowy predators.

"It's ridiculous," Costello told his American counterpart, "that we have to disclose our position but they don't have to report their positions. Hedge funds are taking advantage. It's very hard for a country to defend itself." He said that markets in the long run were correctly priced, but that in the short run there were times when markets moved beyond any pricing justified by fundamental economic information. The Australian dollar had fallen from 65 US cents at the beginning of 1998 to a low of 55 in August. There was a strong case for governments to play a part in managing these dislocations. Costello didn't ask that the US try to control the funds, but he did ask that US authorities impose basic disclosure requirements.

He also asked that the US require that hedge funds publish annual reports and disclose their major investment positions. His request met with a flat no from Summers. The US Treasury secretary told Costello that there was no need to regulate hedge funds, that they were useful in correcting any pricing anomalies in global markets, and that they were a force for good in the world. "In his view," Costello recounted, "if a country's exchange rate was plummeting, it had only itself to blame. It had nothing to do with speculation or regulation. He made it clear that if it was a problem for little countries like us, then we were on our own."

This rebuff from Australia's great and powerful friend made a big impression on Costello. It raised the level of risk that he saw Australia facing in the world, and it lowered the level of reassurance.

"If they were not prepared to do something on this, we could not expect US assistance if we got into real trouble. We were on our own. We had to make sure we could look after ourselves."

He didn't discuss the experience publicly, but it changed the way he did his job as treasurer for the next eight years. By the time of the Summers encounter, Costello and his leader, John Howard, had already taken the federal budget into surplus after inheriting a $10 billion deficit from the Keating government. Indeed, Howard and Costello achieved their first surplus in 1997–98, a respectable $1.2 billion surfeit, equal to 0.2 per cent of GDP. But after being turned down by the superpower, Costello decided he would need to go further.

"I realised it wasn't going to be enough to go into surplus. We would need to run a surplus big enough to pay down the Commonwealth debt, and, if possible, pay it off altogether." Net federal government debt in 1999 was $72 billion, or 11.6 per cent of GDP. "I had just seen all these countries attacked … No one was going to help us. Just as China decided to build foreign exchange reserves, we had to build an impregnable financial defence. And that would involve retiring debt and building a sovereign wealth fund."

Other countries in the Asia-Pacific drew similar conclusions from the Asian crisis. Not only did Washington stand aloof as Western speculators attacked one country after another, the Clinton administration also decided against putting any US funds into the emergency support package for Thailand, supposedly a US ally. The IMF's rescue package was bolstered by separate loans from Japan and Australia, but not from the US.

The US Treasury's Tim Geithner used America's great heft at the IMF to impose completely wrong-headed and counterproductive conditions on IMF support to the countries in crisis, notably Indonesia. Geithner thought that the crisis countries of Asia – Thailand, South Korea and Indonesia – were suffering a problem of government debt, à la the Latin American debt crises of the 1980s. They weren't. Their governments had sound finances. The true problem was that tsunamis of private money had gushed in then gushed out again. Geithner's prescription was to force savage cutbacks to government spending programs. Millions of people were forced into pointless penury.

The IMF later admitted its error. Geithner went on to become Barack Obama's Treasury secretary and the man who decided to allow Lehman Brothers to collapse, precipitating the viral phase of the global financial crisis.

China, in particular, drew hard conclusions from the IMF's mishandling of the Asian crisis. It decided that it would never allow itself to be dependent on the IMF, or the US, or the West generally, for its international solvency. Instead it would build the biggest war chest the world had ever seen. Its foreign exchange reserves were $US3.2 trillion in June 2011. And Beijing decided not to allow China's currency to be freely traded on foreign exchanges, so it cannot be attacked by speculators, part of its own "impregnable financial defence." The former deputy governor of the Reserve Bank of Australia, Stephen Grenville, observed: "After the Asian crisis, the countries of east Asia decided that they would never go to the IMF again. The IMF is taboo in east Asia. Look at the evidence. The revealed preference of the region is that no one has gone to the IMF since, even when they needed the money."

Costello delivered surpluses in nine years out of eleven, paid back the entire national debt and started a series of national investment funds, the biggest of which was the Future Fund. This marked a fundamental divergence between Australia and the countries to which it has traditionally looked for leadership. The US and UK ran deficits through the good years. The US under Bill Clinton ran surpluses in only two years out of eight; under George W. Bush, the US did not manage to produce even one surplus in eight years. Britain under Tony Blair also failed to produce a budget surplus. These countries were unable to live within their means. And in each year that they ran deficits, the US and UK were adding to their stock of national debt. So both America and Britain entered the global financial crisis with poor public finances. Australia, by contrast, entered the crisis in a very strong position. Australia was not unique in its ability to exercise fiscal self-control. Canada, like Australia, enjoyed surpluses in nine of the eleven years leading into the crisis. New Zealand produced surpluses in fourteen out of fifteen years. Running responsible public finances in a democracy is not an impossible dream. It can be done. It was done.

So while Australia did implement the Thatcher–Reagan pro-market revolution, this was a key difference in the Australian version. The governments of Bob Hawke and Paul Keating had marked the Australian project as different from the British and American ones with three important features: Hawke was more inclined to consensus than confrontation; Hawke and Keating negotiated an explicit power-sharing arrangement with the unions, the Prices and Incomes Accord, to manage change; and they were more deft in reforming social spending. John Howard and Peter Costello carried to fruition the Hawke–Keating project. The Liberals continued the Labor program of stripping back some of the main rigidities in the economy. They dispensed with the Accord and took a confrontational approach to the unions. But they also added an important new feature to the Australian model – they built an "impregnable financial defence" by paying off public debt. The Howard–Costello government braced up the newly open Australian economy with this important precaution against economic vulner-ability. It was only after they had been thrown out of power, only when the global financial crisis struck, that it became starkly clear just how important it was to the economic health of the country.

In the moment of crisis, when money was the hardest thing to find, Australia didn't need to borrow any. Fiscal independence turned out to be indispensable to true sovereign independence. Even the superpower has learned this lesson. As the US Secretary of State Hillary Clinton remarked to Kevin Rudd on the subject of dealing with China, according to a US cable released by Wikileaks: "How do you get tough with your banker?"

Another Howard–Costello reform that turned out to be central to the country's success was one of its very first. The Reserve Bank had always set official interest rates in consultation with the government of the day. But five months after taking office, Costello formally increased the independence of the Reserve Bank. In an exchange of letters with its new governor, Ian Macfarlane, he committed it to a fixed target for inflation, keeping it between 2 and 3 per cent on average over the course of the economic cycle. It was right in the middle of this range at the time, but had been in the realm of 7 to 9 per cent in the late 1980s.

Independence, which was about to become extremely chic around the world, was an excellent idea because politicians were the worst people to set interest rates. They always cut rates too low in time for elections. Why? So as to generate a spurt of growth that made the economy look good. But the problem was that, for politicians courting popularity, there was rarely a right time to raise them again. It's always popular to cut rates, to give people cheaper mortgages and lower credit-card bills, to pump up the stock market and house prices with cheap money. It's never popular to take all that away. So money was usually too cheap for too long, and that meant inflation was usually too high as well.

Today the arrangement of an independent Reserve Bank and an inflation target sounds unremarkable, but Labor was furious. Its leader at the time, Kim Beazley, threatened to appeal to the High Court to have it overturned. Why? Because requiring the central bank to "pursue a hard-line inflation-first strategy seems inconsistent with the clear obligation and guarantee to protect jobs" as set out in the Reserve Bank charter. And the bank's previous governor, Bernie Fraser, had also opposed the idea of an inflation target. In a famous moment of indiscretion during the life of the Keating government, he had said that he would resist any such proposal by an incoming Liberal government: "I won't go just to appease some dickhead minister who wants to put Attila the Hun in charge of monetary policy."

The incoming Liberal treasurer, Peter Costello, of course, was to be the "dickhead." It so happened that Fraser's term expired just a few months after the Coalition won the election. Why did Costello go ahead and fix the target? First, because he didn't think the status quo was working to create jobs or to keep inflation low. Of course, unemployment had been at 10 per cent at the height of the recession and the Reserve Bank charter had been helpless to do anything about it. In the neoliberal playbook, the bank was best deployed to keep inflation in check. This would improve the climate for investment and growth, which would, in turn, be a much better jobs incubator than a high-inflation economy. Second, because his talks with fund managers and investors in London had uncovered a perception that Australia was an inflation risk. Inflation had already moderated, especially after Keating's 1992 introduction of a more flexible industrial relations system, enterprise bargaining. But the perception of Australia as a high-inflation risk remained. The Reserve Bank's independence was in doubt, Costello discovered, and no wonder. The bank set rates in consultation with the government, its decisions being announced by both the bank and the government, and Keating had boasted of having the bank "in my pocket." New Zealand had led the world in establishing a rigorous inflation target. It had signed a formal contact with the governor of its central bank to keep inflation between 0 and 2 per cent. "I was shocked to be lectured about how far we were trailing behind the Kiwis," Costello wrote in his memoirs.

Soon after Costello's agreement with Ian Macfarlane on the new set-up, John Howard illustrated exactly why it was necessary. Costello tells the story:

> Early on in our term, when we were having trouble with unemployment, Howard suggested that we cut interest rates. I told him this was beyond the Government's control since we had ceded this power to the Reserve Bank. "When I was Treasurer, we used to set the rates," he told me.

When a government wanted a quick fix, it was always too tempting to meddle with rates for short-term advantage. And it was generally a poor outcome for the national interest. For this reason, interest rates were best put beyond the control of politicians. Doing so required a serious act of political self-abnegation; Australia was lucky that it got a treasurer who was prepared to do it. Later, Paul Keating would argue that it was not much of an accomplishment for the Liberals because he had already given the Reserve Bank de facto independence. Maybe so, but if he had, no one noticed. The bank's last rate change under Keating was still announced as occurring in consultation with the federal government. A formal agreement on independence and an explicit inflation target were indispensable to the prosperity that followed.

John Howard believed that there were just five big economic reforms that liberalised the Australian economy: "Two were reforms carried out by the Labor Party, with our help; the other three carried out by us in the face of their opposition." And these were? Deregulating the financial system, phasing out tariffs and quotas on imports, privatising government-owned businesses, reforming the tax system to impose a smaller tax on incomes and a bigger tax on consumption, and deregulating the labour market.

In the Howard version of the story, Hawke and Keating can take credit for the first two – deregulating finance and stripping away industry protection. He takes credit himself for the latter three – privatisation, tax reform and labour-market liberalisation. But, as the old adage says, success has many fathers and failure is an orphan. Hawke and Keating make their own claims to paternity of some of these reforms.

In truth, Labor did begin the privatisation push when it sold Qantas and the Commonwealth Bank. But Howard took it much further. As soon as he was elected, his government privatised fifty-seven state-owned enterprises, including the national shipping firm Australian National Line, Australian Defence Industries, all the capital city airports and the first part of Telstra, which fetched $14 billion. When conditions allowed, the Howard–Costello government sold the rest of Telstra. In proportion to the size of its economy, Australia was one of the world's most aggressive sellers of state assets, second only to New Zealand. The proceeds of the Australian sales were mainly applied to paying down the national debt. So, like most of the pro-market economic reform, the work was started by Labor and finished by the Liberals.

Labor also carried out the first big deregulation of the labour market. It was Keating in 1992 who introduced enterprise bargaining under the Accord with the ACTU. This major change moved many workers from collective to enterprise agreements over the next few years, and by 1999, 48 per cent of workers were covered by enterprise deals while fewer than half as many remained on collective ones.

This was the liberalisation that Howard wanted to press forward. Not just by extending the reach of enterprise bargaining, but by adding more flexibility to the scheme. As soon as he was elected, he tasked Peter Reith with producing further deregulation. The 1998 dispute on the waterfront, an ugly confrontation between Patrick Corporation and the Maritime Union of Australia that turned violent, has clouded the public memory of Howard's broader first-term reform. Howard did not propose radical change. He could not have imposed it, since Labor was opposed to any encroachment on the existing laws and the powers of the unions, and the Australian Democrats under Cheryl Kernot held the balance of power in the Senate. Reith and Kernot instead negotiated a modest and incremental set of changes. The key difference between the successful Reith reform and the failed WorkChoices effort a decade later was that the Reith changes included a guarantee that no worker would be worse off: the "no disadvantage" test. The Reith reforms reduced to twenty the maximum number of award conditions that could apply to workers. And he introduced a new form of individual contract between worker and employer, the Australian Workplace Agreement. These were used mainly in the mining sector and only became controversial after Howard removed the "no disadvantage" test a decade later. The AWAs then became an emblem of his much-loathed WorkChoices. Rudd and Gillard abolished them. Howard later conceded that his zeal had inadvertently set his cause back. He said in 2011 that there had been nothing wrong with the original AWAs: "We made a mistake in 2006 in taking away the 'no disadvantage' test."

Labor believed it was unnecessary to go any further. Keating put it best: "The wages system is running like a Swiss watch," he said in 2005. "The key point is the labour market fundamentally does not need reforming. The move to enterprise bargaining was completely successful. We've had rising real wages and falling unit labour costs ever since and, of course, low inflation. The proof of the pudding is in the eating. In the fourteenth year of the expansion, with high levels of employment growth and real supply constraints, we're still turning out moderate wage increases – 3.3 per cent last year – without industrial disputation." In the end, Labor got its wish. Rudd and Gillard later reintroduced some modest regulatory restrictions on labour market flexibility to appease their trade union constituents.

With tax reform too, Labor made a start, and the Liberals took it to a deeper level. Indeed, Howard and Costello succeeded where Keating had been blocked. Keating had wanted to impose a major new simplified tax on consumption. With the extra revenue, he wanted to make big cuts in income taxes. But his plan, known as Option C on a three-option menu, was confounded at a tax summit when the Business Council of Australia vetoed it and Hawke refused to force the issue. Keating's next-best solution was to broaden the scope of other taxes – notably by imposing taxes on fringe benefits and capital gains. He used this revenue to cut income tax rates in 1986 and 1994. His Holy Grail of a wide-reaching consumption tax would be realised by Howard and Costello a decade and a half later.

It was a masterwork of modern politics that the Liberals got away with it. Howard publicly declared his plan, then took it to an election in 1998. And won. The proposed new 10 per cent goods and services tax (GST), with offsetting cuts to income taxes, met a ferocious Labor resistance and hysterical fearmongering. The energy minister in the Queensland Labor government warned that Australians would not be able to afford their GST-inflated increased electricity bill: "Cold baked beans for lunch, cold fish and chips for dinner could become part of the Australian staple diet." We're still waiting for that one. Similarly absurd claims would be made a decade later about the plan to introduce a carbon tax. And because the Howard plan would cut the tax on trucking fuel, the left-wing Australia Institute claimed that the GST would kill "at least 65 more people each year" because of extra air pollution and traffic accidents. The National Tax and Accountants' Association predicted that 200,000 jobs would be lost in the first year. Of course, none of this came to pass.

"Our win rewrote the rule book," Costello observed in his 2008 memoirs. "It was the only time until then (and possibly since) that a party in the Western democratic world had won an election proposing to introduce a new tax." Howard and Costello had campaigned with conviction, determination and relentless energy. They lost seats at the election but held enough to win.

But surprises remained. To get the tax reform bills through the Senate despite Labor's opposition, the government negotiated a deal with the Australian Democrats in seven days of intense discussions across the cabinet-room table. One of the demands of the Democrats' leader, Meg Lees, was that the government create a greenhouse-gas abatement program. Costello tells the story:

> This was 1999. Neither Howard nor I had much of an idea of what a greenhouse gas was, let alone how to abate it. Trying to co-operate without blowing the financial position, I whispered to Howard, "Offer her four hundred."
>
> "Okay," he said. "Four hundred million." She accepted.
>
> I tapped him on the shoulder and whispered in his ear, "That's not what I meant. I meant we should offer her four hundred thousand."

Howard had misunderstood and increased the offer by a thousand times.

Costello continues: "Howard having inadvertently offered four hundred million he felt he couldn't withdraw it. It was the largest single expenditure measure in the negotiation and way out of line with comparable programs. It was how four hundred million got expended by mistake."

Howard and Costello got their GST reform. Australia had been one of the higher-taxing countries of the OECD and its corporate tax rate had been uncompetitive. Now it was one of the lower-taxing ones, and its corporate tax rate was below the average. But it was to be the last breakthrough rejuvenation of the Australian economy. Howard and Costello transformed from reformists to caretakers. Their government lost its policy ambition as it aged, just as Keating's had. Australia's outstanding productivity performance in the 1990s, which had transformed it from one of the least productive countries to one of the most productive, was flagging. By 2003–04, it had slumped back to its long-term under-performance.

Only when Howard won the 2004 election in an unexpected landslide was he jolted into action. In emphatically rejecting the alternative prime minister, Labor's Mark Latham, the Australian people had reposed an enormous new level of trust in Howard. He had not only enlarged the government's majority, his government now controlled the Senate for the first time. It was untrammelled power over the parliament. Howard decided it was too good an opportunity to miss. He later reflected that he had gone into politics "to be a participant and a fixer and a change agent, rather than just a spectator or an academic." He decided to make "a breakthrough reform on IR." He knew he was taking a risk, but industrial relations was his primary policy passion. "This is a big reform," he recalled reasoning with himself. "Do I err on the side of caution at a time of prosperity? Or do I use the high prosperity when it is the right time to introduce reforms that obviously are going to be attacked?" He would drive the pro-market revolution further than anyone had thought possible with a sweeping new deregulation of the labour market. The opportunity of unhindered power called forth Howard's daring. The spark of opportunity had rekindled ambition in him, the work started, and WorkChoices was born.

In the twelve years before Hawke and Keating took power and the reform era began, Australia had suffered four recessions. When Howard left office, Australia had enjoyed sixteen years of continuous economic growth, on the way to at least twenty years of unbroken expansion. Through the Asian crisis of 1997–98, through the US recession of 2001, through the worst drought in a century, Australia continued to grow and prosper. Average protection for manufacturing had fallen from 25 per cent at the beginning of the Hawke–Keating era to under 5 per cent. Manufacturing exports had trebled from being valued at less than 1 per cent of GDP to over 3. Trade openness was estimated to have directly added $2,700 to the annual income of the average working family, which increased to $3,900 with indirect benefits, according to the Centre for International Economics. At the beginning of the reform phase, unemployment was 9.9 per cent. When Howard left office, it was 4.5 per cent. The profits share of national income had grown under Hawke and Keating and did so again under Howard from under 20 per cent of GDP to 27 per cent. The wages share had fallen from around 56 to 53 per cent. Yet wages had gained strongly. Average wages, after adjusting for inflation, were stagnant in the Hawke–Keating years as the Accord had imposed restraint. But in the Howard–Costello years they grew by a total 21 per cent.

When the reform era ended in 2007, Australian official interest rates were held at a disciplined level of 6.75 per cent by an independent central bank. If an emergency should happen along, it had plenty of scope to cut rates to stimulate growth. It was a potential that countries such as the US and UK, which had almost reached the limits of their monetary policy, did not enjoy. Likewise, Australia had plenty of fiscal firepower in reserve to stimulate the economy through government spending. With no national debt, only assets, Australia was in a very strong position. Many other countries had almost exhausted their ability to borrow. In the reform phase of 1983 to 2007, under Labor and Liberal governments, Australia had realised that it was on its own in the world. It started to make its own way. This was just as well. Australia had no idea how severely it was about to be tested.

12

I EXPECT YOU TO DIE

The villain Goldfinger shackles James Bond in the prone position, legs held wide apart, with a burning red laser beam poised to slowly cut the hero in two, starting at his crotch. Goldfinger bids Bond farewell and moves to leave the room. The secret agent, transfixed by the inexorable movement of the deadly beam as it inches towards him, calls out: "Do you expect me to talk?"

Goldfinger retorts: "No, Mr Bond, I expect you to die."

The global financial crisis was the economic death ray, apparently inevitable, that flared an angry red, first in the US and then moving outward, threatening to cut through every major developed economy in the world. Or, as the International Monetary Fund put it, "the global economy is in a severe recession inflicted by a massive financial crisis and acute loss of confidence ... by any measure, this downturn represents by far the deepest global recession since the Great Depression."

SmartCompany, a business news site, reported: "Australian entrepreneurs have started 2009 with one word ringing in their ears: Recession." The consultancy Access Economics predicted that the mining-led economy "will unwind scarily fast" in 2009. "This is not just a recession. This is the sharpest deceleration Australia's economy has ever seen."

The world economy seemed to fall away under the forecasters' feet, so that every pessimistic forecast was soon followed by an even gloomier one. At the end of a staccato series of frantic cuts to its forecasts, the IMF said that Australia's economy would go backwards by 1.4 per cent in 2009. The stock market dipped, the currency slumped, a quiet run on the banks began. Like all the other major, rich economies tightly intertwined with global financial and trading systems, Australia, economically speaking, was expected to die.

The remarkable fact is that it did not. It was the exception. Like 007, it eventually outwitted its tormentor. "The economy has recently passed a stress test that all other rich countries' economies to some degree failed," the *Economist* magazine reported in 2011. "The global financial crisis did not pass Australia by, but neither did it drive it into recession."

Australia's chief economic officer was as amazed as anyone. When Wayne Swan was told the official result of the economy's performance in the first quarter of 2009, the treasurer uttered a single word, with feeling: "Fuck!" The economy had shrunk in the earlier quarter, by 0.5 per cent. If it had done so again, this would have been widely regarded as a recession. Instead it grew, by 0.4 per cent. Unemployment, which the official forecast said would reach 8.5 per cent, stopped rising at 6. The difference between these two figures in human terms? A quarter of a million jobs that had been expected to be lost were instead retained.

Swan noticed that, from then on, he was treated differently. Whenever he went to an international meeting of finance ministers, he was "moved up in the speaking order." Not because of his eloquence but because he was regarded with a newfound respect. An international collection of essays on the global crisis, *What's Next?* edited by David and Lyric Hale, includes one on the Australian experience. Its title? "It didn't have to be that bad – the counter-example of Australia." The remarkable performance gave a touch of celebrity to Australians in economic policy circles worldwide. One prominent business leader, Heather Ridout, chief executive of the

Australian Industry Group, felt the force of Australia's fashionableness when she arrived at a major global gathering in Seoul in November 2010. "There was huge interest in Australia from the business people there" for the meeting of leaders of the twenty major economies, said Ridout. "There was a lot of admiration for what Australia had done. Australia's twenty years of growth is just seen as remarkable, and then on top of that there was the fact that Australia managed to avoid a recession in the global financial crisis." Business leaders from all countries were "curious about how Australia had done it."

And that is the question. How did it happen? What set Australia apart?

Many of the business people in Seoul had the impression that it was the mining boom. In this, they were merely reflecting the casual assumption you'll often hear from Australians, and especially members of the federal opposition parties, that "it was all China" or "it was just the mining boom." Both contributed – indeed, they are pretty much the same thing in terms of their effect on Australia. It is China that accounts for most of the new demand for Australian minerals. But if the success story were only about China and the mining boom, it would have had a very different ending. Australia would have suffered a recession. No one would regard the Australian experience as anything unusual. More importantly, hundreds of thousands more people would have suffered.

Six stand-out elements differentiated the Australian story. There were three acts that provided critical support to the economy through the crisis. And there were three things that didn't happen, dogs that didn't bark, elements of the crash elsewhere that did not occur in Australia. The federal government's response was central to several of the key parts of the story.

Prime Minister Kevin Rudd called a meeting of officials and advisers in Sydney at the nondescript Commonwealth parliamentary offices in Phillip Street on October 10, 2008. It was the day dubbed Black Friday. The storm had been gathering in fury for a year now. In the preceding year, Britain had nationalised a bank, German banks had teetered, Iceland had nationalised several banks, the US had seized control of two vast quasi-public mortgage lenders (Fannie Mae and Freddie Mac), and the IMF had stated that total worldwide losses stemming from US mortgage debts turned bad could reach $US1 trillion. The UK chancellor of the exchequer, Alistair Darling, had warned of the worst crisis in sixty years, and global central banks had injected $US180 billion in emergency liquidity into the banking system. Ireland officially fell into recession.

Twenty-five days before Black Friday, the US Treasury had allowed the investment bank Lehman Brothers to collapse. This decision marked the threshold from manageable turmoil to uncontrolled panic and distress. Lehman failed owing $US613 billion, the biggest bankruptcy in American history. It was counterparty or guarantor to transactions running into trillions. This meant that the international banks that had loaned money to Lehman were likely to lose it. This, in turn, meant that those banks might not be able to repay their creditors. Every loan suddenly became an act of speculation. Abruptly, no one would lend to anyone else. And now that the US had shown it would not save every institution, nothing was safe. The entire global financial system was in the process of freezing in panic.

Two of the storied investment banks of Wall Street, Goldman Sachs and Morgan Stanley, gripped by fear, meekly surrendered their buccaneer investment-banking status and applied to become regular commercial banks. After plundering the world for high-risk profits for a century, they were now sheltering from the storm in the lee of an implicit government guarantee.

In the fortnight before Black Friday, the US Congress approved a $US700 billion emergency fund to save US banks. In the process, the US Treasury secretary, Henry Paulson, "literally bent down on one knee as he pleaded with Nancy Pelosi, the House Speaker," to support the bill, the *New York Times* reported.

Then, in the week before Black Friday, Britain announced a £500 billion deal to save its own banks. To forestall runs on their banks, governments including those of Germany, Denmark, Ireland and Sweden reassured bank depositors that they would not lose their money. And the London stock market suffered its biggest one-day fall, measured in points on the benchmark FTSE index. Two days before Black Friday, Glenn Stevens chaired a meeting of the Reserve Bank board. The bank's earlier intention, just a few days before, had been to cut interest rates by half a percentage point. Instead, it announced a cut of a whole percentage point, the sharpest cut in sixteen years. In media reporting of the decision, the most common adjective was "shock." The cut carried an emphatic message – we know this crisis is serious, and we are prepared to act aggressively to offset it. Jubilant share investors bid prices up by an initial 3 per cent, though half of this effect had faded away by the end of the trading session.

But fear was afoot in the world and it was running from the wholesale market to the retail. Investors were selling everything they could to protect the value of their capital. On Black Friday, a global stock-market rout began, and – because of world time zones – it began in the Asia-Pacific. Australian shares lost 8 per cent of their value on the day. It was the sharpest one-day crunch since the 1987 share market collapse. The resources sector suffered in line with the overall market; BHP Billiton and Rio Tinto both lost about 7 per cent of their share values. Hardest hit were the banks. The National Australia Bank share price, the worst affected, was cut by more than 12 per cent. Prices across Asia moved similarly. The average loss in share prices across the Asia-Pacific, excluding Japan, was 7.7 per cent and the fall in Japan was over 9 per cent on the day. The Australian dollar spiralled, falling from 71 US cents to 66 in the course of a day. Punctuating the news from the financial markets came a development that affirmed the connection between the financial markets and the real world. Singapore declared recession. Wall Street, opening after the Asian trading day had closed, mimicked the losses, falling by 8 per cent.

There was speculation that the Group of Seven – the principal economies of the world, comprising the US, Japan, Germany, Britain, Canada, France and Italy, which were meeting on the coming weekend – were about to announce new joint emergency measures, leaving everyone else out in the cold. The periphery of exposed nations would include Australia. The weight of troubling evidence had reached critical mass and Rudd resolved to prepare Australia's response to the crisis on the same weekend. As Rudd talked, he and his officials noticed that, unusually, the Sydney sky was an ominous grey.

The next day, Saturday, October 11, Rudd convened his kitchen cabinet, or Gang of Four. They met all weekend in the cabinet room in Canberra. The so-called Strategic Priorities and Budget Committee consisted of Rudd, his deputy, Julia Gillard, Wayne Swan and the finance minister, Lindsay Tanner, attended by their top officials. But, for this critical weekend, Swan had left for IMF and World Bank meetings in Washington, checking in by phone when he could. The advice that the politicians had been getting from the Treasury was that Australia was facing two chief problems: a liquidity crisis and a demand shortfall.

The first meant that the economy was going to seize up because of a lack of bank finance. The international bank crisis had frozen the system. Australia's banks rely on overseas banks for most of the funds they raise and, in turn, loan out to borrowers in Australia. But none was lending any more, paralysed by the fear that they would not be repaid. The second problem meant that, even if the finance problem could be overcome, the coming crunch in global demand would leave Australia without enough overseas customers. Demand would fall, and so output would fall. In other words, recession was inevitable, and it would be a sharp one. Global trade was shrivelling at a rate without precedent since World War Two.

Rudd and his coterie of advisers decided that they needed to put a decisive end to the liquidity crisis. The Australian government had the highest possible credit rating of any entity in the world, courtesy of the sound finances built during the Howard–Costello years. Rudd decided that the government would stand behind the banks. Whatever the Australian banks borrowed from offshore banks, the Australian government would guarantee. This reduced the credit risk of lending to an Australian bank to zero. This, in turn, restored full international confidence in the Australian banks. They could continue to stand in the market and borrow. And they did. In effect, Rudd had pledged the entire future income of the country as collateral for the banks. One of the most powerful lessons of the crisis, both in Australia and abroad, is that there is no such thing as private debt. In a crisis, private debt becomes a public obligation.

But what about confidence at home? The Reserve Bank reported that ordinary customers were increasingly pulling their money out of the banks. The second-tier banks, Suncorp and Bankwest in particular, were haemorrhaging cash as people moved money into the big four banks or put cash in shoe boxes under their beds. The Reserve Bank was receiving requests for inordinate quantities of high-denomination bank notes, fifties and hundreds. Seeing a raft of foreign banks collapse, depositors feared the same at home. There was already an implicit government guarantee of bank deposits. Evidently, this was not enough.

Rudd decided to make it explicit. There was an internal debate – how much should the government guarantee? The US, for instance, guaranteed deposits of up to $10,000. What should be the Australian limit? Ten thousand? Twenty? Fifty? The higher the limit, the bigger the contingent liability on the government's balance sheet. The officials wanted a small limit. But Rudd wanted to send the strongest possible signal. "We need to send a strategic shock across the system so people will relax and know their deposits are safe. We can't take half-measures. It has to have a strong psychological impact," Rudd insisted. Against the advice of officials, he decided it would be an unlimited guarantee on both deposits and lending. This was overdoing it and caused complications because investors pulled money from other institutions to put into the banks; the government revised it a couple of weeks later to impose a cap of $1 million, and a fee for guarantees on amounts bigger than this.

The guarantee was effective. And it captured the four key characteristics of the government's decisions in response to the crisis: it was anticipatory and did not wait for the problem to become damaging; it was very much dominated by Rudd personally; it was forceful and emphatic to produce maximum effect; and it worked, with some complications and unintended consequences. In the approach to the 2007 election, Labor had aired TV ads so that Rudd could declare: "A number of people have described me as an economic conservative. When it comes to public finance, it's a badge I wear with pride." And he had followed through by announcing a budget surplus in the first year of the government's life, although the financial crisis demolished this plan before it could be delivered. Yet in this moment of crisis, he was quite prepared to act boldly, regarding the public finances less as a resource to be guarded and more as an active tool of economic management. Rudd and Swan announced the banking measures on the Sunday, October 12, before going back into the kitchen cabinet to plan their response to the second problem.

The second problem was the looming slump of demand in the economy. The Treasury explained the size of the problem to Rudd and his ministers. It was inevitable that Australia would go into recession, officials said. Unemployment, which was 4.1 per cent at the time, would likely increase to 8 to 9 per cent. "Fuck that," Rudd rejoined. "What can we do to prevent that happening?" He said he was concerned that not only would a recession inflict a lot of direct harm, but also that it would hit confidence and set off a second-round effect of cutbacks. Given that it was October, Rudd was worried that employers would use the opportunity of the Christmas break to lay off large numbers of workers. The Treasury secretary, Ken Henry, responded: "If you really want to make a difference, go early, go hard and go households," in creating a stimulus package. Rudd took him up on it. He asked Henry to go away and work out what it would take to keep economic growth above zero.

Two days later Rudd and Swan announced an urgent government package of stimulus spending measures. It was the first major fiscal stimulus move by any government. Others would soon follow, but Australia was a trendsetter. The so-called Economic Security Strategy totalled $10.4 billion, or 0.9 per cent of the country's GDP. Of this, $4.8 billion was to be paid as a cash bonus to Australia's 4 million pensioners just before Christmas. Another $3.9 billion was to be paid as a cash bonus to families, also just before Christmas. These measures were indeed going early, going hard and going households. Retail sales increased appreciably, despite the onrushing global crisis. In the following months, Deutsche Bank's chief economist, Tony Meer, estimated that of the $8.5 billion immediate cash handout component of the December spending, recipients spent $1.8 billion in shops in December and January and used $2.5 billion to pay down debt.

Further, to support domestic house-building activity, the Treasury suggested doubling the grants paid to first-home buyers.

Rudd decided to treble them at a cost of $1.5 billion. The number of first-home buyers entering the market surged immediately. Finally, the government added $187 million to its programs for training and retraining workers. Two months later, Swan announced a further measure, to target a third component of demand: private fixed capital investment. An additional investment allowance, in the form of a bonus 10 per cent tax deduction, would apply to investments made over the next six months. This idea was proposed by Rudd and garnered from a dinner he'd had with the Australian Chamber of Commerce and Industry. The cost to the budget was $1.6 billion, bringing the overall cost of this first stimulus package to $12 billion, or 1 per cent of GDP.

Governments are usually too late in enacting stimulus. Why did Australia act earlier than other countries? The Treasury's head economist, David Gruen, said that there were two reasons. Usually, said Gruen, "only when the downturn is well advanced does it become clear how severe it is turning out to be. Furthermore, as economic conditions deteriorate, it is rare for any specific event to provide a clear, unequivocal signal that a serious downturn is coming." This time was different. The collapse of Lehman Brothers was the clear signal. But that was equally evident to all countries. It still doesn't explain why Australia acted earlier. Gruen said that Australia's officials still smarted from the experience of the 1990s recession, where there was an "inordinate delay" in the fiscal response. We "were determined not to repeat it when another recession loomed." The analysis and resolve at the bureaucratic level was one thing. Political will was another. Rudd supplied it.

By being early and decisive, Rudd not only kept the economy from falling into recession, colloquially defined as two quarters of negative growth, he also snapped the country out of a gathering mood of gloom. It turned out to be crucial. David Gruen remarked that in the early stages of the crisis, "both consumer and business confidence in Australia fell in a similar manner as in the rest of the OECD." But then, as registered by Wayne Swan's expletive, Australian optimism bounced back. "Consumer confidence rebounded sharply, and kept rising, so much so that the cumulative rise over the four months to September 2009 was the largest four-month rise in the 35-year history of the series," said Gruen. The government's intervention "was able to generate a favourable feedback loop in the economy," where "policy supported economic activity, which in turn convinced consumers and businesses that the slowdown would be relatively mild. This in turn led consumers and businesses to continue to spend, and led businesses to cut workers' hours rather than laying them off, which in turn helped the economic slowdown to be relatively mild." Beyond the mechanics of dollar-in-dollar-out economic stimulus exercises, Rudd had happened upon the special alchemy of economic growth, the formula for confidence.

When they had finished putting together the $10.4 billion "cash splash" handouts, Rudd thanked Ken Henry for his efforts with a gift. He handed him an inscribed copy of one of the most famous and influential books of the last century: *The General Theory of Employment, Interest and Money*. The British economist John Maynard Keynes published it during the Great Depression in the 1930s. And as Rudd gave it to Henry in front of a small gathering of officials, he remarked: "We're all Keynesians now." What does this mean? Lord Keynes, a terrible toff who disdained ordinary people as "the boorish proletariat," was the man who gave governments the intellectual authority to stimulate economies with spending. Until Keynes, centuries of classical economic doctrine paralysed governments. The Depression went on and on, unemployment hit unprecedented levels, yet governments sat back and watched. Economies were supposed to be self-correcting.

The suffering was supposed to be morally sound. Pain was a purgative. Keynes challenged the doctrine with his opus. Economies were not self-correcting, he argued. And it was the legitimate role of governments to raise aggregate demand in the economy to restore equilibrium. Under the force of Keynes' work, governments started to spend money on a grand scale specifically to create jobs. The most immediate beneficiaries? The dirty proletariat. But entire economies ultimately benefit. It's now unthinkable that governments could sit idle and watch unemployment soar to 30 per cent.

The comprehensiveness of Keynes' triumph seemed complete when Richard Nixon, a Republican, uttered the famous words that Rudd was quoting – "we are all Keynesians now." Indeed, during the Christmas break, as Rudd worked on an essay response to the global financial crisis and got gloomy about the world economy, he had been reading a biography of Keynes, written by Lord Skidelsky. He had been comprehensively gearing himself up for the new advent of Keynesianism that he was in the process of embracing.

On the same weekend that Rudd and Swan announced the dual bank guarantees, the G-7 countries did indeed, as expected, announce a joint plan to stabilise the world financial system. A moment of market euphoria followed, only to be dashed. The measures were inadequate and not properly co-ordinated. The storm intensified. Within two weeks, three countries appealed to the IMF for emergency solvency funds: Pakistan, Hungary and Ukraine. Central banks across the world now engaged in a blur of bank rescues and interest-rate cuts. Within the same fortnight, the governor of the Bank of England, Mervyn King, conceded that "it now seems likely that the UK economy is entering a recession." The IMF warned that more banks worldwide would fail because private funding had become "virtually unavailable." And the man who, more than any other individual, had been responsible for the entire crisis, the former chairman of the US Federal Reserve, Alan Greenspan, admitted that he was in a state of "shocked disbelief." He said he had "found a flaw" in his ideology that the best way to regulate banks was to allow them to regulate themselves.

Other countries soon followed the same Keynesian script as Australia. Most notably, in November, China announced mammoth stimulus spending of $US586 billion over two years. This turned out to be, proportionately, the biggest emergency spending package among the world's ten largest economies. It was the equivalent of 3.1 per cent of China's GDP. But Australia's initial package was soon followed by a second, much bigger, stimulus announcement. Altogether, this would rank Australia's stimulus spending as the sixth biggest in the world, in proportion to its economy. Using the consistent approach and results of the IMF, the effect of Australia's total stimulus spending on the economy in 2009 was the equivalent of 2.9 per cent of GDP. Next came Japan with 2.4, the US with 2, Canada with 1.9, Germany and Britain with 1.6 each, France with 0.7 and Italy with 0.2. Why did Australia produce so big a stimulus?

As they considered a second package over the Christmas break at the end of 2008, Rudd and his officials became increasingly gloomy. Importantly, their main streams of information were coming from the US and the UK. As part of his holiday routine of a daily swim in the 18-metre pool at Kirribilli House, Rudd read the London *Financial Times* and the main US papers. He spent some time most days working on his 7,700-word essay for the *Monthly* magazine on how the crisis marked the defeat of the neoliberals and the triumph of social democrats. This helped stoke his personal anger at the man-made disaster that US policy had now delivered to the world. As an intellectual, Rudd was always conscious of the climate of ideas in which practical policy was crafted. He was seeking to adjust it accordingly: "From time to time in human history there occur events of a truly seismic significance, events that mark a turning point between one epoch and the next, when one orthodoxy is overthrown and another takes its place," he wrote. "There is a sense that we are now living through just such a time … barely 30 years since the triumph of neo-liberalism – that particular brand of free-market fundamentalism, extreme capitalism and excessive greed which became the economic orthodoxy of our time." Rudd was declaring a new era of an enlarged role for the state, and he was living it out. His economic adviser, Andrew Charlton, was on the phone regularly to two of the more pessimistic US economists, Nouriel Roubini and Joseph Stiglitz.

At the same time, officials at the Treasury in Canberra were on the phone regularly to Washington and hearing the economists at the IMF become ever more pessimistic about the world outlook. A senior Australian Treasury official described it as looking at a map of the world where only countries expecting economic growth were illuminated. One by one, the lights were going dark. Australia was still lit but, without government action, the lights would go out in 2009.

So when Rudd returned to the office on Monday, January 19, he, his personal advisers and the Treasury were filled with a sense of impending doom. If they had given more weight to the view from China, India or Brazil, their mindset might have been a little less black. The Reserve Bank's Glenn Stevens would later label the downturn "a North Atlantic crisis" rather than a global one. It was the North Atlantic mood that Australia's policy-makers imported. While Rudd and the government were preparing to return to the task of economic policy-making, Stevens was busy announcing a second dramatic official interest-rate cut of a full percentage point. And the two arms of officialdom did not work in isolation from each other. The Treasury and the Reserve Bank have a permanent point in common. The Reserve Bank board always includes, by custom, the secretary of the Treasury. So there is a formal mechanism for communication, as well as plenty of informal chatter within the "official family." Rudd and Swan also took care to visit Stevens and discuss their plans before announcing their stimulus spending. He raised no objection.

Work on the stimulus package started immediately on Rudd's return to the office. His kitchen cabinet met near daily for a total of about sixty hours over the next fortnight. At their first meeting, Ken Henry told the gathering that demand in the economy was falling so steeply that there was no way government spending could support economic growth at its typical rate of about 3 per cent a year. But there was a case for government spending to fill some of the gap. Without any stimulus from the government, the economy would have delivered scant growth in the 2008–09 financial year – 0.5 per cent – and none the next.

The bare minimum of extra government spending, Henry advised, was the equivalent of 1 per cent of GDP for each of the next two years. The political palatability of Henry's advice was immediately obvious – this should create enough extra activity to keep Australia's economic growth above zero for the next two years, through to the next federal election. Henry's advice set the starting point – 2 per cent of GDP over two years was to be the bare minimum. Australia's GDP was $1.2 trillion, so 1 per cent is about $12 billion. That amount – $24 billion – is a huge sum, equivalent to adding just under a tenth to the annual federal budget. It's more than the total annual economic output of about eighty countries. Yet, for the times, it was still reasonably conservative: the IMF was calling on governments around the world to add stimulus of 2 per cent in 2009 alone.

Rudd took the same approach to Act II as he had to Act I. He wanted a package that would keep growth above zero. But, not content to think about spending year-to-year, the ministers wanted to analyse the likely patterns of growth in the economy quarter-by-quarter. The reason? They wanted to match their performance to the scorecard, seeking to prevent even one quarter of economic contraction. Growth is measured quarter-by-quarter in the national accounts, and the ministers wanted to avoid two quarters of shrinkage in a row. Why? Most of the media, based on a hardy misapprehension, likes to report that this is the definition of a "technical recession." This is a kind of urban myth, but it is an enduring one. The ministers did not want to bet the reputation of their government as economic manager on the media's ability to educate itself. So the stimulus was crafted to deliver a continuous stream of adrenaline into the economic system, quarter-by-quarter. An old conundrum runs, "Do we measure what we do, or do what we measure?" In this case, there was no conundrum. Rudd decided the program according to what was to be measured, the actions matching the metric.

The short-run jolt was to be a repeat of the October package, $12.2 billion in "bonus" payments, most of it in $950 wads for families, in the first half of the year. The medium-term hit was to be a school-building program of $14.7 billion over three years, a Gillard initiative, and $3.8 billion for home insulation, a Rudd proposal. The longer term stimulus was to be a $22 billion program of major projects, roads, ports and rail. When the package was finally assembled, it was $42 billion over four years.

Rudd & Co. were extremely active, perhaps hyperactive, alert for any suggestion of "market failure," trouble that might require further government intervention in the market. Apart from the two stimulus packages, Rudd and his ministers also granted $6.2 billion to the car industry, $300 million to local councils, $15.2 billion to the states, and a $4.7 billion "Nation Building Package" announced in between the two larger stimulus packages. They committed $8 billion to buy mortgage-backed securities from small banks and credit unions and other institutions that might have had trouble selling them into the market.

And there was more. They crafted a plan for the government to supply credit to the car retailing industry, the plan that gave rise to the Godwin Grech affair. This was the fabrication by a politically partisan Treasury officer that Rudd was seeking to use the scheme to gratify the interests of a caryard-owning comrade in Queensland. That affair damaged only Rudd's accusers, Grech – who turned out to be not only partisan but possibly disturbed – and his dupe, Malcolm Turnbull, while leaving Rudd politically stronger.

Rudd also put together another plan, for the government to supply credit to the commercial property sector, the so-called Ruddbank. The government put $2 billion into a new fund and pressed the banks to commit another $2 billion. It had potential to create credit of up to $30 billion. It was at this point that the opposition really started to worry. If Rudd would prop up property developers, who would he not prop up? In the end, Ruddbank was defeated in the upper house and never issued a dollar in loans.

In five months, the Rudd government created economic and industry support with a measurable value of $90.7 billion. That's the equivalent of the total annual economic output of Luxembourg or Libya. It was equal to 7.5 per cent of GDP. If anything, Rudd was embracing the crisis with a little too much enthusiasm. There was no market failure, real or anticipated, that he wasn't ready to deal with. Wherever the market seemed poised to fail, Rudd positioned the government to respond. The crisis defined Rudd's prime ministership. It gave him a grand purpose and an urgent challenge. And the polls revealed an appreciative public. The prime minister was having a good crisis.

Certainly, the federal government was not constrained by any shortage of money. The Howard–Costello government had bequeathed Rudd a government with no net debt, only assets.

After eliminating the deficit, and paying off the national debt entirely in 2006, the conservatives put money into a series of investment funds. The biggest was the Future Fund, which was created to cover the looming liabilities of Commonwealth public service pensions. For two years, instead of having to pay interest on debt, the Australian government was actually receiving net interest instead. So Rudd enjoyed a strong starting point, unique among the major developed economies, unconstrained by existing debt or deficit.

From a pre-crisis forecast budget surplus of $22 billion in 2008–09, Rudd ended up delivering a deficit of $27 billion. It was to be the first of at least four. The Rudd deficit peaked the following year at $55 billion, a very big 4.3 per cent of GDP, making it proportionately the biggest since the end of postwar reconstruction, before beginning to taper off as stronger growth delivered more taxes. The cumulative federal net debt was projected to blow out to a maximum of $107 billion, or 7 per cent of GDP, in 2011–12. Compared to its inheritance from the Howard–Costello government, this was a reversal of $150 billion or 11 per cent of GDP, an extraordinary turnaround in just four years.

Nonetheless, looking abroad, the Australian debt level was remarkably modest by comparison. In 2010, when Australia's federal net debt was 6 per cent of GDP, the average for the OECD countries was 48 per cent. The US economist David Hale observed: "Most other G-20 governments are deeply envious of Australia's fiscal situation."

Even before he announced Act II, Rudd worried that the stimulus plan would lead the government into serious debt and wanted a plan to help it out again. He asked the Treasury for some fiscal rules. Henry came back with a number of alternatives, and Rudd adopted the Treasury's preferred option. This was a pair of guidelines. The first was that once growth returned to its long-run trend of 3 per cent, any extra revenues would go towards reducing the deficit. The second was to limit the rise in government spending to 2 per cent in real terms once the crisis had passed. The successor Labor government, headed by Julia Gillard, kept to those rules and promised a return to surplus in the federal budget by 2012–13. One piece of research the Rudd government did not conduct? A cost–benefit analysis of the various parts of its spending plan.

The Rudd kitchen cabinet considered many scenarios and hypotheses, but only one event took Rudd and his ministers completely by surprise – the opposition decided to oppose the stimulus package. The opposition did endorse the initial $10.4 billion stimulus, but baulked at the second, $42 billion one. The opposition leader, Malcolm Turnbull, argued that it was excessive. He said he could support something only half as big. The government countered that the opposition would condemn the country to recession. The conservatives seethed with envy, frustration and anger. The Liberals were envious that it was Labor that got to spend the treasure piled up by Howard and Costello. It would accrue to Labor's political benefit to stave off recession, not theirs. They were also frustrated that they were unable to prevent Labor spending. Labor controlled the lower house and won the support of the Greens to get its spending plans through the upper house as well. Finally, the Liberals were angry, and some of them quite genuinely so, because they felt that Rudd was being reckless with the national finances. For practical purposes, however, the opposition move raised the political risks for Rudd and brought an end to thoughts of further government intervention.

It was a near-run thing, however. Malcolm Turnbull had taken his early position to support the government in the crisis, putting the national interest ahead of the temptation to make political hay from tormenting the government in difficult times. The opposition had supported the first stimulus package. Presented with the second, bigger spending package, Turnbull had to make a threshold decision: "In terms of the political options there were really only two – to oppose it and present a Plan B – which is the approach I always favoured – or waving it through criticising it as we did," Turnbull later explained. "The problem with that approach is that you don't have the courage of your convictions and would be seen as such." While there was no real consultation on the stimulus in the Rudd government beyond the inner Gang of Four, the Liberal opposition reached its position through a broader process.

> We formed the view in my office prior to the shadow cabinet meeting that we should oppose it on the basis that it was excessive. We also recognised that to do so would be enormously unpopular and that a lot of heat would come our way as a consequence. This was a decision therefore that I needed to ensure my colleagues owned – that it was not something imposed on them by the leader. So we had to have an open and frank discussion in the shadow cabinet and we did.

But while Turnbull might have made up his mind before throwing the subject open to his colleagues, he seemed equivocal to some of his senior colleagues. He convened three meetings without declaring his position, as the deputy leader and shadow treasurer Julie Bishop recalled. "Malcolm called a special shadow cabinet meeting to discuss our position on the stimulus. There were no papers for the meeting" for fear of leaks, she wrote in a later email to her colleague Joe Hockey to settle a difference over who had supported what.

> Malcolm opened the meeting by setting out the government's proposal and then asked me for my view. I said we should vote against it, that the package was too big and not well targeted,

that the first stimulus had yet to take effect and that it would massively drive up government debt.

Warren Truss [leader of the National Party, the junior partner in the coalition] agreed but was cautious. Nick Minchin and Chris Pyne spoke in support of the package – for different reasons – and we went around the room. Many spoke against the package including Dutton, Ciobo, Keenan, Abetz and you. Most said that if we didn't oppose debt, then what did we stand for?

One name that Bishop didn't cite was that of Tony Abbott. His position? The future leader did not turn up for the meeting. He was in his post-election funk, mourning the political demise of John Howard and missing high office. He phoned Turnbull's staff to say that he thought the party should oppose the stimulus. The matter was not finally decided at that meeting. Bishop said, "There was a party room meeting, and then another shadow cabinet meeting and while the majority were in favour of opposing it, Malcolm went back to his office without confirming what he would do."

But in Turnbull's own mind, it was clear-cut. "There was no equivocation on my part following the party room," he recalled. "The only debate was what our alternative stimulus package should look like." Either way, the opposition made its choice. The position of national unity on stimulus in the crisis was now broken.

The day after the second stimulus package announcement, the Reserve Bank made its third mega-cut of 1 percentage point to official interest rates. The central bank had now cut official interest rates from 7.25 to 3.25 per cent since March 2008. One final cut of a further 0.25 percentage point in April 2009 completed the monetary contribution to the national stimulus effort. Taken together, the government's stimulus spending and the Reserve Bank's monetary loosening boosted economic growth by a combined total of 5 to 6 per cent of GDP in 2009, according to Stephen Anthony of the consultancy Macroeconomics. This was a tremendous shot of economic adrenaline. The monetary and fiscal branches of policy had come together to deliver a tremendous boost to the national economy. And it worked.

The opposition argued that the Rudd stimulus didn't keep the economy out of recession – that it was all due to the China factor. The Treasury disagreed. In the absence of the stimulus spending, the economy "would have contracted not only in the December quarter 2008 (which it did), but also in the March and June quarters of 2009, and therefore that the economy would have contracted significantly over the year to June 2009, rather than expanding by an estimated 0.6 per cent," David Gruen reported in the Treasury's post-crisis analysis.

It is entirely possible that the government spent more than it needed to. Certainly, one well-credentialled economist argued so. Professor Warwick McKibbin of the Australian National University, who was a member of the Reserve Bank board at the time, thought the government overreacted. "The government panicked, and now they have to work out a way to pull back some of the spending. The stimulus spending did play a role in avoiding recession, but it was just too big. Everything was a political program and it was brought forward in the guise of a stimulus."

The $42 billion package was 75 per cent bigger than Ken Henry's recommended starting point. Rudd had seriously exceeded what the Treasury regarded as the minimum required. And the North Atlantic expectations of Armageddon did turn out to be a little overdone. In July 2009, six months after Rudd's two-year $42 billion stimulus was announced, the IMF started revising its forecasts upward: "The global economy is beginning to pull out of a recession unprecedented in the post–World War II era, but stabilization is uneven and the recovery is expected to be sluggish. Economic growth during 2009–10 is now projected to be about ½ percentage points higher than projected in ... April ... reaching 2.5 percent in 2010." A month later the Reserve Bank started revising its forecasts upwards too. And in October it began raising official interest rates to match.

Still, it is an Australian luxury to wonder whether the country overreacted. In the US, nearly three years after Lehman Brothers was allowed to collapse, with unemployment at 9.2 per cent compared to Australia's 4.9, some prominent American economists were still arguing that their economy needed more government stimulus spending.

Kevin Rudd's crisis-fighting did not stop at the water's edge. He threw himself into trying to shape the global response. The first reaction in Washington was to convene an emergency meeting of countries excluding Australia. The Bush administration reached reflexively for the Group of Eight as its mainstay. This is the cluster of rich industrial countries that dominated the world economy postwar – the US, Japan, Germany, Britain, France, Canada, Italy, plus Russia. The Bush White House then debated inviting other countries. There was a clear case for adding the big, newly thrusting developing nations, including China, India, Brazil, Mexico and South Africa. But Rudd lobbied hard, with leaders of some other countries, to make the Group of Twenty the cockpit for steering the crisis response. This group did include Australia.

Britain's prime minister, Gordon Brown, recalled his initial negotiations with the US president, George W. Bush:

> The G-20 hadn't yet been properly constituted. There had been some discussion of whether there should be a G-8 plus 5, or a G- plus a number of countries, and a lot of suggestions did not include Australia, of course. I was the one who negotiated it with George Bush. I had pressed for the G-20 – obviously

that was in Kevin's interests because he wanted Australia to be part of it. The first big decision we made was whether the group we convened was going to be the G-8, or the G-8 plus, or the G-20.

Rudd got his wish. The main reason was that the bigger the group, the bigger the impact. But only up to the point of holding cohesion. The G-20, which includes all the G-8 plus the European Union and the biggest developing countries, also embraces a more representative spread of mid-sized economies. Three are important Islamic geopolitical powers: Indonesia, Turkey and Saudi Arabia. Argentina, Australia and South Korea make up the rest. Peter Costello had been one of the prime movers in the creation of the G-20 years earlier. Now Rudd worked to make it the main global crisis-response mechanism. After an initial summit in Washington, the G-20's decisive moment arrived at its London summit in April 2009.

Packed into Number 10 Downing Street for a leaders' dinner, the twenty presidents and prime ministers were elbow-to-elbow around the dining table. The world economy showed no signs of stabilising. The sense of crisis was real. Some of the leaders later recalled looking around the table at their peers that night and seeing fear in their eyes. The London summit pledged $5 trillion in stimulus spending, 2 per cent of global GDP, to create demand. They pledged a further $1 trillion in funds for the IMF to expand its emergency lending. And they promised new and improved supervision of the world banking system.

It worked. Markets steadied and activity soon stabilised. "Our prediction would be that in coming years, the London G-20 Summit will be seen as the most successful summit in history," wrote Colin Bradford and Johann Linn in a paper for the Brookings Institution in Washington. Gordon Brown's conclusion: "Until

April 2009 the world was probably heading for as bad a set of problems as we saw in the Great Depression. That was cut short by the dramatic action that never happened in the 1930s but did happen with the world community coming together." He shared the credit with the Australian leader. "Kevin played a big part," Brown said in 2011.

> He'd been active in making proposals for financial stability. As we prepared for April, we had a number of key leaders who were in close consultation with me and the teams we had working on it and obviously Australia was very much part of that. At that stage Australia was much less affected by the crisis. It played a major part in bringing people together and making it a success.

Costello had helped develop the G-20 and Rudd had helped deploy it effectively in a moment of crisis. Like much of the history of Australian economic success, it was a bipartisan project.

So what were the six standout elements that differentiated the Australian story? There were three positive acts that provided critical support to the economy through the crisis. First was the Reserve Bank's deep and decisive cut to interest rates. Cutting official rates from 7.25 to 3 per cent was powerful. For the typical homeowner with a mortgage, this cut their annual interest bill by about $9,000. Even in the middle of a crisis, many households managed to feel reasonably comfortable. While aggregate salaries and wages fell by 2.6 per cent in 2009 as firms cut back on hours, household disposable incomes nevertheless rose by 3.5 per cent at the same time because of the lower interest rates.

Second was the federal government's early and aggressive use of stimulus spending. Third was the fact that these other two factors generated a critical mass of positive psychology: confidence.

Employers were disposed to cut workers' hours, not workers. Shoppers kept shopping. It was probably helpful to national confidence that the loudest potential critic and fearmonger was silent in the early stage of the crisis. The opposition leader, Malcolm Turnbull, made a deliberate early decision to support the government where possible and to be silent where he could not. He put his political interest aside temporarily in the national interest.

And there were three potentially disastrous forces that did not come into play, elements of the crash in other countries that did not occur in Australia. First, there were no bank failures. Bank collapses led the crisis in the US, UK and Europe. The four major Australian banks, by contrast, were sound and profitable throughout. No Australian financial institution required a government-funded rescue. As some of the world's most famous banks teetered and toppled, all four of the Australian banks were among the exclusive club of top-rated institutions. None was downgraded during the crisis. Only a dozen private-sector banks on the planet qualified for membership in that club in 2011. So Australia accounted for a third of all rolled-gold private banks in the world, even though its economy represents less than 2 per cent of global GDP.

How did this come to be? The politicians and regulators get a lot of the credit and bank management gets the rest. Like the success of the Australian economy itself over the last twenty years, the strength of the banking sector was a bipartisan accomplishment, years in the making. Paul Keating has claimed credit for the soundness of Australia's banks because of his decision as treasurer to create the "Four Pillars" policy in 1990. This requires that the four big banks remain separate, barred from taking each other over. This prevented them "cannibalising each other," in Keating's words. As a protected species, they had no need to mount risky takeovers to bulk themselves up defensively.

But Four Pillars was followed by "Twin Peaks," a second key policy decision made seven years later by Peter Costello as treasurer. Until 1997, the Reserve Bank was responsible for two separate functions. It set interest rates to manage the economy, but it was also responsible for policing the banks to keep them sound. Costello split the functions. The central bank was to be responsible for rates only, and a new agency was created to supervise the banks. The Australian Prudential Regulatory Agency (APRA) was born. "The RBA opposed this decision," Costello wrote in his memoirs. "I proceeded with it. I think it was the right decision." He believed that it meant the Reserve Bank did a better job: "With an exclusive focus and enormous resources, the bank is better placed to make monetary policy decisions." Canada had earlier pursued this same separation of functions. And Canada was the other developed country whose banks stood rock solid during the crisis.

These are two decisions that the US did not make. There is no prohibition on takeovers and mergers of the biggest banks. There is no separation of monetary policy from bank supervision. In America, the Federal Reserve does both. And it did both dreadfully in the 2008 crisis. The Fed was responsible for the total breakdown of prudential policing of the banks, leading to the disastrous collapses that set off the crisis. And the Fed was also responsible for the ruinous run-up of cheap money that generated the housing bubble. The Fed's failures and culpability were complete. It is hard to imagine a greater failure. The response of the US political system? Instead of splitting the Fed's functions, the US actually intensified its powers and increased its scope. In the US, failure has been rewarded and risks compounded.

There is a special risk when putting control of interest rates and bank policing together in one institution, as the US does. And that risk is a conflict of interest. When a central bank is using interest rates to try to create growth in the economy, it will be tempted to use its other power to do the same. That is, it will be tempted to allow banks to lend money more loosely than they should, because this will help pump up growth. But to do its other job properly, to keep the banks sound, the central bank should be resisting this temptation. It was a temptation too strong for the US Federal Reserve. The Fed under Alan Greenspan conflated its loose money policy and its loose banking supervision to generate a monstrous bubble in the US housing market. If Greenspan had enjoyed control of only one aspect, the damage might have been reduced.

Costello's decision to create a dedicated bank police force, APRA, was one of the Twin Peaks. The other was his decision to expand the national corporate regulator, the Australian Securities Commission, to supervise investment products offered to the public. This became the Australian Securities and Investments Commission (ASIC). These two institutions, one regulating banks and the other regulating financial products offered to investors, constituted a system unique to Australia.

Australian banks were also healthy because their managements avoided reckless lending and speculative investments. Paul Keating is no fan of the quality of Australian bank managers – he described them as no better than "counterhopping clerks" who had managed to work their way up the bank hierarchies. But he did allow that they had learned well the lessons of risky speculative lending in the 1991–92 recession. Bankers concurred. Saul Eslake, former chief economist at the ANZ Bank and now at the Grattan Institute, added that "very few Australian households took out mortgages that they were unable to service as interest rates rose. Lending at very high loan-to-valuation ratios did not become as commonplace as it was in the US or Britain, partly because a much smaller proportion of mortgages are securitised in Australia than in the US." When a loan is securitised, it is packed up as a part of a bundle of loans and sold to an investor on the open market. In other words, the bank that issued the mortgage sells it. It no longer cares whether the homeowner keeps up the repayments. So it has less incentive to control the quality of its lending decisions in the first place. The loan becomes someone else's problem.

Finally, the number of loans turning bad was minimal because the overall economy remained strong. Borrowers could meet their repayments. The cumulative effect of these various factors? The proportion of US mortgages classified as seriously delinquent hit 9.7 per cent. In Australia the comparable figure was less than 1 per cent.

Second on the list of absent problems was that Australian exports did not collapse. The Australian dollar absorbed a lot of the shock of the global downturn – it lost about a quarter of its value in 2008–09. This meant that the country's reduced income didn't look so small to us because we were counting it in shrunken Australian dollars. And Australia was protected from the worst part of the global trade collapse, the crunch in manufactures. Trade in manufactures, together with finance, was one of the main neural pathways that economic pain travelled along from one country to another, spreading the crisis.

Worldwide, as recession hit and demand fell away, international trade fell more sharply than at any time since hostilities broke out in World War Two. The volume of global trade shrank by 12 per cent in 2009. But within that, the hardest-hit sector was manufacturing. Global manufactures trade was down by 23 per cent in the year to October 2009. The car trade, for instance, suffered a brutal 36 per cent crunch. Manufacturing is not a very big part of Australian exports; it makes up only 16 per cent of the total. So its impact on Australia was minimised.

Because Australian exports were dominated by commodities, it was a prime winner from China's economic stimulus spending.

In 2008–09, the price of Australian commodity exports fell by almost 40 per cent. But as the Chinese stimulus kicked in, these prices started moving back up again. By the end of 2010, the price loss had been completely regained. Even though China buys only one fifth of Australian exports, it's the price-setter for most commodities. So it dragged prices up as it sucked commodities in. And Australia benefited.

Third, Australia's real estate market did not collapse. House prices looked vulnerable. They'd risen by 150 per cent in the dozen years before the crisis. That made them even more inflated than US and Canadian house prices. An Aussie "Chicken Little" emerged to dramatise the danger for the media. The economist Steve Keen, of the University of Western Sydney, sounded a dire warning that prices would fall by 40 per cent or more. That would carry unspeakable consequences. At the time of his warning, US house prices had fallen by 20 per cent, and that was enough to wreak personal and economic havoc on a vast scale. Australian house prices were supported by so much unsustainable debt, he argued, that the collapse was inevitable. His prediction won him a lot of prime media time. It fitted perfectly the big narrative unfolding in the global crisis, it gave the media an Australian angle, and it was so big that it was sensational.

Keen did not go unchallenged. Another economist offered him a bet on his apocalyptic forecast. Macquarie Bank's Rory Robertson bet him that if Keen turned out to be right in the year after his prediction, Robertson would walk from Canberra to the top of Mt Kosciuszko. That's about a 200-kilometre stroll followed by a 2,300-metre climb. But: "If Dr Keen turns out to be less than half right, as I expect, and home prices drop by (much) less than 20 per cent, he will take that long walk. Moreover, the loser must wear a t-shirt saying: 'I was hopelessly wrong on home prices! Ask me how.'"

Keen, needless to say, lost the bet. He made the long walk in good grace and has a novel t-shirt and smarting ego as souvenirs. A year after striking their highest pre-crisis point, in March 2008, the average house price across the eight capital cities fell by just 6.7 per cent, according to the Australian Bureau of Statistics. And a year further on again, they were 13.3 per cent higher than at their pre-crisis peak. Rather than falling in the downturn, house prices had actually risen.

The question is: why? How did Australia manage, once again, to confound the expectation that it would die? Australian house prices were, no doubt, overpriced. But four key factors kept them aloft. First was that Australia's housing "bubble" had already had some of the air squeezed out of it in 2002 and 2003. The Reserve Bank had raised interest rates and its then governor, Ian Macfarlane, had preached loud and long about the dangers of overpriced real estate. These monetary and psychological factors held the craze in check. Second, Australia's mortgage market was well disciplined and the banks well supervised. Third, the basic balance of supply and demand remained a very tight one. Largely because of restrictive planning and land-release policies, supply of new housing had trouble keeping up with demand from a growing population. There was no major oversupply. This was terrible for housing affordability, but worked as a positive factor in the crisis. Finally, the Reserve Bank had plenty of scope to cut interest rates, and it did. This meant that housing finance grew cheaper. More people could suddenly afford to buy. And people already paying off their homes found the mortgages to be much more manageable as interest repayments fell.

All of this really only means something if it helps the lives of people at the human level, rather than at the macroeconomic indicator level alone. These were the central pillars that held Australia's economy aloft when others were falling in the Great Crash of 2008

– the three positive factors of decisive Reserve Bank interest-rate cuts, aggressive government stimulus and buoyant confidence, together with the absence of three negative ones: bank failures, an export collapse and real estate distress. But what was the overall effect on the lives of citizens in whose name the country is run?

Two researchers at the Social Policy Research Centre at the University of New South Wales ran a survey of people's lives in 2006 and then again in 2010. They asked a random sample of about 2,600 Australians detailed questions about everything from their access to warm clothing and dental care to their regular social contacts and computer skills. And they asked how they felt about their wellbeing. Peter Saunders and Melissa Wong reported their provisional conclusion in May 2011. The results "paint a picture in which most Australians were better off (and felt so) in 2010 than they were in 2006, although many were adversely affected by the [global financial crisis], particularly younger Australians. Many reported that the GFC had no effect on them, and most forms of deprivation declined somewhat," they reported. "Overall, the results suggest that the resilience of the Australian economy and the decisive fiscal actions taken by government protected many people from experiencing the adverse social outcomes that might otherwise have occurred when global financial markets imploded."

So Australia successfully flicked the switches in response to the crisis – the right switches at the right time. The switches worked because they were attached to powerful engines. In other countries, notably the US, even when their authorities pressed the same policy switches, they met a different response. The engines turned over, but gave little power. Why? Because the Australian policy engines were kept in robust good order during the good times, while the engines of US policy were run down badly. A precondition for effective crisis response is a well-maintained machinery of policy. We will see more on this in a later chapter.

Almost as remarkable as the Australian economic experience was the Australian political experience. While Australia enjoyed prosperity in the midst of international hardship, its government signally failed to win credit for the accomplishment. The Rudd government enjoyed very high levels of popularity during the acute crisis phase of 2008–09, but it failed to carry this into the recovery phase in 2010.

Two things happened. Rudd's opponents cleverly turned a tale of extraordinary economic success into a political narrative of incompetence. The opposition successfully latched onto implementation problems of the home insulation program that was a component of the second stimulus package. The shadow environment minister, Greg Hunt, doggedly pursued problems of hasty and ill-managed installation, including fire hazards in thousands of suburban ceilings and four dead installers. As Hunt put it: "The government said we will multiply the size of this industry twentyfold – everything flows from that." The problems were a media staple for weeks and then months. The Pink Batts became a symbol of Labor incompetence.

And the *Australian* newspaper decided to campaign against the school-building component of the same stimulus package, the so-called Building the Education Revolution. The newspaper applied a level of detailed daily scrutiny that it did not apply to any other area of federal, state, local or corporate investment. It elevated the issue to a regular front-page story and portrayed it as an unmitigated waste of public funds. The program's budget was less than 1 per cent of annual federal outlays, but a casual overseas visitor reading the *Australian* would have been forgiven for assuming that it was the dominant share. And there were problems with the program. A government-appointed audit found that 3 per cent of schools had complained about the projects. Some of the state governments implementing the program allowed chronic overcharging. The federal government had hoped that every new school project would lead to a ribbon-cutting revelry for local Labor politicians. The opposition picked up on the *Australian*'s campaign to turn the program into a liability instead of an asset, and talkback radio amplified the level of outrage.

These two programs were shorthanded into Pink Batts and school halls. Together they became the popular symbols of Rudd's stimulus. They chimed with a long-standing stereotype of Labor as the party of fiscal incompetence. Rudd's economic triumph in managing Australian growth through the global crisis was widely reduced to a lampooning. The opposition magnified the federal debt that fuelled the stimulus to add a further level of outrage. It campaigned for years against Labor debt and deficits, and held it up as the confirmation of every fear that anyone had ever held of Labor's budgetary recklessness. All of this took a great deal of the shine off the Rudd government's economic success in the public mind. The Rudd government never succeeded in finding a concrete symbol of its success, never managed to compete with the Pink Batts. And it never managed to win wide recognition of its own version of events. It was a government that paid enormous attention to the legerdemain of daily media presentation – "spin" – yet failed to win this critical argument.

But this was only an awkward inconvenience for the Rudd government, not a fatal misstep. Polling showed that it was heading for comfortable re-election. The truly serious damage was self-inflicted. The government's decision to defer its plan for addressing climate change, its emissions trading scheme, was the threshold moment. The speed of the collapse in Labor's support showed not a drift but a rupture – Rudd's popularity concertinaed from 59 to 41 per cent in two months, according to the Nielsen poll. And the government's standing suffered accordingly. The pollster John Stirton observed at the time: "It looks like a protest against Kevin

Rudd." He had avowed that climate change was "the greatest economic and moral challenge of our time." Rudd's commitment to action on climate change was a deep part of his political persona. By so easily abandoning it, he raised an existential question in the public mind – if he doesn't stand for this, what does he stand for? If we can't believe his commitment to this, which commitment can we believe? Labor moved abruptly from being ahead in the polls to being behind. Seriously weakened, Rudd's party deposed him in a lightning coup and replaced him with his deputy, Julia Gillard. It was the first time since the war that a party had brought down its own prime minister during his first term in office.

The economy survived the most savage global economic crisis since the Great Depression, but the prime minister presiding over this success did not. The economy was expected to die, yet lived. The prime minister was expected to survive, yet was dispatched. Australia's economic success was the envy of the world, yet it seemed to hold its achievement in little regard. The new Australian model, more than two decades in the making, had been put through a brutal stress test and emerged, unscathed and untroubled. As at the end of every 007 adventure, it was off enjoying itself with the champagne and the girls while the audience was still catching its breath.

13

THE THIRD PHASE

History must have a sense of humour. How else to explain the fact that Australia started its historic shift towards the free market under a Labor prime minister, and that it came to a halt under a Liberal one? The Thatcher–Reagan pro-market revolution was brought to Australia by Bob Hawke, a former trade union leader. And it was brought to an end by John Howard, a man who'd devoted his prime ministership to crusading for the advance of the free market.

Howard didn't intend to have this effect. Quite the opposite. But his WorkChoices policy turned out to mark the point beyond which Australia would not go. The policy proposed a deregulation of the labour market. It was deliberately designed to allow the dismantling of working conditions that had been painstakingly protected for a century. It was a frontal assault on the entitlements of workers and the power of unions. Howard didn't need to lose an election to grasp that he had overreached.

With the utmost reluctance, Howard picked up the phone to his minister for workplace relations, Joe Hockey, on April 6, 2007. The Australian Council of Trade Unions had been campaigning against WorkChoices for almost two years, long before it was even legislated. The campaign had been devastatingly successful. It would be almost another eight months before the federal election. Howard was calling Hockey in a bid to head off defeat. It was Good Friday. But Howard didn't want to be a martyr. He wanted to stay in power.

Hockey had been urging his leader privately for four months to amend WorkChoices, almost from the moment Howard gave him the portfolio. The government had lost the argument and was shaping to lose the election. Hockey thought he was swaying his leader but couldn't be sure that Howard would take his advice until the prime minister's voice came down the phone line: "Well, how do you think we should do it?" With those words, Howard declared surrender in the 23-year bipartisan campaign to drive Australia further in the direction of the free market.

Hockey replied: "How far can we go?" In the short run, the answer was to change the law so that all existing entitlements would be protected. In the argot of industrial relations, it was to restore the "no disadvantage test" to workplace agreements. It was a policy reversal but not enough to constitute a political recovery. Howard and his government went the way of history at the election. This confirmed the existing evidence: Australia would not tolerate another major deregulation of the labour market. Even one of the canniest and most successful politicians of postwar Australia had been unable to win this reform. But in the longer run, it was another prime minister who would answer the question "How far can we go?"

The research of both main political parties concurred that voters switched from Howard to Rudd for three main reasons. One was WorkChoices. It had broken the relationship of trust that Howard had established with the electorate. Even Howard's retreat on the policy made no difference to public opinion. WorkChoices, it turned out, was not a transactional proposition. It had changed fundamentally the sentiment toward Howard as a leader. "It was when Howard went from being a reassuring Daddy to being a nasty Daddy," in the words of Michael Cooney of the progressive think-tank Per Capita. Another reason was that the people wanted action on climate change and trusted Kevin Rudd over John Howard to take this task seriously.

Third was that Howard had simply been in power too long, that there was a public appetite for something new. There was no appetite for radical change. That's why Labor spent precious party dollars to screen a TV ad so that – as we have already seen – Kevin Rudd could reassure Australia of how boring he was: "Some people have called me an economic conservative. And when it comes to public finances, it's a badge I wear with pride."

There was desire for a new face and a new emphasis. The Liberals' pollster, Mark Textor, summed it up in a presentation to Howard and the party campaign team before the 2007 election. The Howard government was seen as "out of touch, too old, and too tired." Each of these three central Liberal liabilities was self-inflicted. In essence, the election was about the rejection of Howard rather than the embrace of Rudd. The opposition leader himself grasped this. Speaking of the electorate's view of the two competing leaders, Rudd said: "They think I'm all right. They are really critical of him."

Rudd's guiding mantra was one he had lifted straight from Britain's Tony Blair, when the Englishman was coaching some Australian Labor visitors on how best to approach the task of persuading voters to unseat the conservatives. Blair told the Aussies he had a three-part formula, and it was "reassurance, reassurance, reassurance." Rudd hewed so closely to Howard on most areas of policy that he was much derided for his policy "me-tooism." Howard put it this way: "His policy was to sound as much like me as possible, except for those one or two areas where of course he had to be different – such as IR [industrial relations] and climate change." The online satirist Hugh Atkin said that Rudd was campaigning according to the "clever principle of similar difference." But the best quip was Peter Costello's: "The more I hear from Kevin Rudd, the more I wonder whether even Kevin Rudd wants a change of government." In essence, the electorate's choice of Rudd over Howard was a decision for Howard minus the nasty bits. Rudd did not have a mandate for radical change. But there was a new emphasis.

The new emphasis was to give greater weight to fairness, to equity. And so, in the great trade-off between equity and efficiency, Rudd gave less weight to efficiency. Rudd talked a great deal about efficiency-related issues, especially productivity. He promised surplus budgets and tax cuts and appointed Lindsay Tanner not only the minister for finance but also made him the minister for deregulation. Rudd was no economic radical.

But his government's decisions, social and economic, did unmistakeably shift the emphasis. It was no secret: "John Howard's neo-liberal experiment has now reached the extreme, the time has come to restore the balance in Australian politics," Rudd, as opposition foreign affairs spokesman, wrote in his essay in the *Monthly* where he labelled Howard's Australia a "Brutopia." He continued: "The time has come to forge a new coalition of political forces across the Australian community, uniting those who are disturbed by market fundamentalism in all its dimensions and who believe that this country is entitled to a greater vision than one which merely aggregates individual greed and self-interest."

Once in the prime ministership, he badged the change by describing himself as a leader occupying the "reforming centre." If you missed this, you certainly didn't miss the symbolic acts by which he clearly advertised himself to be more interested in equity than his predecessor was. Among these were the apology to indigenous Australians, the pay freeze for members of parliament and the appointment of the first female governor-general.

And then there were the hard-policy acts of equity over efficiency. Rather than any further privatisations, he started a big-government intrusion into a private-sector market with a $42 billion government-built National Broadband Network. Rather than any further cuts to tariffs, he gave the car industry a $6 billion grant under the rubric of a "green car" initiative. The luxury car tax was raised from 25 to 33 per cent. Rather than any further deregulation of the labour market he reimposed protections for workers. He took the federal government into an area traditionally the province of the states with a prominent policy on homelessness. And he appointed the deputy prime minister as not just the minister for industrial relations and education, but also the minister for social inclusion.

The Rudd government made some big, expensive commitments to the cause of social equity. The biggest, the one that rang alarm bells in the Treasury, was the decision to raise the pension for 3 million age pensioners in the 2009 budget. It was not just a one-time increase. The Treasury would have been content with that. It was a permanent improvement in the formula by which pensions are calculated. Instead of getting a pension equal to 25 per cent of the average wage, Rudd Labor raised the base ratio to 27.7 per cent. That meant an extra $1700 a year extra for single pensioners and $500 extra for couples. The cost to the budget was $14.2 billion over four years. The Treasury's concern was that this was a structural increase in spending, and that it was destined to grow in proportion to revenue as the population aged. It was for this reason that Julia Gillard challenged the increase in the Rudd inner sanctum. But Rudd and Swan pressed ahead regardless.

There were other major social equity decisions under Rudd. One was the introduction of paid parental leave, a benefit of about $10,000, at a cost to taxpayers of $700 million over five years. Another was the increase in the childcare rebate. The rebate, which had been stuck at 30 per cent of out-of-pocket expenses, was raised to 50 per cent. For a family, this change makes the rebate worth up to $7800 for each kid, each year. And there was the hospitals reform plan, which, in its latest iteration under Julia Gillard, is to cost $16.4 billion over five years from 2014.

But it was only when the global financial crisis struck that Rudd really answered the question "How far can we go?" Facing global market failure with potentially catastrophic consequences, and writing of "a turning point between one epoch and the next, when one orthodoxy is overthrown and another takes its place," Rudd put concerns of efficiency aside. The man who had advertised himself as an "economic conservative" now became a radical interventionist and one of the world's most devoted Keynesians. In proportionate terms, he engineered the world's second-biggest stimulus spending package, second only to China's as a percentage of GDP, as we saw in the last chapter.

The Rudd government intervened, as many governments did, in the banking sector, to guarantee the banks' borrowings as well as depositors' funds up to $1 million per account-holder. But it also intervened in the car retailing and commercial real-estate sectors by offering to supply emergency credit. And one of its stimulus measures was to commit funds for something that the federal government had always left to the states: 20,000 new units of public housing.

The stimulus package was an extraordinarily big intervention. Most of it was temporary. And Rudd had not forgotten concepts of efficiency and limiting the size of the state. He committed the government to a fiscal straitjacket to keep post-crisis real increases in spending to 2 per cent, a discipline which the Howard government did not meet in four of its budgets. This would eventually return the budget to surplus.

But much of the Rudd government's spending has added permanently to the size of the federal government. The best way to measure this is to estimate the size of the "structural deficit." This is different to the topline deficit that the Treasury publishes and that all political debate focuses on. The published deficit is, of course, hugely influenced by the economic cycle and by one-off decisions that have no persistent effect. The structural deficit, or structural surplus, is the underlying state of the public finances in the absence of cyclical forces, after taking account of one-off decisions. The Treasury does not issue an estimate of this figure, so we must rely on non-government economists. A former budget analyst at the Treasury and the Finance Department, Stephen Anthony of the consultancy Macroeconomics, publishes regular estimates. He calculates that the structural deficit in Rudd's first budget in 2007–08 was $25 billion. In 2010–11, it had blown out to $65 billion and would reach $77 billion the year after, in his estimate. He called for "urgent remedial action." Anthony warned: "Unless Australian governments act now to address their budget deficits and prepare for leaner and more volatile times, they are failing in their duty of care."

Another vital measure of efficiency is national productivity. Contrary to popular impression, productivity is not a way of measuring how hard a country works. It's the key way of measuring how smart a country works, in getting maximum benefit from the same amounts of human labour and invested capital. We will hear more about this in chapters to come, but it is the true key to national prosperity. Australia performed poorly for a long time on this key measure, with a long-run average of 1.2 per cent annual improvement. This almost doubled during the 1990s, thanks to the economic reforms of the 1980s and '90s. Then it slumped again in the last decade. For the last five years, it's been below zero.

Australia has moved into a new phase. In its nation-building phase from federation in 1901 to the election of the Hawke–Keating government of 1983, Australia gave priority to equity over efficiency in crafting the so-called Australian Settlement. It was a fairly rigid construct designed to bring a sense of fairness to a new country.

In its reform phase from 1983 to 2007, the Australian Settlement was dismantled and Australia concentrated on improving its competitiveness. The emphasis in Australian policy switched emphatically to efficiency as Australia tended to its relative wealth in the world and a new Australian model of political economy took shape.

In 2007, the pendulum reached the limit of its sweep and started to swing back. The motive force was the idea that a corrective was required, that the market had been allowed to intrude too far, that it was time for a return to greater equity. The advent of the global financial crisis in 2008–09 pushed it yet further in the direction of equity over efficiency. By mid-2011, there was no evidence that this phase had yet run its course.

14

FREE-MARKET HONG KONG OR SOCIALIST FRANCE?

A leading American newspaper threw down a challenge to Australia in 2010. Declaring that the country faced a "tipping point," the *Wall Street Journal* claimed that it had to make a choice: "Does Australia," it posed, "want to philosophically go the way of free-market Hong Kong or socialist France?" A dramatic choice indeed. The particular issue at stake was Australia's proposed mining tax. The venerable journal of US capital thought the planned tax to be pure socialism. But the larger point that the newspaper failed to comprehend was that Australia had already made its choice. And it was not one that the *Journal*, permanently on an ideological war footing, could understand or even recognise.

Australia has chosen to be neither Hong Kong nor France. Yet it enjoys the best of both types of society. Hong Kong is the archetypal low-tax, low-benefits, laissez-faire state. It is consistently rated as the freest economy in the world, but it is also one of the most unequal societies in the world. Income tax is a maximum 15 per cent and the tax on corporate profits is 16.5 per cent, making it the least taxed society in the developed world. Its overall tax burden of 13 per cent of GDP puts it between Uganda and the Congo in the world rankings. Hong Kong puts a high premium on efficiency over equity. It has high growth and low unemployment. In the world of the *Wall Street Journal*'s right-wing editorialists, it's the ideal.

Hong Kong also benefits from its romanticised image in the Western imagination as the exotic Orient's freewheeling centre of trade and traffic, legal and illicit, the centre of the opium wars, the entrepot where the great British trading *hongs* of Jardine Matheson and Swires made their fortunes, and where Europeans could do as they pleased in the face of an enfeebled China. With its dramatic harbour and noisy bustle, even today Hong Kong is a city where Europeans can feel at home in an exotic locale, where the infrastructure of expats' clubs and English-language service caters to the needs of the foreign executive, where apartments on the Peak and the yacht club's access to leisure provide a pleasant sanctuary for the monied. And a foreign passport lifts entirely from the mind the background concern that most locals live with, the risk that its great-power overseer, China, might one day change its mind about the liberties of its small southern possession. The charm of Hong Kong, low tax and manageably exotic, to the expat is seductive, and to the aspiring billionaire it is even more alluring. Hong Kong, with a population of just 7 million, was home to thirty-six US-dollar billionaires in 2011, more than Japan with its vast economy and its 130 million people.

That gave Hong Kong, with 0.1 per cent of the world's people, 3 per cent of its billionaires. It ranks one-hundredth in the world by population but seventh by billionaires. The rich of Hong Kong all have the reassurance of multiple passports. Citizenship for the super-rich is no more burdensome than any other lifestyle accessory.

But Hong Kong also has the greatest gap between rich and poor of any society in the developed world, on par with Nicaragua in 2008. And it has the highest level of poverty. The US is generally regarded as the most impoverished of the developed countries, with 15.4 per cent of households, almost one in six, living in poverty. The definition of poverty is less than half the national median income. But Hong Kong is worse at 17.9 per cent.

The economy has enjoyed vigorous growth for many years, though it shrank in 2009 in the global crisis. It is a high-income economy. But the growth has not improved conditions for ordinary people. The convenor of Hong Kong's executive council (the equivalent of the senior minister in a cabinet), Leung Chun Ying, pointed out in April 2011 that GDP per head had grown by a very respectable 34 per cent in real terms in the decade since 1996, which was the year before the Asian economic crisis hit. Yet in spite of that growing prosperity for the city overall, 1 million workers – 30 per cent of the workforce – had suffered a fall in their incomes. Leung said that Hong Kong's experience had debunked the "trickle-down" effect, where the rising riches at the top of the income distribution are supposed inevitably to trickle down to improve incomes at the bottom: "It is a unique phenomenon in Hong Kong when wages of the higher level soar high, the lower level wages fall even more quickly."

Average household incomes have yet to recover to their level of 1997. That level? About $HK29,200, or about $A3,500, a year. So in nearly a decade and a half of strong growth, the average, already pitiful, has actually fallen. Leung added: "I believe the reason is we do not have a minimum wage." This was, he said, the biggest cause of fury for the people of Hong Kong.

And so, after years of debate and much anger and many dire warnings from the business community, Hong Kong introduced a minimum wage in May 2011. The wage is $HK28, or $US3.60, per hour. The US federal minimum wage is regarded in other developed countries as very low. And the US wage is $7.25 an hour. Hong Kong's is exactly half as much. Are the people of Hong Kong satisfied?

Two months after the minimum wage was introduced, the annual day of ritual anti-government protest arrived. This July 1 event has been a fixture on the Hong Kong calendar since the end of British rule in 1997, when some citizens wanted to let Beijing know that they would insist on their civil liberties under China's rule. Rather than any easing of popular anger, the crowd in 2011 represented the biggest outpouring of frustration since 2003 and 2004, when there was anger at a proposed new security law, subsequently dropped. The police estimated that 51,000 protesters set out at the beginning of the march from Victoria Park, and the organisers estimated that 218,000 people arrived at the end. This was four times the organisers' estimate of the previous year. Many banners demanded an early move to full democracy, but media reports emphasised that many of the protesters were complaining about unaffordable housing and other living conditions. Some carried coffins to represent the cramped housing conditions of the poor, where it's common for a small apartment to be partitioned into three or four tenements. Hong Kong has the most unaffordable housing in the world, according to the 2010 Demographia survey of 325 housing markets. The price of the median dwelling in Hong Kong is 11.4 times the annual median household income, the highest ratio anywhere. Australia also features in the list of countries with "severely unaffordable" housing with its ratio of 7.1 and Sydney was the second-worst market in the world at 9.6. It is a serious problem for Australia, but in Hong Kong it is worse still.

"Most people are very angry at this government," said Michael DeGolyer, director of the Hong Kong Transition Project, interpreting polls conducted by his non-profit outfit. The big issues were economic, he said – zooming housing prices, inflation and the growing disparity between the rich and the rest.

The question of democracy hangs over everything in Hong Kong, or the Hong Kong Special Administrative Region of the People's Republic of China, as it is formally known. Its people's civil liberties are protected under the Basic Law, its made-in-Beijing constitution, for fifty years from 1997. The people's political rights, however, are limited. The chief executive is quasi-elected, and ultimately appointed by Beijing. There is a plan to introduce a fully elected political system by 2020, but, as with everything in the city, this is subject to the will of Zhongnanhai, the walled compound in Beijing where China's leaders live. As the July 1 demonstrations show, the 7 million people of Hong Kong do have much greater freedom than their 1,300 million counterparts across the border. This is the "one country, two systems" formula at work.

But because the freedoms of one of the systems are entirely dependent on the goodwill of the other, there is always a tension. In December 2010, for instance, Beijing made it clear that Hong Kong's freedom of speech ends at the border.

When a mainland Chinese court sentenced Zhao Lianhai to two and a half years jail for speaking up on behalf of parents whose infants had been killed or sickened in the 2008 contaminated milk scandal, there was an outcry in Hong Kong. Twenty-eight Hong Kong people, delegates to the Beijing pseudo-parliament, the National People's Congress, wrote a letter to the Supreme People's Court in Beijing asking for clemency. The response from the top Beijing official responsible for Hong Kong, Wang Guangya, was clear: "Others should not interfere. Moreover, I understand that this incident has already been properly settled." Asked whether the joint letter from the Hong Kong NPC members to the court amounted to interference, Wang said: "Under 'one country, two systems,' well water should not intrude into river water." The proverb is redolent with history. After the massacre of the Chinese students calling for greater accountability in government in Tiananmen Square in 1989, it was exactly this form of words that a former Chinese president, Jiang Zemin, used to discourage protests from Hong Kong.

Because Hong Kong's system is the most economically free in the world, it is very kind to business and very harsh on humans, unless, of course, they happen to be wealthy. The wealthy can live well in any country. This is not the test of a society. Is Hong Kong really a desirable society? Even Hong Kong itself doesn't seem to think so. The introduction of a minimum wage shows that even in a quasi-democratic system, giving rein to the untrammelled rights of capital over people is intolerable. Hong Kong wants what Australia already has.

Even if we put aside the geography of having to live in an overcrowded city, the economics of hanging on the teat of its great-power overlord, and the geopolitics of the permanent risk that its liberties could be extinguished on the whim of a remote ruler, does the *Wall Street Journal* really think that Australians should embrace a socioeconomic system with a six-day work week, a minimum wage just one-fifth of Australia's, poor working conditions, a miserable welfare system, falling average real wages, sub-standard health care and a ranking of twenty-one on the UN's Human Development Index, the same index on which Australia ranks first? Surely not, and it's hard to imagine that the *Journal* would seriously propose it for the people of America, either. Hong Kong is not an attractive model. It could only be the suggestion of an ideologue who doesn't have to live there on the same terms as the local people. For the *Wall Street Journal*'s editors it may be some kind of ideal, but for a rational person it is not a model but a caricature.

*

France is at the other end of the *Wall Street Journal*'s spectrum, the antithesis of Hong Kong. It's a high-taxing, high-benefits, rigidly regulated state. France is also subject to a lot of romanticising. The land of Napoleon and the Revolution, of the Louvre and Notre Dame, inventor of the cinema and the guillotine, Chanel and champagne is consistently the world's most popular tourist destination.

In 2010 it was visited by 76 million people, which gave it 11 million more tourists than residents.

Paris is the only city in the world that Hollywood's unwritten rules will permit to be portrayed as being as desirable as New York.

In the *Wall Street Journal*'s world, however, France is held in disdain because it puts a higher value on equity than efficiency. It has twice in the last twenty years been ranked by the World Health Organization as offering the world's best overall health care, and for most people suffering disorders such as cancer or AIDS, treatment is free. With the longest life expectancy in the European Union and the lowest rates of obesity, France delivers a high quality of life to most of its people.

Where income tax in Hong Kong is a maximum of 15 per cent, the French system includes an additional tax on wealth. This tax, named the "solidarity tax," is powerfully symbolic and controversial beyond its fiscal significance. It's levied on anyone with wealth of €800,000 or about $US1 million, and it includes the value of property owned. At the top rate, people with taxable wealth above €16.79 million pay an additional 1.8 per cent of their holdings in tax each year. The tax collects only 2 per cent of the national tax revenue, but is fiercely debated. Whereas Hong Kong has thirty-six billionaires, France is home to twelve. While Hong Kong is the least taxed society among rich countries, France is the seventh-most highly taxed, with the government collecting the equivalent of 42 per cent of GDP in tax in 2009.

The *Wall Street Journal* is right that France has serious problems. Like most of Europe, it has sluggish growth, persistently high unemployment and a debilitating national debt. France's traditional attachment to equity has gone too far, creating an entitlement mentality, burgeoning government spending and a loss of economic vigour. A proposal for modest, prudent change usually produces paralysing strikes and truck blockades that commonly force the defeat of the proposal. Fairness has come to be redefined as the permanent entrenchment of existing privileges, the status quo above all else. But how is unemployment of 9 per cent good for equality? Is youth unemployment of 22 per cent fair? Both rates are around double the comparable rates in Australia. The minimum wage, incidentally, is €9 an hour, or about $US13 or $A12. It's more than three times the Hong Kong equivalent, yet still below the Australian minimum wage of $A15.51 an hour.

Those in union-protected jobs have been likened to the "aristocrats" of modern France. When dockworkers at a Marseilles oil port went on strike in 2010 over the privatisation of some unloading operations, their managers rebuked them by publishing a spoof ad for their jobs. Titled "The Best Job in the World," it stated that their conditions included a work week of 18 hours, annual pay of $US66,000 and guaranteed employment for life.

Economic sclerosis produces social and political frustration. France declared a state of emergency to control weeks of race-based riots in suburban Paris in 2005, where up to 1,408 cars were torched and hundreds of people were arrested in a single night. Riots flared in France's other major cities, too. "There is a problem and that problem is one of equality of opportunity and respect for everyone in the republic," said the then president, Jacques Chirac.

In the first half of 2011, the leading candidate for the 2012 French presidential elections was Marine Le Pen, leader of the ultra right-wing Front National Party and daughter of Jean-Marie Le Pen. The main difference? Where the father was anti-immigration and anti-Semitic, the daughter is anti-immigration and anti-Muslim. She is an economic protectionist who wants France to reimpose the trade barriers it abandoned to join the European Union. She has said that there is "a desire for a revolution in France." Frustration among the French with social injustice and the gap between rich and poor had led to an anger comparable to that of the demonstrators who overthrew governments in the Arab uprisings of 2011: "We're in a pre-revolutionary situation here. What's happening today resembles what was happening before the French revolution. I think the desire for a revolution like those on the other side of the Mediterranean exists here. Of course, I'm appealing for a democratic revolution – and that's also perhaps the role of the Front National – for a peaceful revolution by the ballot box, a patriotic revolution."

Nicolas Sarkozy, France's president, took office promising to change the "French model." It had created a "malaise" in the country, he said in 2005: "The best social model is no longer our social model." He wanted to junk France's traditions of big government and a big social welfare net. Instead, he sought a more Anglo-Saxon, market-based economy: "Work more, earn more," was one catch-cry.

But when the 2008–09 global crisis struck, the French model surprised Sarkozy and many others. It slowed, certainly, and it suffered a recession. But its downturn was shallower, more fleeting, than that of any other major European economy apart from Germany's. The French daily *Le Monde* puffed out its chest in a moment of national pride: "In the crisis, the French model, formerly knocked, finds favour once more." Even one of the most strident critics of the French model, Britain's *Economist* magazine, conceded, "The French way of doing things looks pretty good – at least in these troubled economic times." Sarkozy relented: "The recession has brought the French model back into fashion," he told a joint sitting of both houses of Congress. "The French model has its chance once more."

Why did France prove so robust during the global financial crisis? Part of the reason is that it didn't suffer a major home-grown financial crisis because its banks were more conservative than those of the US, Britain or even Germany. First, thanks to regulation and bureaucracy, troublesome and frustrating in normal times, it's a long and arduous process to obtain even a prime mortgage for real estate in France – and you can forget subprime. Second, French households had a relatively high savings rate of around 12 to 15 per cent, compared to the US rate which hovered around zero pre-crisis. Meaning? When the trouble began, households in many countries suddenly started to worry about their spending and began to save more. And when you save more, you spend less, and consumer spending falls. But the French, already saving at a high rate, saw no need for sudden extra saving. Third, the French government was quick and effective in adding stimulus spending to the economy.

But the central explanation for France's resilience, according to the head French analyst for the OECD, Hervé Boulhol, is something else: "The main feature is the size of the automatic stabilisers, which cushions the shock." This is simply the way that a country's government finances react when the economic growth rate changes. The more unemployment benefits and other welfare payments increase, the greater government spending becomes. Because this happens naturally with a slowdown, it's called automatic. And because it offsets the fall in private activity in a slowdown, it's called a stabiliser. The average size of the automatic stabiliser in the Group of Twenty countries was 1.8 per cent of GDP in 2009.

That is, without governments needing to do a thing, public spending rose by an average of 1.8 per cent during the recession. In France, it was 2.5 per cent. (In Germany, it was 3.5.)

In Hong Kong, where the automatic stabiliser is small because the size of government payments is small, the economy took a big hit but bounced back quickly. The overall impact? Hong Kong's economy suffered a much greater loss of economic activity, ten times as great as France's, but it was briefer. The Bank for International Settlements reported Hong Kong's output loss at 10 per cent in 2008–09.

France was in recession for two years, however, while Hong Kong suffered only one year of recession. Nevertheless, on the face of it France fared better. But a key part of the picture is what effects linger after the crisis has passed. Hong Kong, which entered the crisis debt-free and didn't spend much more public money in the bad time than it did in good, was left with a tiny government debt of only 4.5 per cent of its GDP by 2011. But France entered the recession with a big debt, which grew much worse in the recession.

In France, Hervé Boulhol put it this way: "We have this big social net which in a crisis is a good thing. The question is, in the long term, is it good or not?" He worried about the long-run implications for national public debt. As government spending has increased with the automatic stabiliser, so has the government deficit. "France's government debt has been increasing continuously – in the 1970s it was 30 per cent of GDP, and pre-crisis it was 70 per cent. In 28 years the debt take has increased by 40 per cent of GDP, so the annual average increase has been 1.4 per cent of GDP. This social safety net is not financed. The cost has been pushed on the next generations. When we think about a [French] model, that's what we think about."

Government debt in France was a record 81.7 per cent of GDP in 2010. (As a passing curiosity, the EU treaties set a legal limit for members' debt of 60 per cent.) "That will put us into a snowballing effect of debt and interest," Boulhol predicted. "The problem is, we have no restraint." Sarkozy tried to impose some. He proposed raising the earliest retirement age gradually by two years, from 60 to 62, and the full retirement age by two years from 65 to 67, in line with most European countries. This would extend the income-earning years of the workforce – two extra years when workers would pay taxes instead of being paid pensions. In an aging society, this would be an important curb on runaway deficits. The proposal brought a fierce yet predictable response, with millions marching in protest and strikes breaking out across the country. Marseilles won worldwide attention for its stinking garbage mountains piling up in the streets while the garbage collectors were on strike.

Union leaders claimed that the entitlement to a pension at the age of 60 was a "birthright." The threshold had been lowered from 65 to 60 in 1983. The national "birthright" was an innovation that was all of twenty-seven years old. The leader of a major French trade union, François Chérèque, said: "We have several million people in the street who support us and believe in us. The only one blocking the country is the government." The president's approval rating fell to its lowest point, yet Sarkozy pressed on in the face of the protests. The then finance minister, current IMF director Christine Lagarde, made the argument that gradually lifting the retirement ages would be less painful than raising pension contributions or trimming benefits for the 15 million people in France already on pensions. The retirement age would rise by four months every year until the full two-year increase took effect in 2018. The French congress, where Sarkozy's party enjoyed a comfortable majority, accepted the gravity of the national condition.

The reform passed. It exhausted Sarkozy's political capital and his will. He said it would be his last major reform before the 2012 election. The problem with the French model, designed to deliver equality and generous benefits, is that it has failed to deliver equality, especially to the one in four young people who cannot find work, and its benefits are offered at a level of generosity that can only be purchased by mortgaging the incomes of future generations. It is not working, and it is not affordable. And the French have started to search for a solution.

France is the fifth-biggest economy on earth, and has a very high average income. Yet on the leading indices of quality of life, France fails to make it to the top tier. It may be the world's favourite country to visit, but it is not the favoured place to live.

It is ranked fourteenth on the UN's Human Development Index and eighteenth on the OECD's Better Life Index. Australia is ranked first on the OECD index and the Human Development Index. Hong Kong is ranked twenty-first on the Human Development Index.

The *Wall Street Journal* argued that Australia needed to choose the philosophical direction of either Hong Kong or France. Hong Kong's people are dissatisfied with the practical results of its governing philosophy of low-tax and low-benefit laissez faire. The introduction of a minimum wage is a way to moderate the harsh effects of the most unequal system in the developed world. Similarly, France's government has realised that its philosophy of high-taxing and high-benefit *dirigisme* is leading it to national disaster. Both countries, from opposite ends of the ideological spectrum, are seeking to correct somewhat, to adjust by shifting to the centre. As Hong Kong improves benefits for its citizens to make life more tolerable, France curbs benefits for its citizens to make life more affordable.

Why would Australia want to choose either model? It has the third freest economy in the world with strong levels of opportunity and unemployment below 5 per cent. Yet it has good working conditions, universal health care, a solid social welfare system and, overall, the most desirable living conditions in the world. It also has a greater level of equality than the average of the rich countries, with low crime and a well-funded system of pensions and superannuation.

Indeed, Australia under Kevin Rudd raised the public pension age from 65 to 67 in 2009. But because it acted long before any anticipated crisis point, it was able to do it in a very gradual way, phasing it in over fourteen years, to take full effect in 2023. The threshold age of 65 had been in place for a century. No one claimed it as a "birthright." There were no strikes. The country was not traumatised. The change was accepted as a prudent preparation for the financial burden on the state that looms with an aging society.

Australia has a two-part retirement incomes policy. The public pension, to which this threshold age will apply, is fully funded from the public purse at 27.7 per cent of the average wage. It is really a poverty-prevention measure. The other part is a privately funded system of superannuation savings. Employers are required to pay the equivalent of 9 per cent of workers' salaries into their superannuation accounts. The accounts are personal and portable. Workers are free to top up their accounts from their own pockets. Superannuation is taxed at concessional rates to encourage retirement saving. In 2009, the Rudd government announced that it would gradually increase this compulsory employer contribution from 9 to 12 per cent over seven years, from 2013 to 2020. This would add an estimated $108,000 to the final retirement balance of a worker on the average wage and today aged 30.

The Washington-based Centre for Strategic and International Studies has rated the readiness of twenty key countries to face the aging of their societies. It has created two measures within its Global Aging Preparedness Index. One measures the ability of a country's government to pay its projected pension burden. The other estimates the adequacy of the likely size of the retirement incomes of its citizens. In 2010 it ranked Australia second among developed nations in the first measure, behind Poland, and fifth among developed nations in the adequacy measure, after the Netherlands, the US, Germany and the UK.

And Australia manages to do all this within its means. It had no recession and the average income per head of $US44,000 in 2009 was higher than in either Hong Kong ($29,000) or France ($42,000). These fetishes of the extreme Right and the extreme Left are not useful examples for Australia to follow. Rather, they demonstrate the problem of excessive attachment to ideology over practicality. The choice is a false dichotomy. Australia has worked out a model that allows it to enjoy the best of both with the worst of neither. It is not a tipping point. It is a culminating point of synthesis.

SUPERMODEL KRYPTONITE

For half a century it was said that when America sneezed, Australia caught cold. But in 2008, America came down with pneumonia and Australia went out to play cricket with the kids. "As an American, it's quite disconcerting to come down here and discover that in Australia the recession is over, housing prices are firm, the auto industry is solid, and the economy is growing. Even your banks are sound," observed an adviser to the US Democratic Party, Bruce Reed, in an after-dinner speech during a visit to Melbourne in late 2009. "Have you learned nothing from us?"

Reed at the time was the head of a think-tank, the Democratic Leadership Council, and later became the chief of staff to the US vice-president, Joe Biden. Although he has a serious job, he has a natural comic flair. He told his Melbourne audience of a remark he'd heard from Peter Costello at a conference: "Costello proclaimed that 'the US has lost its bragging rights.' You know you've hit bottom when Peter Costello is telling you you've lost your bragging rights. Peter's predictions are often spot on, but on this point he was engaged in wishful thinking. We Americans were born to brag. Bragging rights are in our constitution. If you think we're going to be humbled by bollixing a war and bringing the global financial system to its knees, think again. We're Americans – we don't have to be rich or successful to be insufferable."

His wit takes the edge off a harsh truth, but it's a harsh truth nonetheless. Australia has looked to America for the very definition of modernity ever since World War Two. If something was American, it was the latest, it was the best, it was the coolest. This applied not just to US pop culture or technological advances, but also to nation-building ideas and problem-solving flair. Above all, Australia looked to America for its might. And the source of that might is its economy. As Australia's former top defence planner, Hugh White, has observed: "In the long run, economics is what counts in power politics. National power has many manifestations – military, political, cultural – but only one ultimate source. No country in history has exercised great power without great wealth, and the country with the most wealth always ends up with the most power."

The made-in-America crisis of 2008–09 marked the turning point, the moment that made it impossible for Australia to look to America for economic leadership. As noted in the last chapter, Hong Kong and France have never provided any kind of model for mainstream politicians and policy-makers in Australia. In the last thirty years, Australians on the centre-Right looked to America for leadership and example, and on the centre-Left to Europe and, more than any other European country, to Sweden. They looked to these countries because they embodied the ideals of the Right and Left respectively and they were demonstrably successful. Both sides took occasional counsel from London. Overall, however, because of its thrusting economy, because of its military might, because of its leadership of the West in the Cold War, because of its centrality in world affairs, America was the single most important foreign influence on the thinking of Australian politicians, intellectuals and officials. But after the Great Crash of 2008 and the Great Recession of 2009, it was no longer plausible for America to hold itself out as the Great Model.

Although, as Reed quipped, that might not necessarily stop some Americans from trying. Reed wasn't finished. He claimed to know the key to the Australia–US relationship: "I believe I have discovered the secret to our friendship: Americans run the global economy into the ground, then get ourselves invited to the only country doing well enough to have a good laugh about it."

The American model had lost its appeal for some even before the crisis. It seemed to be failing the broad mass of its people, the lower- and middle-income groups. "The economy's shortlived expansion after the 2000–01 recession was the only postwar expansion during which the real income of the median family declined," observed Laura Tyson, a professor of business at the University of California and the chair of the Council of Economic Advisers during the Clinton administration. And if you're an Australian struggling to recall the 2001 recession, it's not your memory failing. That was one of the three big economic dislocations of the last twenty years that Australia's main trading partners suffered, but that Australia did not.

Tyson continued: "For many Americans, the first decade of the 21st century was a lost decade for the economy. A second lost decade has already begun. No wonder they think the economy is still in recession – for them, it is," she wrote in mid-2011, when the US economy was two years into recovery, yet unemployment was stuck at 9.2 per cent. This was an improvement on the peak rate of 10.2, but still far above the pre-crisis level of 4.9 per cent. At the time she wrote, Australia's rate was 4.9.

America has proved to be very good at generating growth and jobs over many decades, but lousy at dealing with hardship, poverty and disadvantage. The sky is the limit for the talented, the hardworking and the lucky. But if you slip, it can be a bottomless pit for the sick, the poor and the unfortunate. The US doesn't offer its people a social safety net so much as a highwire. Perhaps the most serious American failing has been in providing for the health of its citizens.

If you've ever looked into the details of living in America, you might have noticed how eye-wateringly expensive it is to buy medical insurance. It's vastly more costly in the US than for any other developed country. Why? Because while the US has lots of companies vying to provide high-cost, high-quality health care, it has no government intervention in the market to support a reasonable level of care for the broad mass of people. The result is that America has by far the world's most expensive health system and, at the same time, the worst health outcomes in the developed world.

The poor cannot afford to buy health insurance in America. And that means that they cannot afford to get sick. One result is that an estimated 18,000 to 45,000 Americans die every year because they are uninsured. This is, of course, a scandal for one of the world's wealthiest nations. In Western Europe, in Japan, in Australia, in New Zealand, in Canada, no one dies from lack of health insurance.

Another result of America's expensive and ineffective health system is that Americans live shorter lives than average for people living in the developed world. With a life expectancy of 78.3 years, the US ranks thirty-sixth in the world. This is identical to Cuba, a country with one-fifth America's per capita income. Americans live, on average, three and a half years less than citizens of the five countries with the highest life expectancies: Japan, Hong Kong, Iceland, Switzerland and Australia. A baby born in America today can expect a shorter life than that of a baby born in Malta, Ireland or Costa Rica.

If the US spent the same amount of money on health as the average of the countries of the developed world, and achieved the same outcomes, it would save $US988 billion every year, and its citizens would live an average six months longer. Of course, it's not so simple, but this does illustrate the dysfunctional way in which the US deals with health. The US determination to preserve a free-market free-for-all in health care sets it apart. It is the only developed nation that does not provide universal health care for its people and is content to watch them die needlessly by the thousand each year.

President Barack Obama's attempt to make modest reforms to the system sent US politics into paroxysms of outrage. This anger helped give rise to the Tea Party movement and a thrashing for Obama's Democratic Party at the US midterm elections in 2010. The so-called Obamacare plan, legislated to take effect in 2014, will not offer universal health care either. But it is designed to make sure that nearly all Americans will, at least, have health insurance.

Equality and fairness were never America's long suit in its attractiveness as a model for the world. For most of the twentieth century, the US was the standout model for countries seeking fast growth, big profits and low unemployment. So the moment of despair for even America's staunchest admirers came with the multiple and concerted failures of US policy that led to the financial and economic collapse of 2008–09. Faith in the US dollar as the world's reserve currency was one barometer of the world's crisis of confidence in America. When geopolitical shocks struck, such as the Arab uprisings or the Japanese earthquake of 2011, the price of traditional safe haven assets – gold, the Swiss franc – jumped, but the US dollar did not.

Even serious and sober US experts began to suggest that the world should edge away from their country's currency. The president of the World Bank and a former US deputy secretary of State, Bob Zoellick, proposed a new global monetary mainstay of a basket of currencies plus gold. The Nobel Prize–winning economist Robert Mundell suggested that the US dollar and the euro could be fixed to each other, and to gold as well. Gold, said Mundell, "has a strength and a confidence that people trust." The implication, of course, is that the greenback no longer does.

America spent the good years squandering its good fortune as the world's only superpower after 1989. And although Washington was never reticent in "sharing," to use the favoured US euphemism, its views about the pernicious influences of other countries, its downfall was squarely homegrown. The greatest single cause of America's economic collapse was not a policy but an attitude. Complacency.

"Everything is perfect yet improving," was the phrase conjured by Jim Grant, publisher of *Grant's Interest Rate Observer*, to summarise the mainstream sentiment towards the US economy and markets in the years while the disaster was building. The Bush administration presided over seven years of economic growth and one of downturn. Yet it was guilty of running eight consecutive budget deficits and adding inexorably to the stock of government debt. This was not just happenstance: "Reagan proved deficits don't matter," the vice-president, Dick Cheney, told the then Treasury secretary, Paul O'Neill, during a cabinet meeting. "We won the [2002] midterms. This is our due." This vignette, recoded in O'Neill's memoirs, is telling. Cheney interpreted electoral victory as a licence to run up the national debt.

When Bush and Cheney arrived in the White House, the federal government had outstanding debts of $US5.6 trillion. When they left eight years later, the debts were $US10.6 trillion. It's more meaningful to express the failure as a proportion of the US economy. Clinton cut the federal debt from the equivalent of 66 per cent of GDP to 56 per cent. Bush, however, ran it up from 56 to a whopping 84 per cent. This meant that the federal debt in proportion to the US economy was bigger than at any time since the early 1950s, when the US was still paying for World War Two and the Korean War. So when the good years ran out and the crisis arrived, the US had limited fiscal firepower left with which to fight it.

The other weapon in the armoury, the Federal Reserve's interest rates, had also been enfeebled. Interest rates are like a medieval knight's lance – to be potent, they need to be lowered. But the Fed under Alan Greenspan had kept the key official interest rate so low for so long that there was limited scope for big cuts. Greenspan's Fed had held the policy rate at between 1 per cent and 4 per cent for five of the seven years preceding the global financial crisis. The peak rate was 5.25 per cent, and it was held at that level for all of three months. Meaning? The neutral level for the Fed's policy rate, where it is neither stimulating nor subduing the economy, is generally agreed to be about 4 to 5 per cent. Greenspan mostly held the rate below that level in the years leading up to the crisis. He had the economy on a permanent feed of adrenaline even when it didn't need any. So when it really needed it, the hit had a much-reduced impact. He spent years finding every possible excuse to avoid raising rates, willing the good times to roll on. In a famous 1970 quote, the longest-serving chairman of the Fed, William McChesney Martin, said that "The job of the Fed is to take the punch bowl away just as the party gets going." Greenspan kept the US intoxicated with cheap money for years.

Yet it was clear what was required from the White House, the Congress and the Fed. Greenspan's predecessor as Fed chairman, the legendary Paul Volcker, the towering figure who famously broke the back of US inflation, could see what was wrong and what needed to be done with both national spending and official interest rates. "What is required is a willingness to act now," said Volcker, "and to act even when, on the surface, everything seems so placid and favourable. What I am talking about really boils down to the oldest lesson of economic policy: a strong sense of monetary and fiscal discipline." The US got neither.

Greenspan's institution, the Federal Reserve, which was responsible for supervising the banks, in the meantime allowed the creation and runaway growth of the sub-prime mortgage market. The combination of cheap money and a regulation-free zone saw the most extraordinary boom in house prices in the country's history. The total value of all house prices in the US was worth the equivalent of about 80 to 100 per cent of GDP from the mid-1950s to the 1990s. In the Greenspan speculative frenzy, this zoomed to 140 per cent, way out of line with all historical experience. It was a bubble waiting to burst.

And when it burst, when the financial system froze and house prices collapsed and the economy headed for a brutal recession, the Fed had limited scope to lower interest rates to stimulate the economy. So when the US pressed the buttons of the twin economic engines of fiscal and monetary stimulus, both engines responded feebly. They had been allowed to run down in the good years so that they had little left to give in the bad.

Summing up pre-crisis American complacency, the US economists Carmen Reinhart and Ken Rogoff put the dangerous delusion like this: "The US, with the world's most reliable system of financial regulation, the most innovative financial system, a strong political system, and the world's largest and most liquid capital markets, was special." Strikingly, America's self-imagined unique strengths were precisely its greatest vulnerabilities. These were exactly the components of its failures. The ancient Greeks believed that Hubris was always followed by Nemesis.

A British politician, Stuart Agnew, reported this startling fact in May 2011: "I was recently asked if young people growing up in the UK should consider emigrating elsewhere to avoid having to take responsibility for our ever increasing national debt." Agnew, from the small right-of-centre UK Independence Party, sits as a British representative in the European Parliament. He decided to look into the matter: "I have undertaken some rudimentary research into the subject and the results shown below have surprised me. With the notable exception of Australia, most First World Western economies are creating worrying burdens for future generations."

He worked out the burden of national debt per person in seven countries, the ones that a Brit might find desirable. This is what he found, presented here in Australian dollars. National debt per citizen in Britain was $24,750, in Canada $16,280, in France $33,750, Germany $30,070, New Zealand $30,900, the US $42,350 and Australia $5,670. In other words, only two of these countries, Canada and Australia, had lighter debt burdens weighing on them than Britain. And he considered only Australia's debt to be small enough to be an attractive "welcome" present for the new citizen.

Was he overreacting to alarmist constituents? Not at all. The governor of the Bank of England, Mervyn King, has pointed out one of the simple truths of the post-crisis world for the British people: "In 2011," he said at the outset of the year, "real wages are likely to be no higher than they were in 2005. One has to go back to the 1920s to find a time when real wages fell over a period of six years." Three years after New York and Washington led the world financial system into its paralysis of fear, the principal economic powers – the US, the UK, the EU, Japan – were still suffering from serious problems of unemployment and debt.

The debt will weigh on their living conditions for decades. "The average gross general government debt-to-GDP ratio for advanced economies is projected to rise from almost 91 per cent at end-2009 to 110 per cent in 2015, bringing the increase from pre-crisis levels to 37 percentage points," said the International Monetary Fund in May 2010.

How serious is this? The World Bank has estimated that debt becomes a drag on a country's economic growth when it reaches the equivalent of 77 per cent of its GDP. And debt begins to snowball once it hits about 80 to 90 per cent of GDP, unless corrective surgery is performed. Among the G-7 countries of the US, Japan, Germany, Britain, Canada, France and Italy, the "ratio is rising to levels exceeding those prevailing in the aftermath of the Second World War." And for what? The West has not recently fought an existential war against the forces of fascism so that liberty may survive. It's for the indulgence of politicians and regulators who betrayed the trust of their people, and for the venality of financiers and investment bankers. The top staff of just the five major Wall Street investment banks were paid $US38 billion in bonuses in the year before their creation collapsed, taking the livelihoods of billions of people and the prosperity of the West with it. The poverty rate in the US rose to 15.1 per cent in 2010, its highest in seventeen years. One of the more extreme of the many accounts of hardship of the unemployed in post-crisis, minimal-welfare America: "My family is eating stir-fried dandelions out of yards to keep from starving. I am college-educated and cannot pay rent. I have not had a penny income so far this year. We were turned down for food stamps. We are natural-born US citizens."

The US had never put much emphasis on equity, placing its trust in efficiency, interested in growth and opportunity above all. Increasingly, it seemed unable to provide much of any of these.

*

While Europe as a whole has been suffering so-called Euro-sclerosis for so long that it is not an attractive model for Australia, one Northern European country has managed to capture the imagination of the Australian centre-Left for decades. Sweden is credited with inventing the social democratic welfare state. For the moderate, non-socialist Left, it has been a guiding light.

Sweden was one of the poorest countries of Europe in the mid-1800s, its economy heavily agrarian and cottage-based. But the government engineered the creation of a modern capitalist economy with banks, corporations and an emphasis on technology, and by 1890 it was one of the world's fastest-growing economies. It was open to trade with the world and emphasised exports. Unharmed in both of the world wars, when it remained studiously neutral, it stayed one of the fastest-growing economies in the world until the 1950s.

As early as 1936, the London-based journalist and broadcaster George Soloveytchik wrote that Sweden had found a "middle way between collectivism and individual free enterprise," forming a "unique example of a controlled capitalism that works." When he wrote this, the Social Democratic Workers' Party had been in power for four years. It would remain in power for fifty-nine of the next seventy-five years. The Swedish model was very much the project and the creation of the Social Democrats.

By 1970 Sweden was the fourth-richest country in the OECD, measured by income per capita. In the century to 1975, income per capita in the world economy grew at an annual average of 1.5 per cent and Western Europe's at 1.7 per cent. In the US it grew at 1.8 per cent. Sweden's averaged an impressive 2.4 per cent. And while labour and capital clashed in most capitalist societies, in Sweden's corporatist model there was close and harmonious co-operation between the unions, business and the government.

Wages were high and so was welfare. Taxes represented 50 per cent of GDP from the 1960s to the mid-1990s, double the proportion in the US, making it one of the most heavily taxed countries on earth. Yet this didn't crush the private sector, which was highly efficient. Sweden had the benefit of rich natural resources, including timber, iron ore and gold. It tapped plentiful hydroelectric power. Timber products, especially paper and steel products, remain among its biggest exports. But it also managed to produce big and successful exporting manufacturers, like Ericsson, Volvo, Electrolux and Scania.

Puzzling over how a country could enjoy high growth with such a heavy tax burden and high wage costs, a visiting economist from the IMF dubbed Sweden a "bumblebee." Its body seems far too big and cumbersome for its tiny wings, yet it somehow manages to fly. Swedish manufacturing ran into the same problems of competitiveness as most of Europe did in the 1980s – steel, shipbuilding, pulp and mechanical engineering were in dire trouble. Shipbuilding disappeared. The rest upgraded and moved on to a more technology-heavy, knowledge-intensive plane. New industries in information technology, biotechnology and pharmaceuticals appeared and flourished.

With the advent of the Thatcher–Reagan revolution, Sweden also followed the fashion. The government pulled back on state intervention to allow market forces greater play. The financial markets were partly deregulated, centralised wage negotiations ended, and income tax rates were cut. Even as Euro-sclerosis descended on Western Europe in the 1980s, Swedish unemployment remained impressively low at around 2 to 3 per cent. The Swedish model had adjusted, moved to the right a little, and powered on. Compared to the rest of the developed world, it remained heavily taxed, with high wages, big unions, high welfare benefits. And, maddeningly to conservatives, it kept growing and remained prosperous.

The happy picture fell apart in the early 1990s. A housing bubble burst, dragging Sweden's banks into a crisis and its economy into a deep recession. The government assumed a quarter of the liabilities of its failing banks, the so-called Stockholm solution to the banking crisis. The government deficit ballooned. In 1994 it was a substantial 15 per cent of GDP. The krona was sold off in a panic. To support its value, the central bank briefly raised interest rates to 500 per cent. Unemployment hit 9.3 per cent. Sweden, in short, was a mess. The recession of 1991–94 was Sweden's deepest and longest since the Great Depression.

The people voted the Social Democrats out, one of their rare interludes on the opposition benches, and elected a conservative government to deal with the crisis. It shifted Sweden further towards the market. The central bank, the oldest in the world, was granted independence from the government. Most markets were deregulated, except for labour and housing. The state sold out of many corporate shareholdings. The government moved to keep welfare payments viable by cutting the generosity of pensions and creating private retirement accounts. All of these steps will be familiar to Australians from their own pro-market reform drive. The Swedish model had been adjusted and growth resumed. The government eliminated its deficit and balanced the budget by 1998. To its admirers, the Swedish model seemed to be as attractive as ever.

But as the crisis faded, so did reform. Complacency set in. Sweden's greatest strength, its proudly generous and egalitarian system of welfare and benefits, was in the process of becoming its greatest liability. Within a decade, it became an intolerable burden. By 2005, two-thirds of adult Swedes either worked in public service jobs or received government welfare, living on tax revenues generated by the other one-third. There was no growth in the number of jobs in the private sector. In fact, said the chief economist at the Confederation of Swedish Enterprise, the group representing 80 per cent of the country's private sector, Stefan Folster: "The number of jobs in the private sector in 2005 was lower than it was in 1950."

This was not because Swedish companies were not hiring. Sweden's big multinationals were profitable and hiring, just not in Sweden. Two-thirds of all the jobs they created were in other countries. The big Swedish entrepreneurial success story, Ikea, moved its base to the Netherlands and its tax domicile to the Netherlands Antilles, a tax haven. Perversely, small business was paying higher taxes than big business, and with an onerous set of obligations for every staff member, the small business owner had little incentive to hire. Folster said, "The statistics show Sweden with relatively low unemployment," of about 7.6 per cent in 2005, "but Sweden is unique in that the unemployed people are mainly on sick leave." Real unemployment, according to economist Jan Edling who formerly worked for the powerful union body LO, was around 20 per cent. His disclosure was momentous because LO was one of the architects of the Swedish model. Yet now one of its top people was admitting that its vaunted success was much exaggerated.

In a country with a workforce of 4.1 million people, 1.5 million – nearly 40 per cent – were not going to work on any given day. This was the combined number of the jobless and the notionally ill.

And why would they go to work? The sickness benefit was paid at the rate of 90 per cent of their normal wage, for about 70 per cent of people. The cost of paying the benefit was shared between the government and the employer. It was a form of disguised unemployment. Earlier in the century, when the unions paid for unemployment and sickness benefits, a union official would drop in at the home of the absentee worker to check up on him. Now, even though there was a government system for monitoring people on benefits, it broke down under the weight of numbers.

The prime minister of the day, the Social Democrats' Göran Persson, wanted to perpetuate the system. He argued that taxes needed to be raised to keep up with the number of people on sickness benefits. Sweden was already the most heavily taxed country on earth. He wanted more of the same. The system had created such a big constituency of people on benefits that he dared not offend them by proposing reform.

"But are people really sick?" asked Marietta de Pourbaix-Lundin, a politician from the Moderate Party in Sweden's conservative coalition, the Alliance. "Our systems are really generous and it doesn't pay to work. You have almost as much money to not work. With the costs of going to work, you can actually lose money by going to work." The system, she said, had lost legitimacy and was "cracking." And Swedes, she said, "do not protest on the street, but they are quietly protesting against the tax system." How? The workers who were officially ill, home collecting sickness benefits, were surreptitiously taking up cash jobs on building sites or cleaning houses, she claimed, entering the black economy. Sweden needed to restore an incentive to work in the mainstream economy.

Even the king and queen agreed. Carl XVI Gustaf, asked in 2005 for his opinion of the state of the Swedish model, first deferred to his wife, Silvia, the daughter of a German industrialist, who said: "It needs to be modernised." The king concurred: "It's worked well for Sweden but there is a feeling that it needs to be updated." (In 2011, he would be accused of excessive familiarity with models in advanced stages of undress, but it was not clear whether any of them were Swedish.)

Sweden's per capita income had fallen from fourth to fourteenth in the OECD by 2005. After outperforming other rich countries for a century, growth in Sweden's income per person had fallen back to 1.7 per cent from 1975 to 2005, underperforming the US and underperforming the average for Europe. And productivity growth had slumped from a very respectable average 2.1 per cent a year over the previous quarter century to just 1 per cent a year from 1975 to 2000. "Bumblebees fly, and Sweden can still fly, but we have the potential to fly like a sparrow hawk and move up to the top," said Folster.

Swedes agreed that their model needed renovation. And again, they reformed only at the point of crisis. In 2006, the Social Democrats lost power and the centre-right coalition won. The Moderate Party's Fredrik Reinfeldt became prime minister as leader of the

Alliance by a modest margin of seven seats and 2 per cent of the vote. His government set about cutting and tightening eligibility for unemployment benefits, sick leave and early retirement plans to encourage work. With the changes, the number of people on these benefits fell by 150,000. The government relinquished its monopoly ownership of pharmacies. The Social Democrats' ban on private hospitals, and other hyper-regulatory excesses, was relaxed. The government cut property taxes and abolished the wealth tax. It created a system of income-tax credits so that a worker on average income keeps the equivalent of an extra month's wages each year.

When the global financial crisis hit, Sweden had the advantage that its government was in surplus. It still took a serious blow. Sweden trades intensely with the world. The value of its exports and imports equals 100 per cent of its GDP. That ratio for Australia is about 40 per cent, and for the US even less, around 25 per cent. So Sweden is a small, open economy where trade has huge sway. This has been a source of prosperity in the good years, but in the bad its exports were badly hit. And its banks had no serious exposure to the US banks from which the financial contagion initially spread, but they did have a lot of exposure to the Baltic banks that did. The authorities steadied one bank and took over another to prevent its collapse.

The central bank responded decisively, floating the krona and cutting interest rates from 4.75 to 0.25 per cent in the course of ten months. The government announced emergency fiscal stimulus equal to 2.7 per cent of GDP. It added a further 3.4 per cent of GDP as investment in transport, mainly public transport, from 2009 to 2011. And its automatic stabilisers, thanks to the size of its welfare state, are the biggest in Europe, offering a natural buffer against volatility.

None of this was enough to prevent Sweden from taking a battering. From economic growth of 3.3 per cent in 2007, Sweden fell into a gentle recession, with a contraction of 0.6 per cent the next year and then a sharp shrinkage of 5.3 per cent in 2009. This made the Swedish economy one of the hardest-hit in the EU-15, after Finland and Ireland. The EU as a whole contracted by 4.2 per cent in that year. Unemployment in Sweden reached a peak of 8.3 per cent.

So Sweden's economic growth suffered greater damage than the US's, which had zero growth in 2008 and contracted by 2.6 per cent in 2009. But Sweden's unemployment rate held up much better than America's. While the kingdom's rate jumped from 6.2 to 8.3 per cent, the republic's leapt from 5.8 to 9.7 in one year. This divergence is exactly what you'd expect from the two models, with one emphasising equity and the other efficiency. In Sweden, even though the downturn was sharper, it threw many fewer people out of work.

Sweden's experience of the crisis was tough, yet it emerged from the episode in much better shape than most of the countries around it. Growth bounced back to a rapid 5.7 per cent in 2010, against the US rate of 2.6, though the Northern European nation's unemployment was stubbornly stuck at 8.2 per cent. Sweden's government fell into deficit during the crisis, but quickly returned to surplus. Swedes were sufficiently impressed to reward Reinfeldt with a slight increase in his government's share of the vote, which grew by 1 percentage point to 49.2 per cent. But the government lost seats, fell two short of a majority, and resumed power as a minority government with support from the Greens – the first time in almost a century that an elected centre-right government was returned to power.

Disturbingly for many Swedes, the party to enjoy the biggest gains was the far-right Sweden Democrats. They doubled their share of the vote to 5.7 per cent, propelling them into parliament for the first time, with twenty seats in the 349-seat *riksdag*, Sweden's unicameral parliament. The anti-immigrant Sweden Democrats have their distant origin in Swedish prewar fascism. They went from no presence in the *riksdag* to become the sixth-biggest party after the 2010 election, and the only one that is aligned with neither government nor opposition. Their abrupt rise is a reminder to Swedes of the larger stakes involved in creating a successful, prosperous, sustainable model. Where the mainstream fails, extremists are always ready to step in.

The OECD secretary-general, José Ángel Gurría, compared the strength of the post-crisis Swedish economy to that of the Swedish fictional character Pippi Longstocking. This famous creation of Astrid Lindgren was the strongest girl in the world. Gurría described Sweden as "an island of prosperity." The renovation of the Swedish model remained a national priority, nonetheless. As a member of the ruling Moderates, Johnny Munkhammar, wrote: "Challenges such as youth unemployment, inflexible housing markets, waiting lists for health services, and too-high taxes, still plague the country. So reforms that increase economic freedoms should and will continue – the results so far have been more than encouraging."

Sweden is trying to achieve what Australia has already accomplished: balance and competence. Balance between egalitarianism and prosperity, equity and efficiency, fairness and freedom. And competence in maintaining and running good policy. "We are not doing worse than the rest of Europe," said Fulster, "but we compare ourselves to the better performers in the OECD like Australia – Australia has been very successful." The models that Australia looked to for inspiration now look to Australia.

16

HOW TO BLOW IT

In the last months of his life, the man who named Australia "the Lucky Country" was annoyed by one thing more than any other – with the possible exception of his failing health. It was the popular conception that a mining boom was the national salvation. "It's quite appalling to discover people saying today that Australia is still the lucky country because we have all these minerals," Donald Horne said to me in 2005, in his final interview. "There's still a bloody lucky-country mentality!" He saw that Australia had improved mightily since he wrote his 1964 book, but since then the title of the book had also become entrenched as an international byword for Australia, and the more widely it had spread, the more widely it was misunderstood. Horne, of course, meant it ironically. Australia's underground riches, its luck, were its curse. They allowed Australia to prosper without effort.

Horne saw the return of a mining boom as history's whispered temptation to Australia to relapse into national underperformance. It's an invitation to complacency. Japan's consul-general in Sydney, Masahiro Kohara, thinks of Australia as "a man lying on a bed of treasure." The picture evokes a lazy country that doesn't bother to make an effort to improve its situation. If it discovers some sudden need, it can sell a piece of its unearned treasure and go back to sleep. Kohara's metaphor fits neatly with Horne's conception.

In sum, Australia has proved that it can be better than the Lucky Country. It did not have success thrust upon it. It overcame its inauspicious beginnings as a military-run colony stocked with criminal outcasts, a nation founded on racial discrimination in a continent with the world's most fragile natural environment. The settlement that nearly starved in its early years is today a country that is one of the world's ten biggest food exporters.

The new country depended heavily on the concepts and capital of its British settlers for its success. But the increasingly free penal colony ultimately demanded and crafted for itself greater rights than the free citizens of its mother country were enjoying at the very same time. The first country in world history to vote itself into existence was not just a collection of happenstances but the result of deliberate acts of nation-building. "The land called Australia hardly seemed the place that would be remembered for its gifts to representative democracy," wrote John Keane in his history of democracy. Only radicals believed that "the sunburned continent called terra australis could make important contributions to the world," yet nonetheless it did so. The eight-hour day, the secret ballot, the right of women to stand for parliament, the first workers' party to be elected to majority government – in these and the establishment of other rights for the common people, Australia was democracy's champion and history's pioneer. At the time Australia federated in 1901, it was a proudly democratic, egalitarian society with the highest average income per person in the world.

Australia was quite a surprise to natural science. The land of the platypus, the laughing bird and the black swan moved Charles Darwin to remark that "an unbeliever in everything beyond his own reason might exclaim, 'Surely two distinct Creators must have been at work.'" The black swan has since come to be a metaphor for the improbable, the unimaginable. The financial trader and author Nassim Nicholas Taleb wrote a best-selling book on the idea, titled *The Black Swan: The Impact of the Highly Improbable*, without ever having seen one himself. Australia's political arrangements have turned out to be almost as unexpected.

Its early economic success, likewise, was built within a British imperial framework but according to local specifications. The bounty of a pastoral, manufacturing and mining economy was distributed by a carefully constructed system designed to share the benefits around. In crude outline, according to the deal that became known as the Australian Settlement, the empire delivered the country a living through trade preferences, the country delivered industry a living through protectionism, and industry delivered the workers a living through centralised wage-fixing. White Australia kept the troublingly hard-working Asians out, while giving the British a comfortably familiar enclave. Originally designed to create cohesion as a nation-building exercise, the protectionism started to choke competition and enterprise. Mining booms came and went and the country's problems only grew worse. The final mining boom of the protectionist era was the boom of the early 1980s that coincided with Malcolm Fraser's prime ministership. It didn't save Fraser and it was not going to save Australia.

Australia's leaders of both major political parties joined forces for the Australian Unsettling, a 24-year opening of the economy to the world and to market forces. It ended only in 2007. From federation until the advent of the Hawke–Keating government in 1983, Australia had emphasised equity over efficiency. From 1983 to the end of the Howard–Costello era, the balance had shifted to efficiency. The election of Kevin Rudd in 2007 put Australia into a new phase, with priority swinging back to equity.

The national zigzag brought Australia to an especially propitious place. Australians live more than two years longer than the average for people in rich countries, enjoy household incomes one-fifth higher, and work the equivalent of one week per year fewer hours. Income is more equally shared than the average for rich countries, and social mobility is greater.

And when the revitalised model was tested in the great financial and economic conflagration of 2008–09, Australia emerged as the only rich country in the world to have enjoyed twenty years of uninterrupted economic growth. It still continues to enjoy it.

The overall result? In the carefully tallied comparison in the OECD Better Life index, Australia's overall living conditions were the best among the world's thirty-four rich countries in 2011. And, in an even wider sample, the UN's Human Development Index ranked Australia as having the best living conditions of all the countries in the world. In other words, Australia in 2010–11 offered the best conditions for human existence on planet earth, a sweet spot indeed. This does not mean that Australia lacks problems. It does mean that, as the *Wall Street Journal* put it in a report on Australian living conditions in May 2011, "many other nations would love to have Australia's problems."

The *Economist* magazine published this headline in May 2011: "Australia's promise: The next Golden State." An image of a solid gold nugget in the shape of a map of Australia adorned an article that asked its readers to "imagine a country of about 25 million people, democratic, tolerant, welcoming to immigrants, socially harmonious, politically stable and economically successful; good beaches too. It sounds like California 30 years ago, but it is not: it is Australia today. Yet Australia could become a sort of California – and perhaps a still more successful version of the Golden State."

Australia's situation was so outstanding that even this attempt at a flattering comparison didn't quite catch it. Although it's not strictly valid to compare a country to a state, California is routinely described by its local media as being the world's eighth-biggest economy and has a population of 37 million people. At the time the *Economist* published its piece, the average Australian income was $3,700 or 7 per cent higher than that in California, the richest of America's fifty states. And Australia's unemployment rate of 4.9 per cent was less than half California's 11.7 per cent. The Californian governor, Arnold Schwarzenegger, had said in 2009, as the US downturn bit: "Our wallet is empty, our bank is closed and our credit is dried up." The state government made painful cuts to schools, child care and health care, among other things. In an attempt to further reduce its $25 billion deficit, its new governor, Jerry Brown, in 2011 proposed abandoning state responsibility for services including fire and emergency response, court security, and housing for low-level criminals. These would become local government responsibilities. By contrast, the Rudd–Gillard government had doubled federal funding to the Australian states for education and hospitals.

Australia is in the happy but disorienting situation that it is in better shape than the countries to which it has traditionally compared itself, even the countries to which it has looked as models. As discussed, the Australian centre-Right has long looked to the US, and the centre-Left to Sweden. But Australia today, by combining the freedom of America with the fairness of Sweden, has higher income per person and faster growth than both, lower unemployment than either, and better overall living conditions.

"The most interesting aspect of the success of the Australian model is the knowledge that a country can achieve a significant degree of egalitarianism without sacrificing economic freedom," wrote David Alexander, a journalist and former press secretary to Peter Costello. "The fact that it is not *a priori* impossible to achieve a low tax state with a lower level of inequality through policy design is highly significant." The developed countries spent an average of 50.5 per cent of GDP in 2010. Sweden spent more than the average at 53 per cent, making it the fourth bigger spender as a proportion of GDP. The US spent less at 42 per cent, the fifth smallest. Australia spent less again at 36 per cent of GDP, with only South Korea and Switzerland spending smaller shares.

Alexander calls this Australia's "platypus model" of political economy, combining attributes that were thought to be impossible to find in a single creature. The platypus is a super-shy animal, and it was concealed in a far-away land, but when Europeans eventually happened upon it, they were shocked. Till then it was a rule of biology that mammals gave birth to live offspring, while birds and reptiles hatched eggs. Yet here was a warm-blooded furry creature with all the attributes of a mammal, yet it laid eggs. With the bill of a duck, poisoned spurs on its back legs, the tail of a beaver, the feet of an otter and the reproductive system of a lizard, it reduced biologists to incredulity. When the colonists first sent a specimen back to London, some scientists were convinced that it was a hoax. One, a George Shaw, took to a dried platypus pelt with scissors to find evidence of the stitching that, he was sure, must have been used to sew a duck's bill onto a beaver-like animal. But of course it was genuine, and science was forced to rethink. A new order of creature, an egg-laying mammal, the monotreme, had to be added to the classification system. Theory had to make way for reality. "A similarly naive binarism exists in classifying the world's political economies," Alexander wrote. Australia offers a genuine alternative, a low-taxing egalitarianism, "both more successful and more sustainable than other models."

One of the secrets of Australia's balance is that its leaders have not been slaves to ideology. Labor and Liberal prime ministers have employed policy tools borrowed from the ideological toolkit of the other side. Prime ministers drawn from Labor, traditionally the party of workers, have run hard with policies that were highly disruptive to workers. Bob Hawke and Paul Keating ran a pro-market reform agenda because they judged it to be practically necessary to revitalise the Australian economy. Prime ministers drawn from the Liberals, the conservative party that stands for small government, have embraced policies that increase the size of the welfare state. John Howard introduced family tax payments in his first year in office and increased their generosity through his term. Spending on government assistance for families was a hall-mark of his government. When he took power, Australian government spending on family allowances was 1.5 times the average for OECD countries; a decade later it was twice the average. Howard was motivated by a pragmatic political desire to hold the political middle ground. But the effect was to redistribute income and to make household incomes more equitable. This insight will not please ideologues from either side. But it is an explanation for the Australian ability to balance equity and efficiency.

Australia is in the enviable position of being rated not only as the best place to live your life, but also one of the very best places to end it. A charity, the Lien Foundation, commissioned the *Economist* Intelligence Unit to rank countries according to their quality of death. After looking at twenty-four indicators of the quality and availability of end-of-life care, it placed Australia second in 2010, after Britain.

History, however, is strewn with the ruins of once-successful societies and once-celebrated models of political economy. In the last century alone the world alternately admired the German or Rhineland model, the French model, the British model, the American model, the Anglo-American model, the Japanese model, the Swedish model, the Nordic model and even, yes, the Soviet model. There was a phase, in the 1950s, when the USSR was the fastest-growing economy in the world, and its apparent success gave rise to much commentary. It was disturbing to capitalists and exciting to socialists, until it petered out, later collapsed, and finally disappeared from the face of the earth. The Shelley poem "Ozymandias" is always cited whenever the vanity and hubris of a civilisation comes up. A traveller tells of a ruined statue of a once-great ruler with the inscription: "My name is Ozymandias, king of kings: Look on my works, ye mighty, and despair." The broken monument is surrounded only by desert.

History shows that national success can be fragile and fleeting. And smugness or boastfulness will not equip Australia with the attitude it needs to solve its next problems. Yet having achieved the apex of living conditions, Australia's first mistake would be to fail to appreciate what it has and how it was created.

Australians generally have a sense that their lives are good. Asked if they are satisfied with their lives, 75 per cent of Australians said yes, compared to the average in rich countries of 59 per cent, according to the OECD Better Life study. Yet on questions related to economic success, there seems to be a reluctance to accept that it is anything other than happenstance, or luck. This is a curious asymmetry. Australians are ready to blame their governments for any economic problems that might emerge, but unwilling to give them any credit.

When told they live in the world's best-performing rich country, some Australians have a strong automatic reaction. Among the scores who considered this proposition at my request, perhaps three-quarters instantly dismissed it: "No, that can't be right." A few even became agitated when told that their country was doing well. Instead of allowing that Australia could be flourishing, most – professionals and managers as well as students and tradespeople – launched into a list of reasons why it couldn't be so. Or they ran through some reasons why, if it *was* so, the result couldn't be authentic or "real."

The first reason: "It's just the mining boom." The second reason: "It's all just China." These are closely connected. The mining boom's principal driver is Chinese demand. And Australia feels China's economic presence most strongly through mining. So let's take this as a single reason to explain Australia's economic health. It is certainly true that the dramatic increase in the value of mining exports has lifted Australian income. Shareholders in mining companies have enjoyed fatter dividends. Companies that supply the mining industry have also profited. The total effect? The Reserve Bank estimated in 2011 that the mining boom had added about 13 per cent to the national income.

It is a sizeable addition, no question about it, but the mining boom cannot be credited with Australia's overall economic well-being. Australia reformed its economy, enjoyed a record-breaking growth phase and became a standout economic success in between mining booms, not during them, and not because of them. The change happened after the boom of the late 1970s and early '80s and before the boom that began in 2003–04.

By that time, Australia had already enjoyed its longest span of growth since World War Two, thirteen years and counting. Unemployment had already fallen from 10 to 6 per cent. National productivity growth had already doubled its long-term average. The federal government had already balanced the budget and delivered five budget surpluses in six years. It had already paid down net debt from the equivalent of 18 per cent of GDP in 1995–96 to 2.7 per cent, already close to achieving zero debt, which happened in 2006. Australia may well possess a bed of treasure, but it had not been lying on it, or relying on it. "Neither China nor the commodities boom has been central to Australia's economic performance in the first decade of the 21st century," wrote John Edwards in 2006, an economist with HSBC at the time and formerly an adviser to Paul Keating. "They may well matter a great deal in the next five years, but they haven't mattered much in the last five."

Indeed, commodity prices collapsed a couple of years later as the global economic crisis struck. Australia managed the crisis without bank failures or recession, principally because of effective policy. Australian mining exports took off again as China stimulated its economy and the world began a recovery. So neither the mining boom nor China built Australia's successful new economic model, and neither is responsible for its adroit response to the onset of the crisis. China's commodities appetite did help Australia's recovery, but, again, it was not the element that kept the country out of recession.

But even the mining boom's addition to the national income doesn't somehow negate or diminish the Australian achievement. If this were so, it would mean that a country can only be considered successful if it surrenders a characteristic source of national advantage. Do the Chinese have to stop using one of their great national advantages, cheap labour, to be considered economically successful? Do the Saudis have to stop up their oil wells if they want to have their wealth tallied? Do the Belgians have to spoil their chocolates and the New Zealanders plough salt into their soil? Must the Germans keep their cars a secret and the Americans forswear filmmaking and finance? Does Singapore have to relocate to a less convenient location because its competitive advantage is built on its geography as a hub and entrepot?

No one would demand that a nation deliberately surrender a competitive advantage or somehow excise it from its national accounts, if it wants to be taken seriously. To ask Australia to disown its mining sector, to pretend that it's not a legitimate part of the national economy, is nonsensical. Similarly, a surge of profitability in a sector doesn't really mean it has to be discounted in some way, does it? No one considers the German economy less "real" if the profit margin on cars rises, or Singapore less successful if the rates for cargo-handling surge.

Quite the opposite. We shake our heads when we see a country too slow, too poor or too troubled to take advantage of a national opportunity. Thirty years ago it was said of Brazil that it was "a beggar sitting on a bag of gold." In the last decade or so the beggar has stood up and started to take advantage of its gold – not its natural resources, which it has always exported and yet remained poor. What changed? Brazil is prospering because it elected a government that managed to entrench low inflation, responsible government spending and manageable taxes. It created a thriving banking and finance sector, which is able to finance business. All of this, in turn, allowed investment to flow, and output and productivity gains to follow.

In three centuries of imperial rule by Portugal, Brazil was forbidden to set up factories, permitted only to export resources. This kept it at the bottom of the imperial supply chain and prevented Brazilians from posing any challenge to Portuguese manufacturers. Gold and sugar and rubber were its chief exports. It is still a major exporter of resources, and exports even more iron ore than Australia. But some 60 per cent of Brazil's exports are now manufactures, including commercial aircraft. It has moved from chronic current account deficit into surplus. Poverty rates have fallen, education improved. Some important groundwork was laid by conservative governments, but Brazil's flowering into the world's eighth-biggest economy took place under the disciplined stewardship of a former trade union leader, Luiz Inacio Lula da Silva, known universally simply as Lula, in power from 2003 to 2011. Brazil is still a relatively poor country, but it is a lot less poor than it was a decade ago. Like Australia, Brazil has prospered with a resources sector, not because of it. Does anyone consider Brazil's dramatic economic improvement not "real"? Of course not. It's a source of happiness and pride in Brazil and admiration abroad. So why do Australians think that a price surge in mining commodities somehow discounts or disqualifies their country's economic achievements? This tells us more about the Australian mentality than the Australian economy. Australians are famously self-deprecating. It seems we deprecate not only ourselves, but also our country's most important achievements.

John Howard and Kevin Rudd can attest to the reluctance of Australians to give credit for economic performance. The Howard–Costello government presided over the standout phase of prosperity in Australian modern history, eleven and a half years of continuous economic growth and falling unemployment, their entire term in power. Average real wages grew by a fifth. Household wealth doubled. Yet this accomplishment was held in such small regard by the electorate that it dismissed Howard in 2007 and gave power to a leader without any experience of economic management.

Kevin Rudd then took power and presided over the standout national navigation of the worst global economic storm since the Great Depression. Australia suffered no bank failures, no recession and only a mild downturn in employment. House prices continued to rise. Yet even as the economy came booming back, Rudd's popularity with the public fractured and his own party discarded him two and a half years into a three-year term. Voters were quick to blame him for wasting public money on ceiling insulation as part of an economic stimulus plan, yet not prepared to give him credit for the success of the overall plan. The party replaced him with a leader without any experience of economic management except what she had learned at Rudd's elbow. And her party went on to lose its majority four months later, even as the economy continued to strengthen.

Australians customarily tell pollsters that they put great importance on economic wellbeing. It is the orthodoxy that economic credibility is the pre-eminent credential for a political party seeking to win an election. But these events suggest that they will not reward the leaders who deliver it. And this is borne out in the academic research on Australian voting. Ian McAllister of the Australian National University has compiled a careful study of survey data in his book *The Australian Voter: Fifty Years of Change*. He came to four main findings on so-called economic voting. First, the Australian voter gives greater weight to the state of the national economy than to his own economic circumstances. Second, the electorate gives greater weight to the outlook for the economy rather than the past or present. Third, "in general, relatively few voters take an optimistic view of the economy in a year's time, regardless of the objective economic situation at the time that the question was asked." And fourth, Australians are increasingly likely to think that their country's economic performance is beyond the control of the government in any case. Or, as McAllister explained: "The proportion saying that the government would make 'no difference' to the economy in the year ahead has consistently increased from 51 per cent in 1990 to 61 per cent in 2010."

In other words, for Australian voters it's about the future, the future is always bleak, and the government won't make a difference anyway. This is unrealistic and reckless. It's unrealistic because for a generation now, the continuous expectation of gloom has been vindicated only once, with the mild downturn Australia experienced in the global economic crisis. It has been a false expectation. And it's unrealistic because the government is the critical element in good policy, and good policy is the critical element in economic outcomes. It's reckless because it is an invitation to politicians to discard good policy. If the electorate will not reward good performance, why bother performing? This low expectation creates a perverse incentive for a politician. It's much easier to deal in cheap populism than good policy, to run fear campaigns than reform agendas, to demonise the rival party than to propose better alternatives. This, of course, is exactly the problem Australia has in 2011. Yet active and prudent economic management is urgently required. Not because the country lacks a boom but because it has one.

The mining boom that resumed in 2009 and was still underway in 2011 was a big one. In 2003 Australia was shipping half a million tonnes of iron ore each day, a volume so large it's difficult to conceive of. Yet eight years later it was shipping more than a million tonnes a day. Even so, this sum is not sufficient to guarantee Australia's economic success. Why not? For one thing, it's too small. No industry that employs just 1.5 per cent of the workforce could ever be responsible for national success. A sector that accounts for less than a tenth of the national income cannot be a substitute for the other nine-tenths. In the last century mining has never generated more than 11 per cent of national income, which happened in 1911. For another thing, it is a cyclical phenomenon. Australia in 2011 was living through its fifth commodities boom in two centuries. The other four all ended. None lasted more than about fifteen years. Basing a national economy on the expectation of a mining boom would be like planning a surfing trip on the expectation of a tsunami. It's always possible, just very unpredictable. And you wouldn't want to sit around waiting for one to arrive.

One of the big figures in the mining industry of the twentieth century, Sir Arvi Parbo, who was chairman of three of the major resources firms, Western Mining, BHP and Alcoa, reflected in 2011 on his sixty years in the sector: "During my time in the industry the supply and demand of minerals were in a steady state for only relatively short periods. It has been said that history is just one damned thing after another, and this is certainly true of the period I am reflecting on in the minerals industry. Most of the time – the 'normal' environment, if you like – it was either a boom or a bust." The big mining expansions come in a boom and usually end in a bust.

So while the mining boom cannot be the basis for a successful economy, it does have the potential to be the basis for economic disaster. It is a vast, convulsive force that brings big opportunities and big profits but also big risks. The first risk is that the upsurge in mining lifts the economy with it, then smashes it when it falls.

The second risk is that to accommodate the growth of mining, the rest of the economy will be punished. In mid-2011, this was well underway. This is a familiar and well-established phenomenon that goes by several names: the Dutch disease, the resources curse or the Gregory thesis (after an Australian economist, Bob Gregory). Huge world demand for a booming commodity pushes up not just the price of the commodity, but also the currency of the supplier country. The Australian dollar's present strength is exactly what experience and theory predict. The dollar's average value has been at around 77 US cents in the twenty-eight years since its value began to be set by the market. In July 2011 it was trading at around 110 US cents.

This is a happy event for Australians looking to travel abroad, but a terrible trauma for exporters of anything other than minerals. The strong Australian dollar automatically raises the price of the products exporters are trying to sell abroad, attacking their competitiveness. This penalises not only manufacturers but also universities selling education abroad, which was Australia's third-biggest export commodity after coal and iron ore. Education services generated over $18 billion in 2009–10. And the high dollar imposes a big burden on firms selling Australia as a tourist destination, the fifth-biggest export item, an industry which earned $12 billion. A burgeoning, rich mining sector also makes first claim on workers and capital, forcing the rest of the economy to ration these resources.

This tension pulling at Australia was captured in the family of a Perth entrepreneur, Steve de Mol. "I have a son earning $180,000 a year while two of my daughters – an occupational therapist and a beautician – earn $40,000 and $55,000," he told the *Financial Review*. "There's the resource-related income, or nothing. If you're hooked into resources, I think you're going to have a pretty good two or three years ahead of you. If you're not, you're going to be a victim of it." De Mol sold safety gear and electrical switch rooms to mining firms.

The Dutch disease was, in 2011, the Australian disease. Manufacturers were already planning to cut their capital investment by 28 per cent from the levels of the previous year, according to a survey of 530 chief executives by the Australian Industry Group. And companies in the services sector were planning to cut their investment by 2 per cent. Services account for four-fifths of the Australian economy and 86 per cent of all jobs. Mining companies, in stark contrast, planned to increase their investment by 55 per cent.

The Treasury cast ahead to see what this might mean over the next nine years. While its economic modelling found that the rise of Asia would continue to lift Australia overall, creating 1.5 million jobs during the rest of the decade, it concluded that the Asian boom would draw on different sectors unequally and force an accelerated rearrangement of Australia's industrial structure. So while the value of output in mining was expected to surge by 65 per cent, construction by 48 per cent and services by 35 per cent, manufacturing output was projected to grow by 6 per cent. And while the number of jobs in the other sectors was expected to grow, employment in manufacturing was projected to shrink by 17 per cent, wiping out 170,000 jobs by 2020. This would be an acceleration of the long, slow decline of manufacturing employment. It would mean that the sector would lose almost twice as many jobs in the nine years ahead as the 90,000 it had shed in the previous decade. The Treasury's modelling did not include the effects of any new carbon pricing. In other words, this restructuring was underway regardless. It would have economic consequences far beyond any projected effects of a carbon tax. And it would be the dominant disruptive force in Australia for years to come.

Donald Horne's apprehension of an Australian mining-induced complacency would be vindicated if the country simply sat and watched all this happen. The mining boom cannot be stopped and "it would not be sensible to try to stop it," as Reserve Bank governor Glenn Stevens has said. But "the lessons of history," Stevens added, "that booms don't go on indefinitely, are also too great to ignore." The mining boom, and its consequences, must be managed. The country needs to extract the maximum advantage from the surge, minimise the harm and prepare for its ending.

The first lesson of Australia's first two centuries is not to yield to the status quo as unalterable, problems unsolvable, improvements impossible. A successful, democratic, stable, fair and prosperous country can be built. The second lesson is that a country, once built, can be changed. Difficult and unpopular reform can be accomplished. It helps if there is bipartisan convergence, as there was in ending White Australia, deregulating finance or ending the era of protectionism. But it's not a prerequisite. With purposeful and skilful leadership, even tough reforms in the national interest can be argued, fought, won. The Rudd government set out to attempt to manage the mining boom in 2010, only for Kevin Rudd to discover that his government had lost its capacity for important reform in the national interest.

It was John Howard's retreat on labour market liberalisation that marked the end of the great 23-year shift towards market forces in Australia. It was Kevin Rudd who began the new era, returning the emphasis to equity over efficiency. Yet while the emphasis of values zigged and zagged, Rudd kept the policy agenda on the same plane at which Howard and Costello, Hawke and Keating had operated:

responsible national-interest policy with an ambitious agenda of reform. Rudd's rubric for it was the "reforming centre."

It was Tony Abbott and Julia Gillard whose combined efforts brought the era of responsible policy-based leadership and ambitious reform to a shuddering halt. Although they occupied opposite sides of the House of Representatives, their separate political calculations brought them together as the political father and mother of Australia's new populism, an ugly, squalling brat that soon drove the nation to distraction. But they couldn't have done it without Kevin Rudd's acquiescence. If the new populism was the political offspring of Abbott and Gillard, it was Rudd who opened the maternity ward and unwittingly midwifed its arrival.

The advent of Tony Abbott as opposition leader brought an abrupt end to the Liberal Party's mindset of rationality and responsibility. It was the party's mode through the years of the Howard–Costello government. Indeed, John Howard's form even in opposition had been as a responsible political leader. From opposition, Howard had been prepared to forgo easy political advantage by supporting the government on important national reforms in the national interest. Of course, he was skilled in the arts of trickery, inconsistency, distraction and media management. He didn't mind the occasional populist foray, on asylum seekers, for instance. But on big matters of national prosperity he was generally guided by a concern for the national interest. Howard's first two successors as Liberal leader continued in this mindset. Brendan Nelson and Malcolm Turnbull remained committed, for instance, to the Howard government's pledge to implement an emissions trading scheme, even though it was now the initiative of the Rudd Labor government.

Although it is usually presented as a measure to curb carbon emissions and limit potentially catastrophic global warming, carbon pricing is essentially a "no-regrets" measure to drive greater energy efficiency in an economy. In other words, whether global warming turns out to be a dire civilisational threat or just a misreading of temperature trends, the policy will have had the main effect of making the economy more efficient in its use of carbon fuels. This cuts costs and improves competitiveness in a world with rising energy prices. So a country can embrace it with no regrets whether the climate fear is real or imagined. And the Treasury modelling of the Rudd proposal showed that it would cut economic output by a negligible 0.1 per cent a year and add a modest one-off 1.2 per cent to consumer prices.

Tony Abbott had also supported the emissions trading scheme. But when he saw the opportunity to gain his party's leadership by opposing the reform, he took it and began campaigning aggressively against the scheme. Abbott's populism is best illustrated by his own words. As Liberal leader, he refused to accept the advice of climate scientists on the climate, and he refused to accept the word of economists on economics. On the human contribution to global warming, he said, "I don't think we can say that the science is settled here." And on the economics, he said: "It may well be … that most Australian economists think that a carbon price or emissions trading scheme is the way to go. Maybe that's a comment on the quality of our economists rather than on the merits of the argument."

A member of the public at a community forum challenged Abbott's rejection of climate scientists and economists and asked, "Who would you listen to out of the experts?" Abbott replied: "The public. In a democracy in the end the people are sovereign." Abbott even went so far as to call for a "people's revolt" against the government's plan to impose a cost on the right to emit carbon, a deliberate effort to mimic the US Tea Party movement, the epitome of modern populism.

The rejection of expertise and expert knowledge mark a politician who is sceptical of the foundation of the Enlightenment, the pursuit of scientific knowledge over prejudice and ignorance. It was not only Abbott's angry opposition that showed him breaking with the Liberals' style of responsible leadership. It was also the glaring blankness of his policy whiteboard of alternative offerings.

Abbott's easy change of mind in pursuit of power, his exuberant embrace of populism, mark him as an opportunist. The MP Tony Windsor was one of a handful of independents who held the balance of power after the 2010 election. He was courted by both major parties as they struggled to piece together enough votes to command a majority in the House of Representatives and form government. He later recounted what Abbott had told him: "Abbott said, 'Listen, mate, I'll do anything to get this job, I'll do anything' ... And he knows this as well as I do, he left messages on the phone and sent them privately that he would do anything, anything on any issue, anything you want, to become prime minister of this country."

But while the opposition leader is a key influence, he cannot single-handedly change the national political and policy agenda. He needs some kind of succour from the government. Abbott shattered the bipartisan commitment to an emissions trading scheme, but the government could have pressed on and fought for its policy, much as Howard and Costello had fought for their tax reforms in the teeth of Labor scaremongering. But the Rudd government lost its nerve. Kevin Rudd later said that Julia Gillard, his deputy, and Wayne Swan, the treasurer, had argued for the surrender on the emissions trading scheme.

Even so, Rudd was leader. He had the option to forge ahead. But his courage failed him. He postponed the scheme. His popularity ruptured. Gillard challenged him. Rudd capitulated. And Gillard led Labor into a wholesale retreat into populism. She immediately identified three priorities that she wanted to address, political problems for the government that she wanted to fix. Each represented a retreat from policy ambition. She sought to neutralise the emissions trading scheme by promising a "citizens' assembly." She announced that she would deal with the rising number of asylum seekers arriving by boat by arranging a regional processing centre in East Timor. And she sought a quick solution to a controversy over a new mining tax by a capitulation to the demands of the three biggest mining companies.

The mining tax was the Rudd government's attempt to manage the mining boom. The basic concept was straightforward. It was to treat onshore mining the same way that Australia's offshore oil and gas sector had been treated for twenty years. The existing system of state royalties on mining would be scrapped and replaced with a single national tax. In fact, this was what the mining industry itself had requested.

In addition to the normal corporate tax, miners would pay a tax on their super profits. A super profit, which economists call a rent, is simple: "A soccer star may be paid $50,000 a week to play for his team when he would be willing to turn out for only $10,000, so his economic rent is $40,000 a week" is the example favoured by the *Economist* magazine. So taxing the $40,000 super profit, or rent, shouldn't affect the soccer player's willingness to take the field. Super profits can occur in any industry under certain conditions – if there is a monopoly or a cartel, for example. Super profits are fairly common in the resources sector. Resources are essential yet non-renewable – dig them up once and they're gone forever. "A country's economic welfare therefore depends on capturing those rents for its citizens," the OECD pointed out in supporting tax-based policies. In the absence of any extra mining tax, about half of the total profits of the Australian mining boom go to investors, banks and shareholders overseas, the Reserve Bank estimated. Rudd's proposed tax on super profits was expected to raise $9 billion a year once fully implemented. The same tax regime had applied to offshore oil and gas for decades, without controversy. For this reason, most Australians had no idea that it even existed. The oil flows, the firms profit, the government collects.

But the Rudd government made several big mistakes. Biggest was that it announced the plan the week after the government had capitulated on the emissions trading scheme. The government was under heavy criticism for weakness, so now it rushed to look strong. Next was that there was no public prelude, no effort to make a case for a new tax system for mining. So just after breaking a core promise, with public trust in some shock, Rudd announced an unheralded new initiative. Third was that the government had not consulted the mining industry on the design of the tax. All three of these problems of political management meant that the tax was launched as if Rudd had been trying to minimise public support for it and guarantee maximum industry resistance. That was what he got. The mining industry fought the plan with an effective $22 million advertising campaign.

The fourth problem was the design of the scheme. It would have redistributed the mining revenue to a number of causes which were worthy in themselves – a lower rate of corporate tax, more investment in major infrastructure programs, tax breaks for small business, an increase in the superannuation guarantee levy from 9 to 12 per cent. But this money would have been spent in an economy that was already going to be in danger of overheating because of the mining boom. As a leading economist, Warwick McKibbin, put it: "If anything, the government proposal increases aggregate demand because you are taking money that would otherwise go to foreign owners and you're reallocating it to put it inside the Australian economy." Rudd's plan would have been a red rag to the Reserve Bank bull, goading it to increase interest rates to damp down the inflationary effects, said McKibbin, who was a Reserve Bank board member at the time. There was a way around this problem. If the government put the proceeds of the mining tax into a sovereign wealth fund, as Norway does, held offshore in foreign currencies, it would not add to overheating. And the money would be saved against the day the boom runs out.

So the Rudd government's effort to manage the mining boom was rushed, botched, ill timed and badly designed. Together with the emissions trading scheme debacle, plotting within his own party and the miners' advertising campaign, Rudd had precipitated a first-rate mess. Rudd, together with the architects of these misjudgments, Julia Gillard and Wayne Swan, was his own worst enemy. The Abbott opposition campaigned against the tax and reaped political advantage from the government's distress.

The mishandling gave the miners a bonanza return on their $22 million ad campaign. They could take some of the credit for destroying a prime minister. And they brought a new prime minister to her knees searching for a compromise to shut down the public noise. The government's original mining tax would have collected $12 billion in two years. The version that Gillard negotiated projected a tax take of $7.4 billion in two years. The miners saved $4.6 billion for an outlay of just $22 million, a return on investment of 20,800 per cent. This made political activism one of the few activities in Australia more profitable than mining. The Australian Council of Trade Unions' public campaign against Howard's WorkChoices had been powerful and effective in shaping public opinion and obliging Howard to alter his policy. Now, with the success of the miners' campaign, Australia appeared to have declared open season for special interests to wage war on elected governments.

Both major parties were suffering from the trauma of failing in attempting a major reform. The Liberals were bruised and bewildered by the defeat of WorkChoices and the most effective Liberal politician of his generation, John Howard. Now Labor was shaken by the collapse of its emissions trading scheme and the premature loss of the leader who had been the most popular prime minister in four decades, Kevin Rudd.

Abbott and Gillard looked at these events and made a self-interested, rational calculation. Two leaders, Howard and Rudd, had delivered sound economic outcomes as prime minister and campaigned on ambitious reforms. Both had been dispatched. Abbott and Gillard responded to the incentives that they saw in front of them. They gave priority to populism and relegated ambitious reform. They pandered to the ignorance and prejudices of the least politically committed people in the country, the people who are paid to sit in "focus groups." If Abbott's rejection of knowledge was a signature moment of populism, Gillard's was her equivocation over one of the central responsibilities of a prime minister. On her first overseas visit as national leader, Gillard was asked in an interview by Kerry O'Brien on the *7.30 Report* whether she had "found her comfort zone yet?" The prime minister replied: "Kerry, I'm just going to be really upfront about this: foreign policy is not my passion … So, yes, if I had a choice I'd probably more be in a school watching kids learn to read in Australia than here in Brussels at international meetings." The politician who had lunged for the prime ministership and unseated her leader was now announcing that she was reluctant to embrace the full responsibilities of a national leader to represent the country in the counsels of the world. Whether she was playing for the common touch or pre-empting critics of her overseas travel bill, she was not demonstrating leadership but populism.

Just as Abbott had been prepared to change his position on climate change in order to take power as Liberal leader, Gillard was prepared to change hers in order to win an election. And she proved willing to change it back again as a condition of forming minority government with the Greens and independents. From Tony Windsor's testimony, Abbott might have been prepared to cut a similar deal in pursuit of power. Abbott had prepared to run at the 2010 election as the anti–Kevin Rudd. But he now found that Julia Gillard had got there first. The two leaders campaigned not as alternative prime ministers but as a pair of opposition leaders. The country voted accordingly.

Both prime minister and opposition leader had demonstrated that they were prepared to change their beliefs on major policy areas if it would help them procure power. With leaders exposed as opportunists, political debates quickly end up in sterile exchanges, like this emblematic one on Sky News between Gillard's trade minister, Craig Emerson, and a one-time candidate for Liberal preselection who now edits the *Spectator Australia* magazine, Tom Switzer, with a postscript from a former Rudd press secretary, Lachlan Harris. It began with Emerson accusing Abbott of being a fraud:

> SWITZER: What evidence do you have that he's a fraud?
>
> EMERSON: I'll tell you. He has supported in the last two years a carbon tax. He has supported an emissions trading scheme. He has said the science of climate change is absolute crap and now he's supporting a centrally planned Direct Action Plan.
>
> SWITZER: But he took to the election an opposition to a carbon tax and an emissions trading scheme and he stuck by that commitment whereas your prime minister has done a complete and utter back-flip. Who's the fraud?

A despairing Harris rebuked: "I think there's still one voter listening somewhere."

*

The secretary of the federal Treasury, Ken Henry, asked Ross Garnaut to give an address to his entire department in 2010. Hundreds of professional staff of the elite policy-making agency turned out to hear Garnaut, one of the pre-eminent Australian economists. He and Henry knew each other well. Both had been involved in the renovation of the Australian economy under Hawke, Henry in the Treasury and Garnaut as Hawke's economic adviser. Garnaut started unconventionally: "Hands up all those who think Australia has been one of the best-performing economies in the OECD in the last ten years." Ken Henry, sitting in the front row of the Treasury lecture theatre, shot his hand up. It was followed by most of the hands in the room. But a moment later Henry pulled his hand down again. Many others followed suit. After smilingly asking what had happened to the independent thinking for which Treasury officers were supposed to be famous, Garnaut asked Henry why he had changed his mind. "I suppose I was thinking about productivity," replied the Treasury secretary. His implied point was that Australia's productivity performance was the glaring failure of recent years.

Garnaut next ordered: "Hands up if you think Australia will be one of the best-performing economies in the OECD in the next ten years." About a third of the audience raised their hands. Garnaut then recited a famous line from Krugman: "Productivity isn't everything, but in the long run it's almost everything." He asked for a show of hands by all those who agreed with Krugman. Again, about a third of the audience raised their hands. Garnaut: "I hope that's a different third of you who just put your hands up." Garnaut's point was that Australia's productivity performance was so poor that it was dooming the country to underperformance for the next ten years.

Henry and Garnaut shared the same essential concern. Productivity is not about making a country work harder, but about making it work smarter. If it were a military concept, it'd be called a force multiplier. It allows bigger returns from the same quantities of capital and labour. Australian productivity's long-run growth rate of 1.3 per cent almost doubled to 2.2 per cent in the 1990s, the result of the reform era, then tapered off. Australia drew at least one-third of its total income growth over the last couple of decades from gains in productivity growth. From 2003, productivity had been negative, which is unusual and alarming. The Productivity Commission's chairman, Gary Banks, has suggested a list of areas to the government which he called "the sweet spot for policy effort." Among them was a tough review of industry assistance. Another was a new effort to increase competitiveness in protected parts of the economy, like taxis, newsagencies, pharmacies and coastal shipping. Another was extracting better value from existing public infrastructure, including water, transport and energy. And deregulation was another. None of these is new. Productivity gains await political will. Banks said these productivity reforms could save Australia $17 billion a year. Governments need to be creative in finding ways to allow employers and workers to improve productivity without damaging workers' pay and conditions.

Australia has many problems. The mining boom is a source of wealth and an advantage, but it is also Australia's biggest looming economic problem. The division of responsibility between federal and state governments makes some problem-solving very complex. For instance, state governments have failed to nourish their growing cities. The bigger the city, the worse the problems of congestion and declining service quality. The states failed to stay abreast of population growth. They failed to invest in the growth of rail and roads, water supply and hospitals. They failed to create an adequate supply of land for new housing.

State failures were then exploited by federal populism. Instead of working out how to improve the cities to accommodate the people, a newly populist Abbott opposition withdrew six decades of Liberal support for a Big Australia immigration policy, and a newly populist Gillard government panicked and capitulated. For the first time since 1947, Australia's bipartisan agreement favouring a big immigration intake collapsed. It happened in just a few short months. No political leader put up a fight. This was despite the fact that immigration has accounted for about four out of every ten dollars in growth in Australian national income in the last generation.

And despite the fact that immigration is one of the solutions to the looming problem of an aging society increasingly unable to afford its own health care and pensions. And despite three-quarters of Australians holding the view in 2006 that immigration had been good for Australia. Rather than enlarging the country to support its ambitions, Australia shrank itself to match its failures.

Australia continues to chew through its stock of environmental assets. Aboriginal Australia is a parallel universe, suffering Third World conditions. Australia has far too much poverty for a country that has enjoyed a twenty-year boom. Mental illness, burgeoning obesity and binge drinking need intelligent attention. The solution to all of these problems is good policy and good political management. Who supplies these essential commodities? Political leaders. Australia had a long run of skilled political leaders who were able to win and hold power and use the opportunity to make important reforms in the national interest.

The two most successful of those believe that this is still possible. In 2010, Bob Hawke said: "There is no reason to assume economic reform can't go on. The overriding lesson is the importance of consultation." He recalled his own ascension, how he convened a national summit, how he instructed the Treasury to give all the delegates the same economic briefing that it gave the prime minister. "Once they knew the facts, they were prepared to give us the authority to do what needed to be done. The basis for our reforms were public knowledge and public understanding. From that broad canvas of public support we went to consultation with particular sectors – the steel industry, for example. That concept hasn't changed. It would be criminal to adopt the attitude of saying it's too hard. You have to bring people generally, and their representatives, along with you; you have to win their understanding. And I don't need to be theoretical about it."

And John Howard: "I hope all aspiring and current prime ministers understand that economic reform requires involving people in a consultative process. All successful reforms have that as a component. Sometimes your opponents will give you political indemnity for your reforms – that's what we did for the Hawke–Keating reforms to tariffs and financial deregulation. We supported them. When we were in government, we received no such indemnity from our opponents. But you can still achieve economic reform if you're patient and you argue your case over a period of time. Rudd never really explained what the ETS was, and the mining tax came out of nowhere." Australia's most successful reformist prime ministers, who were also two of the three longest serving, agree that reform can be achieved, so long as the government works to carry the country with it. At the time of writing, Gillard had signally failed to bring the country with her on introducing a carbon tax, even though it seemed likely to be legislated. And Abbott was not showing interest in proposing major reform – only in installing himself in power. Leaders change, and perhaps one, or both, can develop the agenda and the skills to lead the country in the national interest. Based on the evidence available in mid-2011, however, neither seems to be the leader to take Australia into its next golden era of national improvement.

Australians created the sweet spot for themselves. The country needs to know that, circa 2010–11, it offers the best living conditions available on the planet. Not because it started out that way, and not because of a mining boom, but through building, through reform and through intelligent, public-spirited leadership. And, yes, through a little luck. But, as Donald Horne warned, relying on luck is an invitation to complacency. And complacency is a dreadful problem-solver. As an anonymous wit once said: "Success is all a matter of luck. Ask any failure."

A British marketing consultant, Simon Anholt, has said that Australia is viewed as the "dumb blonde" of the world. Based on an annual international survey of some 40,000 people in twenty countries, he compiles an index that ranks "nation brands." The survey's overall finding for 2010 was that Australia was among the world's ten most admired countries. It found Australia to be one of a handful of countries to be seen as truly global, and that it passed the "t-shirt test" – if you put the slogan "I love Australia" on the front of a t-shirt, it adds value to the shirt. "People know just a few things about Australia – and it's an enviable reputation to have – but it is just not very broad," said Anholt. Australia is considered to be the world's most physically beautiful country and the most welcoming. "What you have is an image of a country that is considered to be very decorative, but not very useful," Anholt said. If he's to be believed, Australia is the Paris Hilton of nation-states: good-looking, frivolous, enjoying a continuous party financed by unearned wealth. If the country lets its current hard-won success slide, then its reputation will have been deserved. The future that the *Economist* magazine saw for Australia as "the next Golden State" will have proved as elusive as the fabulous treasure of the legendary Ophir. If Australia is to have a golden future, it will not be gilded with the sort of gold that is discovered by digging deeper holes in the ground. The necessary gold is not to be found in the country's pits but in its wits.

17

WHY THE WORLD NEEDS
A NEW MODEL

The US victory over the Soviet Union led to celebration that democracy had defeated dictatorship. It was the End of History. Human affairs had reached their evolutionary endpoint, a Utopian flourishing of free peoples in a free market. The celebration now seems to have been premature. Just two decades later, the forces of oppression have a new champion, and it is a commanding one. It is, of course, China, the world's most successful continuing dictatorship. Or, as it's officially known, the People's Republic of China, named with the same perversity of socialist semantics that George Orwell satirised in 1948. What Orwell thought absurd, however, the Chinese communist party thought splendid. It unsmilingly embraced "doublethink" the following year when it took control of the country and named it the People's Republic when it is, in fact, the Party's.

It is the people's republic only insofar as "freedom is slavery," in the words of the slogan employed by the rulers of Oceania, Orwell's fictitious dystopia portrayed in *Nineteen Eighty-Four*. The regime of Orwell's imagining is known only as the Party. That is exactly the common shorthand that the Chinese people use for their rulers, and it is also the name of a 2010 book by the Australian journalist and China correspondent Richard McGregor: "In modern China, the system runs on seduction rather than repression," he writes. "It aims to co-opt, not coerce the population. But even so, terror remains essential to the system's survival and is deployed without embarrassment when required. An official once told me, 'People need to fear the government in China, otherwise the country will fall apart.'"

The republic does not belong to the people but to the Party. The Party fears the people. In 2010, China spent more money on internal security than it spent on national defence. According to the Chinese finance ministry's figures, the government spent 533.5 billion yuan or about $US81 billion on defending the national borders while outlaying 548.6 billion yuan or $US83.5 billion on internal security. Protecting the regime is evidently judged more important than protecting the country. This 3 per cent gap was budgeted to widen in 2011. So where does the Party see the real enemy?

The Party does not trust the people with information and imprisons people for telling the truth. Zhao Lianhai, for example. When his infant son fell ill in 2008, it turned out he was just one of some 300,000 Chinese babies poisoned by contaminated milk. Six babies died of kidney failure. About 880 were hospitalised. The milk was produced from powder made by a state-owned firm, Sanlu. It emerged that the company had put the chemical melamine, an ingredient in hardened plastics such as Formica, into the milk as a cheap way to bulk it up. It was, according to the World Health Organization, "a large-scale intentional activity to deceive consumers for simple, basic, short-term profits." The adulteration of the milk powder was reported to local authorities as early as 2005, but was ignored. The scandal eventually became public when a major shareholder in the company, New Zealand's Fonterra, was notified. It alerted the NZ government, which, in turn, informed Beijing. Reuters broke the story. The Chinese government sought to downplay the situation and controlled Chinese media reporting of the problem. At the time, the Chinese authorities were anxious to create a happy image of China for the forthcoming Beijing Olympics.

Zhao Lianhai, a former food safety worker, was so angered that he decided to create a central point where families could report and rally. He started a website called "Home for the Kidney Stone Babies." The site published a document from the Henan province health department instructing health workers to under-report the number of kidney stone cases. The Chinese authorities blocked Zhao's website, broke up a press conference, and harassed him and his family. For demanding compensation from the government for the child victims, and for refusing to be silent, in 2010 he was jailed for two and a half years by the Chinese courts. Like all official institutions, China's courts are controlled by the Party. The charge against Zhao? For campaigning for the rights of the poisoned infants, he was jailed for "disturbing the social order." In a free country, Zhao would have been celebrated as a father campaigning for the rights of children against an unscrupulous company and a callous state. In China, he was deemed a dissident and a criminal.

There are many similar cases in China where the rights of citizens are repressed in the interests of profit, power or even, as a possible contributing factor in this case, the propaganda priority of the national image, as defined by the Party.

One ancient right of the Chinese citizen was the right to petition the emperor. Even the humblest of his subjects was allowed to approach the royal court to ask for the aid or favour of the ruler. That right continues to this day. If a petitioner is not satisfied with the response of his provincial government, they have the right, by custom and by law, to travel to the capital and make their case to the central authorities. But the Party has become increasingly impatient with the concerns of its citizens. Beijing has made the control of petitioning a performance indicator for local leaders.

In other words, the provinces are rewarded for suppressing the peaceful and legitimate efforts of their people to seek redress for their grievances from the central government. It has become such an industry that local governments pay private security firms to intercept and deter their people from approaching the capital. One such firm, Beijing's Anyuanding Company, was revealed to be detaining petitioners and holding them in secret, illegal prisons, so-called black jails. The Party is a harsh ruler indeed. Even this ancient right of peaceful redress is now effectively denied.

And the Party certainly does not trust the people with any share in any sort of political power. That is why the security apparatus violently overreacted to even the phantom pro-democracy protests inspired by the Arab Spring in 2011. Some of the responses were comically heavy-handed. When a protest was proposed anonymously on the internet for a particular Beijing street, roadworks sprang up overnight in that exact location, a blue-fenced exclusion zone blocking the street. At other supposed protest sites, hundreds of plainclothes police, police dressed as street cleaners and police with dogs inundated the areas. They were essentially protests without protesters. Apart from the police, almost the only people to turn up were reporters. In the absence of protesters, the police set upon the reporters, beating them and loosing dogs on them. Because the victims included some American reporters, this action drew a protest from the US ambassador, Jon Huntsman, a 2012 Republican presidential candidate. Whether this is the conduct of a paranoid regime or just one with well-founded fears for its own survival, it is not only dissidents who challenge its legitimacy and not only foreign ambassadors who question its legality.

Like the name of the country itself, the regime always presents the forms of the Chinese state as being in the name of the people. It is the "people" in whose name the state exists and whose "democratic dictatorship" is supposed to be sovereign, according to Article 1 of the Chinese constitution. But the former premier, and general secretary of the Party from 1987 to 1989, Zhao Ziyang, wrote: "The democratic systems of our socialist nations are all just superficial; they are not systems in which the people are in charge, but rather are ruled by a few or even a single person." Zhao noted that in the course of history, all the alternatives to parliamentary democracy had failed. He added, in a clear reference to socialism and communism: "For several decades during the 20th century, the so-called 'new democratic system,' the proletarian dictatorship, competed with the Western parliamentary system. But in the vast majority of these nations, it has since receded from the historical stage. In fact, it is the Western parliamentary system that has demonstrated the most vitality. This system is currently the best one available."

Zhao laid out the reasons China needed to democratise: "If a country wishes to modernise, not only should it implement a market economy, it must also adopt a parliamentary democracy as its political system. Otherwise, this nation will not be able to have a market economy that is healthy and modern, nor can it become a modern society with a rule of law. Instead it will run into the situations that have occurred in so many developing countries, including China: commercialisation of power, rampant corruption, a society polarised between rich and poor."

Zhao wrote these words while he was being held under house arrest, the condition in which he spent the last sixteen years of his life. As a proponent of political liberalisation, he refused to agree to send the army to shoot the students in Tiananmen Square in 1989. China's paramount leader, Deng Xiaoping, pushed him aside to allow the massacre to proceed. Deng did not occupy any formal position of political power over him at the time and could not win the support of a majority of the body that notionally runs

China, the Standing Committee of the Politburo. Deng could not even win the acquiescence of the general in charge of the Beijing garrison. So he sidelined them all and asserted his personal power. He found another general, in charge of a provincial force, and ordered him to attack the students. Zhao was purged and put under house arrest for the rest of his life, where he recorded his thoughts, published as a posthumous memoir in 2010. It is not, needless to say, available in China. Tiananmen Square was an inflection point in China's modern history. The hardline oppressors won the argument and consolidated power. Deng was the great economic liberaliser of China. It was he who introduced the pro-market reform program that began in 1978. And Deng was also the force behind the decision to maintain political oppression of the Chinese at the critical moment. Today's China still operates on the Deng model. Deng died in 1997.

The idea of citizens' political rights remains alive, despite the success of the oppressors in holding the line against reform. And it remains alive at the very top of the Chinese system. The premier of China, Wen Jiabao, issued a number of calls for greater political freedom for the Chinese people in 2010 and 2011. Taking up the themes of Zhao, Wen said in a speech in London in June 2011, for example, "Without freedom, there is no real democracy. Without guarantee of economic and political rights, there is no real freedom. To be frank, corruption, unfair income distribution and other ills that harm the people's interests still exist in China. The best way to resolve these problems is to firmly advance the political structural reform and socialist democracy under the rule of law." But if he is the premier, why does Wen not act on this thought? The reason is that Wen has no real factional base in the Party. Despite his formal position in what is notionally the second most powerful post in the land, he is relatively powerless against the dominance of the conservatives inside the ruling party. With his retirement scheduled for 2012, he evidently feels the need to make his case publicly, and repeatedly, before leaving office.

Wen's public remarks are the clearest evidence, but there are other signs, less obvious, that the Party is suffering a crisis of conviction in its dogma. The central mechanism for maintaining control of the state, the Party office responsible for personnel, is the Central Organisation Department. Its own confidential documents, cited by McGregor in *The Party*, report that party members are "losing belief." An internal 2006 report went on: "Some individual party members and even cadres in leadership positions no longer have a clear head and doubt the inevitability of the ultimate triumph of socialism and communism." A former head of the organisation department has drawn a distinction between the postwar generation of officials and the current crop. The younger officials "tend to think about themselves and are mainly after power, salary, status, housing and medical care," said Zhang Quanjing.

Yet despite the deep awareness of its greatest failure, despite the obvious unease at its own lack of legitimacy, the Chinese Communist Party has put the Chinese system forward as a model for the world to emulate. The official mouthpiece of the Party, the *People's Daily*, published an editorial in June 2009, which it translated in its English-language edition:

> The tremendous achievements made by China's reform and opening-up over the past 30 years have amazed the entire world. From Vietnam to Brazil, Moscow to Brussels, the North American prairies to the African grasslands, people everywhere are talking about a prosperous China, and marveling at the country's rapid rise and its bright development prospects. The western media reported that China became the world's third largest economy while western countries were

napping. Half the Chinese population is no longer poverty-stricken. They admitted that the miracle China has created has dealt a severe blow to the statement that the "'America model' is superior to any other," asserted by the famous American political scientist Francis Fukuyama in 1989 in his book *The End of History*. Many western scholars have pointed out that in the process of learning from other countries' development models, China has not only found a path of independent development, but also provided a model for other countries to imitate to strengthen themselves and enrich their people.

And it goes on to proclaim that the China model has displaced and bettered the US as any sort of model: "The 'China model' has created miracles, opened a unique path of development and superseded the belief in a superior 'America model,' marking its demise."

What is this "China model"? It's Deng's model, a system based on economic liberty and political repression. It's founded on the idea that people can have freedom as consumers and producers, but not as citizens and voters. It's sometimes described as "market authoritarianism." Yet while the Chinese power structure depends on the coercion of its citizens, the power of the "China model" relies on attraction. The Party can compel its own citizens, but it cannot compel the rest of the world. It can use hard power – coercion – against its subjects, but generally uses soft power – the power of attraction – to get its way with the rest of the world.

The China model's lure depends on the fact that it promises rapid economic growth with political stability. This is a heady combination for autocrats everywhere. It promises greater national wealth and therefore national power, while preserving the power of the ruler and his claque.

It has found quite a number of foreigners willing to act as promoters and apologists. One influential champion of the China model is an American, Joshua Cooper Ramo, a former foreign editor of *Time* magazine. China leads "by the electric power of its example and the bluff impact of size," he says. While working as a partner for the lobbyists Kissinger Associates in Washington and a professor at the Tsinghua University in China, he invented another name for the China model – the "Beijing Consensus."

"China's new ideas are having a gigantic effect outside of China," he wrote when introducing the concept in a 2004 essay. "China is marking a path for other nations around the world who are trying to figure out not simply how to develop their countries, but also how to fit into the international order in a way that allows them to be truly independent, to protect their way of life and political choices in a world with a single massively powerful centre of gravity. I call this new physics of power and development the Beijing Consensus."

Ramo argues that "it replaces the widely-discredited Washington Consensus," which was "a hallmark of end-of-history arrogance," responsible for leaving "a trail of destroyed economies and bad feelings around the globe." While the Washington Consensus was written by a World Bank official in order to make developing countries attractive to international capital, he writes, China's new development approach is enlightened. According to Ramo, it is "driven by a desire to have equitable, peaceful high-quality growth."

This is remarkable because, if so, China's model would be delivering to others what has eluded China itself. Peaceful growth? Quite apart from the massacre of its own unarmed citizens in Tiananmen Square in 1989, protests and riots, officially known as "mass incidents," have been increasing in number and frequency every year, according to the official statistics from the Ministry of Public Security in Beijing. In 1993 there were 8,700 protests, demonstrations or riots in China. In 1999 there were 32,000, and in 2003 there were 58,000. The published number increased sharply in 2004, the year in which Ramo was writing, to 74,000. In 2008 there were 100,000. And in 2010 there were at least 180,000 such incidents, according to Sun Liping, a professor of sociology at Beijing's Tsinghua University. Liping says that three-quarters of these protests are workers or farmers mobilising to defend, or demand, their rights.

High-quality growth? The environmental cost of China's growth has been brutal. Half the length of China's seven major river systems, including the middle and lower reaches of the Yangtze River and the middle reaches of the Pearl River, is severely polluted, according to Jiang Gaoming, chief researcher of the Chinese Academy of Sciences' Institute of Botany. "Environmental analysis of a 2,000-kilometre stretch of the Huai River found that 78.7 per cent of the water failed to meet minimum standards for drinking water; 79.7 per cent was unsuitable for use in fish farming; and 32 per cent did not even meet standards for use in irrigation." In search of clean fresh water, China is drawing down its aquifers which, once gone, cannot be replenished. China's loss of soil and water "posed severe threats to the ecology, food safety and flood control," the country's vice-minister for water resources, Zhou Ying, observed.

Equitable growth? The income distribution in China today is one of the most unfair in the world, more unequal than that of the US.

But setting Ramo's misleadingly romanticised characterisation aside, what does he think the Beijing Consensus actually consists of? What are the policy planks that comprise the edifice? "It is flexible enough that it is barely classifiable as a doctrine. It does not believe in uniform solutions for every situation. It is defined by a ruthless willingness to innovate and experiment, by a lively defence of national borders and interests, and by the increasingly thoughtful accumulation of tools of asymmetric power projection." If we remove the words "national borders," we are left with a set of behaviours that could equally apply to Al Qaeda. Ramo's essay is nicely written and the term "Beijing Consensus" is catchy and often cited. But its policy content is silly and vacuous, and its normative judgments are misleading.

Others have made more substantial attempts to define a "China model." One is a Chinese academic working at the Geneva School of Diplomacy and International Relations, Zhang Weiwei. Writing in a Party publication, he listed the eight attributes that, in his view, constitute the China model. First is a system that "speaks the truth through facts," meaning that practical facts outweigh ideology. Certainly, the unrealistic adherence to dogma in the Mao era has given way to a more practical approach to national affairs. As the US has hewed to an ever more ideological attachment to the idea of the market, China has become more pragmatic. Beijing under Deng abandoned doctrinal attachments to socialism and adopted a pragmatic approach to make use of the market to raise national income.

Second, Zhang writes, the China model gives priority to the lives of the people, especially through reducing poverty. This, truly, has been the greatest of the achievements of modern China, raising half a billion people out of poverty in three decades. China's economic rise could be seen as the greatest poverty-alleviation project in history. Of every ten people in the world raised from poverty in the last thirty years, seven are mainland Chinese.

But in many other ways, the China model has failed to give priority to the lives of the people, especially when there is contest between the rights of the Party and the rights of the people. The issue of official cars is one illustration. Government officials above a certain rank are issued official cars with drivers. To reach such a position, one needs to be a member of the Party. Axiomatically, this is about the cars that the taxpayers provide to Party members. Because of public indignation at the waste of money and inequities involved, the government announced a reform to contain the growth of the system. It made no difference and the number of cars continued to grow rapidly. By 2007, the number of official cars in China was 5.22 million. It had grown by an average 95,000 cars a year since 1990. The total cost to taxpayers in 2007, at an average cost of 200,000 yuan per car and driver, was 1.04 trillion yuan or about $US152 billion. This was five times the total government budget for health care in the same year.

Third on Zhang's list is "the pre-eminence of stability." He elaborates: "As a civilization-type nation, the complexity of ethnicities, beliefs, languages and regionalism in China are second to no other place in the world. This character has given rise to the collective fear among Chinese of 'chaos.'" This, he writes, is why Deng Xiaoping "repeatedly emphasized the importance of stability, because he understood better than anyone China's own contemporary history … The past 30 years mark the first extended period of stability and development China has experienced in modern times, and only such an environment has made China's economic miracle possible."

This is a clear claim to Chinese exceptionalism, to a unique circumstance which gives rise to unique responses. It is also flawed. Zhang's claim to a "complexity of ethnicities, beliefs, languages and regionalism" that is "second to no other place in the world" is easily punctured by a quick glance north to Russia. Or south to Indonesia. Or east to Brazil. Or west to India. And it's plain that countries everywhere develop better in times of peace than in times of strife. There is nothing special or unique about that.

Fourth on Zhang's list is gradualism in reform. Fifth is sequencing of reforms, starting, for instance, as Deng did, with the coastal areas then moving inland. Sixth is the use of a "mixed economy" approach, combining elements of a state-controlled economy with elements of a market-based economy. Seventh is opening to the outside world. These are all unexceptional concepts. Eighth is having a "relatively neutral, enlightened and strong government." He claims this as the Confucian tradition of virtuous and strong rulers.

Surely most people around the world would desire their governments to be neutral, enlightened and strong. But how can any system guarantee this as a consistent state of affairs? History tells us that no system can. The virtue of democracy is not that it is any better at delivering good leaders, but that it has inbuilt mechanisms for exposing and removing bad ones. How can China achieve this? In a country without checks and balances, where the Party is the state and the state is the Party, where the courts are extensions of the Party, where information is censored, where there are no independent institutions, and the people have no mechanism for removing a bad government, it is impossible. This is no accident. This is precisely the way the Party designed it.

Zhang seeks a way around this inconvenient truth: "Fundamentally, the quality of a political system, including the source of its legitimacy, cannot be measured in its procedural correctness. More important is the correctness of its content, and this content, which is about achieving favourable political governance, must be measured by the people's level of satisfaction. Good versus poor governance is far more important than democratic versus autocratic governance." Even allowing this argument, how is the people's level of satisfaction measured? And by whom? In China, the people are not consulted. As the Party's 2005 White Paper on democracy said: "Democratic government is the Chinese Communist Party governing on behalf of the people." Zhang's own criterion for testing the legitimacy of the Chinese government fails on the circularity of a closed regime.

Even sophisticated justifications to glamorise and justify the China model founder on this unavoidable point. The model rests on the denial of freedom to the people.

When all else fails, the ultimate defence of China's oppression of its people is that it "get things done." Deng Xiaoping said: "One of the greatest advantages of socialist nations is that, as long as something has been decided and a resolution has been made, it can be carried out immediately without any restrictions; unlike the parliamentary democratic process that is so complicated, going back and forth, only talking about it without doing it, concluding without executing. In this respect, our efficiency is higher; we carry things out as soon as we have made up our mind. What I am referring to is the overall efficiency. It is our strength, and we must retain this advantage. We absolutely must not adopt the Western system of tripartite separation of powers."

Many of China's foreign cheerleaders and apologists echo this idea. An American investment banker Robert Lawrence Kuhn, author of books including *How China's Leaders Think*, argues that "for now and for the foreseeable future, the one-party rule of the Chinese Communist Party is the best option. An impractical democratic system would transfer resources to an endless political debate, and long and medium-term economic and social benefit would be sacrificed." Western democracy is impractical, he argues, and would undermine economic strength.

It's notable that Kuhn, and many other commentators, have greater confidence in the Chinese status quo than China's own premier does. It's also important to point out that the arguments of Kuhn, and many like him, are empirically false. Certainly, China's economy grew at an annual average rate of 9.9 per cent in the two decades from 1990 to 2010. This is an extremely high growth rate. But Japan, under a democratic system with a free press and an independent judiciary, grew at an annual average rate of 9.3 per cent in the two decades from 1955 to 1973. In other words, a dictatorship cannot be the explanatory variable in China's high growth, any more than a democracy can be in Japan's. A dictatorship is neither a sufficient condition for high-speed economic growth nor a necessary condition. It is, in fact, a splendid red herring.

And Deng has already been proved wrong on his theory about socialism's key advantage. "I would say that the Americans cannot compete with the Soviet Union. The Soviets can do something after just one Politburo meeting. Can the Americans do that?" No, but it turns out that good governance and national success require more than an iron fist. The architect of Soviet communism, Vladimir Ilyich Lenin, is often credited with saying that the Soviet Union's admirers and advocates in the West were "useful idiots." The quote may be apocryphal, but the concept lives on. Westerners like Ramo and Kuhn and many others, quick to deny the political rights of the Chinese people while enjoying full democratic rights themselves, emphatic in defending China's status quo when even China's premier openly voices doubts, are Deng's "useful idiots."

Yet the potency of the China model grows daily. Why? Chiefly because the principal democratic economies of the US, Japan and Europe have collapsed in economic crisis and remain mired in debt while China booms. One of the West's most important economic proselytisers, the World Bank, has acknowledged the demonstration effect of the China model for other developing countries: "China's efforts created . . . chances for them to acquire abundant knowledge and experience from China in regard to their own development." The bank's chief economist is, for the first time, drawn from China.

And the potency of the model is partly because of its strong lure for autocrats and would-be autocrats around the world. The China model gives a new veneer of respectability to an old urge, the reflex of "strongman" rulers to oppress their people in order to get their way.

Some at the top of the US leadership are keenly aware that the "America model" is under challenge. The US secretary of state, Hillary Clinton, said in an interview during her trip to Australia in November 2010: "There are those who look to China and say, 'Well, gosh, they're growing at 9, 10 per cent a year and they're keeping the lid on.' And if you're of an authoritarian mindset and if your history may be such that that's a more comfortable position for you to assume, then that might be attractive . . . And particularly given the global economic crisis, many in the world looked and said, 'Well, look at the US. They had this great financial collapse. They couldn't control the excesses of the market and they paid a huge price for it.' So there's a clear difference."

This is precisely why the China model now has a more forceful appeal than ever. How does the US counter this? Clinton cautioned countries tempted by the China model: "Economies like ours, which are free and very much focused on entrepreneurial energy and individual initiative, are resilient, dynamic, come back, reinvent themselves, because we don't wait for somebody in our national capital to tell us what we can and cannot buy. We are out there making hundreds of millions of decisions a day that are motivated by a desire to increase productivity, to make a claim for greater profitability, and it has worked. And it is, by far, along with democracy, the winning model. Free markets in democracy have proven themselves time and time again ... if you really care about the development of your country, if you believe in the wellbeing of your people over the long run, then you will have to match political freedom and respect for human rights with economic progress."

This is a remarkable turn. When Hillary Clinton was America's first lady, from 1993 to 2001, it was unimaginable that a US secretary of state would have to make the case for the US model over China's. Today, the onus is on the West to show that free countries can also be thriving economies. Because by 2008 the evidence of real-world performance had turned decisively in China's favour. And the force of reality in economic progress has favoured China with increasing force each year, each month, almost each day since.

Beijing is not content simply to provide an example. It exercises its soft power more actively. It cultivates client states by bestowing aid and investment money, as well as political protection through its veto power in the United Nations Security Council. Burma, for instance, has a burgeoning relationship with Beijing. The generals in Rangoon know that China will never demand that they restore democracy. So Beijing gives dictators money and political support, but also, increasingly, as the China model grows in stature, a veneer of credibility. No longer mere tin-pot tyrants clinging desperately to power, they can align themselves with the "Beijing Consensus" and pretend to be practitioners of a breakthrough international development model.

The China model has strong appeal not just to tyrants but also to democrats in developing countries. When he was the South African president, Thabo Mbeki visited Beijing as part of a Chinese diplomatic initiative to improve ties with Africa, the so-called Forum on China–Africa Co-operation. The leaders of forty-one African nations arrived in Beijing as guests of the Chinese government for the first summit-level meeting in 2006. They were awed by the experience, as Mbeki's account shows: "Like all occasional visitors to China, we could not but marvel at the many signs of progress that are so visible along the streets of Beijing. That progress stands out as the palpable expression of the sustained annual rate of economic growth that we have come to expect of China, of 10 per cent or more." Mbeki concluded: "Africa must recognise and respond to the fact that the Chinese economy is one of the biggest in the world. The South African economy – by far the biggest in Africa – is, relative to the Chinese, very small."

At the summit, China's president, Hu Jintao, made the obligatory pledges of eternal fraternity, Africa and China both being "cradles of civilisation and lands of great promise." Africa also happens to be home to a great frenzy of Chinese mining activity, feeding raw materials into the maw of the Chinese dragon and delivering much-needed revenue for the countries of Africa. Hu then sealed the friendship by making a list of promises. Though still a developing country itself, China would double its aid to Africa over the next three years, provide $US5 billion in preferential credit, set up a $US5 billion development fund to encourage Chinese companies to invest in Africa, cancel all interest-free government debt owed to China by Africa's poorest nations, open up the Chinese market to products from Africa's poorest countries by removing all tariffs on 440 products, help train at least 15,000 African professionals, provide general scholarships for 4,000 African students over three years to study in China, build rural schools in Africa, deploy agricultural experts in Africa, open special agricultural technology centres in Africa, plus a range of other measures.

Mbeki was moved to write that "Africa and China joined together to take the first step in a journey of hope that is as long as a thousand miles." In the same period, the US, Europe and Japan were cutting their overseas aid budgets. The title of Mbeki's article: "At the Heavenly Gate in Beijing hope is born!" Mbeki is no longer South Africa's president, but his account provides an insight into the powerful pull of the China model even for a leader who had been democratically elected.

A distinguished veteran Australian diplomat, Dick Woolcott, thinks that the US already has lost the argument. Woolcott is a former head of the Department of Foreign Affairs who, even at the age of eighty-one, was tasked by the Rudd government with a high-level diplomatic initiative. He remains active and well connected to the elites of many countries, notably those of South-East Asia. He argues: "The US, as the leading democracy, has seen its prestige eroded by crippling debt, two unfinished wars and intense political bickering between the two main parties. It's not now the model that it was in the past. This situation is complicated by the spectacular economic growth of China, which is widely attributed to the main-tenance of firm political control by its government. It's worrying."

The Arab uprisings of 2011 showed that the desire for liberty is a universal one. During four decades of authoritarian stasis in the Arab world, when the number of democracies trebled world-wide and freedom flourished on every continent, it seemed that Arabs were left out of the global trend towards liberty. The stasis went on for so long that some commentators started to develop theories that Arabs were unique, that they were somehow culturally disposed to authoritarianism, even that they loved their oppres-sors. Those theories were swiftly debunked when the presidents of Tunisia, Egypt, Libya and Yemen were overthrown by sponta-neous people's uprisings.

There were once similar attempts to argue that Asians were inherently unsuited to democracy. A pair of South-East Asian leaders, Singapore's Lee Kwan Yew and Malaysia's Mahathir Mohamad, in the 1980s led the "Asian values" school. This argued that Confucian countries depended on hierarchies of power and could not embrace Western-style concepts of political equality. And, they claimed, East Asians operated consensus systems, fundamentally at odds with the adversarial systems of Western democracy. But as the people demanded political liberties in South Korea, the Philippines, Taiwan and Indonesia, as they all moved from autocracy to democracy, it became harder to sustain this argument. It was only ever a cover story to justify the autocratic tendencies of Lee and Mahathir, both of whom ran systems that were only notionally democratic.

The idea that Asians didn't want political rights was patronising and offensive. The argument for "Asian values" is now, thankfully, dead. So is the argument for "Arab values." Only the argument for "Chinese values" remains. Or, as it's usually phrased, the argument for a "China model." Or Beijing Consensus. Intellectually, it was killed in 1996, when Taiwan moved to full democracy. The Taiwanese are predominantly ethnically Han Chinese. If anything, Taiwan, whose population is 98 per cent Han Chinese compared to mainland China's 92 per cent, is more Chinese than China. But Beijing continues to tell the world of its Chinese exceptionalism, even while, internally, it is racked with doubt. "The various theories in opposition to Westernization are always taken up by the ruling authorities as tools for the defense of their interests and leadership status, particularly as theoretical tools in opposing democracy and defending autocracy," says the Chinese journalist and author Yang Jisheng.

China today is the world's greatest force for repression. Of the 2.434 billion people in the world living in dictatorships, almost 60 per cent live in China. And it leads, in Joshua Cooper Ramo's phrase, "by the electric power of its example and the bluff impact of size." In dollar terms, China became the world's second-biggest economy in 2011. And while the US still has a much bigger economy and military, it is also the world's biggest debtor. And guess who is America's biggest creditor? As we have seen, Hillary Clinton remarked to Kevin Rudd in a conversation disclosed by Wikileaks, "How do you get tough with your banker?" Its economic size, the freight-train force of its growth and its propaganda prowess make it a formidable advocate. And it advocates the oppression of human liberty.

This is why the world needs alternative models, countries showcasing economic success in tandem with human liberty in its fullest flowering. The great powers of the free world – the US, Japan and Europe – have shown that they cannot answer the challenge so far in the twenty-first century. Two significant middle powers, however, have demonstrated that sound economic performance is entirely compatible with the full spectrum of civil and political liberties. Countries do not need to embrace repression in order to deliver good economic outcomes. Australia and Canada readily prove the point. They both demonstrated resilience during the global financial crisis. These two Westminster democracies are the living rebuff to the notion that countries need to sacrifice liberty in order to deliver prosperity. Australia, in particular, continued to grow and prosper throughout the crisis, as it has through every international crisis of the last two decades.

So whenever someone like the former prime minister of Malaysia, Mahathir Mohamad, says, as he did in 2010, that democracy is a "failed" ideology and holds the Beijing Consensus up as the way of the future, audiences can ask, "But what about Canada, what about Australia?" Until other democracies are able to rebuild sound policies and point to strong economic performance, it's a peculiarity of history that Australia has emerged as the world's leading model for liberty and prosperity, conjoined in democracy. Australians today live in a sweet spot.

The purpose of a thriving economy is to allow people to live fuller lives. In his magisterial history of democracy, John Keane came to an abrupt conclusion about the essential value of democracy: "Its purpose is to stop people getting screwed." Australia today should provide hope to others that it is entirely possible to deliver a people the prosperity that allows them to live full lives, and, at the same time, the freedoms that reduce their chances of getting screwed.

ACKNOWLEDGMENTS

I'm indebted to my forebears for settling in Australia a century and a half ago. Not all of them chose the Antipodes – at least one travelled as a guest of His Majesty's government – but all chose to stay. History has vindicated their choice. Their gift to me across the generations I have been deeply pleased to be able to pass to my children. To Kate, Dylan, Nina, Carla and Thomas, I thank you for showing me every day the best thing Australia has going for it. You are an antidote to curmudgeonliness and a reminder of my generation's responsibility to leave the place better than we found it. I thank you, my supremely patient partner, Mindanao, for your forbearance with my distraction and preoccupation in writing this book. I thank Marija Taflaga for valuable help with research and Chris Feik of Black Inc. for saintly quantities of faith and hope that this project would one day achieve that sweet spot, completion.

Peter Hartcher,
Sydney.

INDEX